AMERICAN SAIL
A Pictorial History

View of the United States frigate *Constitution*, engraved upon a piece of wood,
taken from one of her live-oak knees, in 1833.

"E. Hawkins 1st officer on board ship Calpe of New York Wm Cranston Master, passing the Jnd of Teneriff on the 16th fry 1816, bound from Hvre de Grace to Rio Janeiro having forty passengers on board."

AMERICAN SAIL
A Pictorial History
Alexander Laing

E. P. DUTTON & COMPANY, INC. • NEW YORK

The blank center of the rare American School Sheet opposite was used originally for a script copy of a
patriotic poem, most of which has faded so much as to be illegible. Traces may be seen around the cut-out
portion. Such school sheets helped to impress upon American youth the nature of their country's partial
success in a war which, perhaps fortunately, was not a clear-cut victory for either side. Since there was
almost nothing to be proud of in the operations by land, except for one battle fought by forces that did not
know peace had been signed, the victories at sea and on Lake Erie were stressed all the more emphatically.
The result was a quickened interest in maritime enterprise, and a vigorous expansion of the somewhat
unorthodox ideas that had been expressed in the building and use of the victorious frigates.

TO

PRISCILLA

AND

LOWRIE

WITH LOVE

This Adventure

into

The American

Past

CONTENTS

AMERICAN SAIL
A Pictorial History

American clipper ship. From *Ballou's Pictorial Drawing-Room Companion*, 1855.

The CONTEMPORANEOUS VIEW

What was it like to be alive in the great age of American Sail?

These pages offer a visual answer: ships, harbors, mariners, events upon the sea, as they appeared to the eyes of contemporaries. I have tried throughout to select the work of competent artists who actually saw what they drew, or who worked from the sketches and accounts of eyewitnesses soon after the occasions their pictures celebrate. Part of the truth of history is taste, which changes constantly. The times are reflected in the artistic conventions of the times.

Charleston, South Carolina, as it appeared in 1837 from across Cooper's River. Painted by G. Cooke and engraved by W. J. Bennett. The publisher, Lewis P. Clover of New York, was offering the series of Bennett's aquatints of American cities at this time for about $4 or $5 apiece. If this print did not happen to be dated, some idea of when it was produced could be got from the facts that the smaller of the two white spires marks a church that was nearing completion in 1837 and that the square steeple at the right was demolished in 1852. To the nautical eye the deep topsails suggest a date prior to 1840, although individual vessels still carried them for another decade or more.

Many illustrated histories are misleading because their compilers, in an effort to present an esthetically satisfying view of each important event, have mingled pictures of uncertain authority with others that stand the usual tests of veracity. Such sequences annoy a few specialists and help to confirm the rest of us in our romantic misconceptions of the past. A picture made long after the event is almost certain to display inaccuracies which may be the result of too much loving care rather than of too little. Some marine painters have scrupulously observed the shapes of ships in their own youth, and the changes made in their own later days, without showing any awareness that change also was occurring in the vessels manned by their grandfathers.

I was once scolded in print by an eminent marine scholar for having alluded in a book review to John Masefield's mention of a ship's flagstaff. No sailing ship, my critic said, had ever had a flagstaff. The spanker boom would work havoc with it. Flagstaffs at sea were the lubberly appurtenances of stinkpots exclusively. When I supplied references to a number of contemporary pictures of ships with flagstaffs (some will be seen in the pages that follow), he was astonished. He apologized in a heart-warming letter, explaining that he had been born at sea, had never seen a flagstaff in a sailing ship of his own times, and somehow had allowed the reality of immediate experience to obscure his observation of pictorial evidence with which he had been dealing for years. I tell the story as a small hedge against fate, because I cannot hope to have escaped similar aspects of myopia in my own use of the pictorial record and should like to be informed of inaccuracies resulting.

With antiquarian skill, a few artists derive details for their work from reliable and closely dated sources. Examples can be seen in the eight color plates in Carl C. Cutler's classic work *Greyhounds of the Sea*. For accuracy these paintings met the scrupulous standards of Mr. Cutler. Yet each raises the question: "Why did no contemporary of such ships see them in these bright colors, through this romantic haze?"

Other colors, another haze, not these.

The contemporaneous Currier & Ives lithograph of the *Dreadnought* off Tuskar Light has a fierce, portentous atmosphere, a power of color, which says: "This is exactly how it was, a few days ago, toward the end of that phenomenal passage." To feel so about it may reveal another sort of romanticism. If so, it is the romanticism proper to the 1850s, and therefore part of the history of the great climacteric of sail.

I have not knowingly included a humdrum picture because it was contemporaneous, but the rough charm of the primitive sometimes has dictated the choice: the primitive, truth seen as best it could be, with large emphasis upon the significant, by the honest viewer of limited artistic skill. One quality of the primitive in art is its way of giving us as much as our eyes can comprehend at once. A subtle, later art lacks this emphatic obtrusion of the essential.

The principle of the contemporaneous view may be made clearer if we remember that it is the quality which gives authority and immediacy to all good photographs. Photography attained the technical standards essential to a flexible art form at about the time when the great era of sail was ending. It was confined to "stills" until about 1880. The first attempt to photograph an ocean race aboard one of the contestants with an "instantaneous machine" was made in 1887. I have included some classic early examples of marine photography. But for the meaning perceivable in motion caught at a moment of dramatic intensity we are dependent upon the interpretive skill of the draftsman almost to the close of the nineteenth century. For many such moments no contemporary pictures were made—or none seem to have survived. This is sadly true of the seventeenth century in America. I have tried to let good pictures speak for themselves, with a minimum of explanation. Where I could find no reliable pictures, words alone have had to serve.

To the rule that pictures should be closely contemporary I have added two others: That the vessels, scenes, episodes, and persons depicted should relate to positive American contributions to the advancement of seafaring under sail; and that the vessels should have been products of what is now the continental United States. A few common-sense exceptions will be noted. It would have been silly to exclude a Scottish fugitive from justice who commanded an unwieldy French hulk in the most famous naval action of the American Revolution. John Paul Jones deserves, and is accorded, special treatment.

As a general plan the pictures of particular vessels are arranged in the sequence of their launching dates, within categories which sometimes require a jog backward in time, for a look at the beginnings of a particular trade. The broad arrangement is chronological.

An indulgent foundation some day may sponsor a pictorial history inclusive of every American sailing vessel that had enough contemporary significance to be depicted at all. Many volumes would be needed, and the work would have the magnificent monotony of a complete stamp catalogue. Even the gathering of pictures covering none but vessels of historical importance presents an esthetic difficulty: ship pictures fall into a few categories, within some of which all examples look very much alike.

This book does not pretend to either sort of completeness. I have tried to interpret a vast subject through the selection of its more significant aspects, saving room at the same time for reconsideration of a number of matters that seem to me to have been misrepresented in other books. Some well known ships will not be found here at all because others adequately represent the type, the trade, the particular experience. It would be a pleasure to claim that most of these pictures have been newly rediscovered. But the ubiquitous Kilroy of World War II—surely a sailor!—has his counterparts in the archipelagoes of research. Again and again I have come

". . . the primitive, truth seen as best it could be, with large emphasis upon the significant, by the honest viewer of limited artistic skill." Lord Nelson is said to have called this Tripolitan episode "the most daring of the age." Francis Kearny, who engraved the scene four years later, probably based his aquatint upon one by Guerrazzi made within a year of the event. If so, he reconceived the scene substantially, increasing the dramatic effect. Kearny may have had other materials to guide him. Some of his 1812–1815 engravings identify the naval officers from whose sketches and advice he worked. As a Philadelphian, with Philadelphians for customers, he had a special interest in the fate of the frigate built in his home city. Within a few years he was doing work that is much more sophisticated.

BURNING of the FRIGATE PHILADELPHIA in the HARBOUR of TRIPOLI, 16 Feb. 180

ashore upon what seemed to be an unrecorded island only to encounter presently the sardonic hieroglyph of some inquisitive Kilroy who had got there ahead of me. I have never rejected the truer or more handsome picture merely to present a less common or a newly unearthed one, but gaps will be noted where no reliable picture could be found. Few vessels are as familiar, visually, as the *Mayflower*—but every existing picture and model is a mere guess. The supposed facsimile which recently crossed the Atlantic was conceived as a scrupulous replica of a typical ship of about the same size and date, but her structure was substantially altered to give tourist visitors headroom between decks which passengers and seamen of the period did not in fact enjoy. Captain Alan Villiers thinks that the change injured her stability. On several such counts the fine photographs which have been taken of the new *Mayflower* have had to be passed over. There are other instances. Several of the last sailing vessels in actual commercial use under the American flag were built in England and northern Europe. Rather than an American contribution to the history of sail, their use reflected little more than the nostalgia of wealthy men for a lost splendor which we as a nation had allowed to disappear while its virtues persisted in memory. There were very few foremasthands who regretted the disappearance of the large sailing vessel.

In a brief survey of historical forces that follows, an attempt is made to define more closely the quality and period of America's principal positive contribution to the development of sailing vessels. All inheritors of the impulse of Diderot work with the echo in their memories of the great encyclopedist's hope that his work would have "the character of changing the general way of thinking" about the subjects presented. Sharing that hope in a very modest measure, I shall be pleased if this book shifts a little more toward the truth our manner of looking at one aspect of our American past.

ALEXANDER LAING

Navigators to America in the sixteenth century sailed upon a sea of marvels, but the once ferocious marine fauna took on a waggish character shortly before they swam over the maps' edges, and vanished. This pleasant encounter occurs in the Ortelius atlas of 1570, a vastly respected work in use throughout the first fifty years of colonial venturing north of the Caribbean.

THOSE GRAND WIND MUSCLES, HER SAILS

The yacht *America* as painted by James E. Buttersworth.

THE LOOK OF A SHIP UNDER CANVAS IS NEVER WHOLLY THE OUT-come of human intent. Air and water have a part in it. Change flickers from moment to moment across what the early American sculptor Horatio Greenough called "those grand wind muscles, her sails." As everyone knows who has stood his trick at the helm, there is no such thing as a steady breeze. The postures of canvas have a multitudinous beauty because in them controlled artifice finds a midway meeting with the unpredictable. Even when the sea is flat, a memory of wind hovers in the peculiar stillness of sails that were not designed ever to be at rest.

By several devices—brush, burin, crayon, lens—artists of a special dedication have kept some of these moments of beauty for the rest of us: beauty, not separate from utility, but central within it. Our now perhaps maturing country has come to a belated general recognition that beauty is one test of practical soundness in design. My scanning of the jumbled pictorial record of America's past has turned up proof after proof that this principle, undervalued or ignored until recently in most of our national preoccupations, has always been respected upon the seas. My book deals with the pictured permanence of the handsomest of America's creative forms. Historical candor calls for the inclusion of other parts of the record as well. The Industrial Revolution made a reeking horror of our waterfronts, one possible reason why so many young Americans turned their lives toward the prairies and the mountains. Inside fo'c's'le and hold it worsened the dark brutalities that had been there all along. But, until sail began to be jettisoned as a source of commercial energy, the external hideousness of the Industrial Revolution did not affect the shaping of ships. The trend was exactly contrary. Both hull and tophamper were coming close to the plain excellence of pure form, stripped of adornment, at the very time when the architecture of the land was entering its gingerbread age.

"The postures of canvas": an American topsail schooner of the 1812 period, shown in an aquatint copied from a painting by the British marine artist William J. Huggins. This picture may have been a study for another by Huggins, celebrating the capture of the American privateer *Gipsey* (page 144).

The "grand wind muscles" of the little *Warner,* caught by James E. Buttersworth just as her three upper topsails relaxed upon their lifts. She deserved the attention of perhaps the foremost American painter of ships. Although she was the smallest of the outright clipper ships she set one of the records of the era that have stood unbroken, for more than a century, by any vessel under sail: 27 days from the latitude of the river Plate to New York. In completing this great run on July 9, 1853, she was also concluding a remarkable passage of only 67 days around the Horn from Valparaiso. The *Warner* was built at Cape Elizabeth, Maine, in 1851. She measured 500 tons. Her dimensions—length, breadth, depth—were 138′ x 28′ x 14.5′. Thus she had a remarkably high ratio of length to breadth for her size, almost 5 to 1. She was owned by William H. Merritt of New York. Her captain on the famous voyage probably was Luther Ripley, Jr., although one authority, on different pages, lists both Ripley and "Capt. Carr," who may have been in command on the outward voyage only.

There were brief offshore lapses such as the early ironclad, aspects of an uneasy retreat from sail. But even the bald-headed towing barge—a last expedient for keeping canvas at work amid the warmer sorts of propellants—retained a vestigial, stark beauty. There has been scant room at sea for anything but the stripped essentials. Much comment has been spent upon the stultifying conservatism of maritime enterprise. The towing barge conserved nothing but the plain core of our experience with the older, more elaborate mechanisms that had derived from sail alone its maximum of practical force.

Experience and common sense, hampered by the effect of tonnage laws and other devices for taxing shipowners, controlled the design of ships' hulls until long after experimental research procedures had come into use in other forms of architecture. But the shaping of the grand wind muscles was less constrained. Experience and common sense together told the shipmaster how much sail, and what sort, he could carry to advantage in various circumstances at sea. The master of a vessel was much more likely to be able to specify her spar and sail plans than to dictate her lines under water. The rigs were changed after the experience of long voyages: from ship to bark; from brig to schooner; from sloop to ketch; or the other way about. Most rigs were drastically reduced in sail area about 1860, when the large crews needed to manage them in emergencies could no longer be found or paid. The vessels in the pictures on pages 2 and 3 have stu'n's'l booms rigged at their yardarms, an old device for extending the sail area dramatically at a risk of calamity if sail could not be shortened quickly before the arrival of a sudden squall. Stu'n's'ls became a luxury that few vessels could afford in the latter days of sail.

The evolution of the grand wind muscles—from rotundity to tenseness to the sparse economy of the true windfoil—can be noted chronologically in the pages that follow.

LEFT. A typical ship of the early colonial period. A structure and rig that had become standard by the time of the Spanish Armada and continued in use with no substantial change for half a century thereafter. From a Hondius map of New Spain, 1630.

". . . monstrosities such as the early ironclad, aspects of an uneasy retreat from sail." The *Roanoke* was an unsatisfactory compromise in design. The earlier turreted ships, such as the famous *Monitor*, were designed as floating batteries for use in estuaries particularly. The *Roanoke* was supposed to be a seagoing vessel. She spent about a year with the Atlantic squadron, but "the great weight of the three turrets made her rolling dangerous and the hull was not found to be strong enough . . . the thrust of the turret spindles . . . always threatening to force out the bottom." The Novelty Works in the background sounds like a toy factory. It built big toys, such as engines for the Collins steamers, and these turrets.

LEFT. This is probably the earliest portrait of an identified particular ship owned in the colonies that became the United States: the *Bethel,* belonging to the Quincy family of Boston. The picture shows her in 1748, the year in which she took a Spanish treasure ship of 24 guns and 110 men. She is credited with having carried at the time only 14 guns and 38 men. In this picture she has a broadside of 10 guns on the main deck. In the case of so sizable a vessel with so small a crew, it is possible that some of the guns depicted were dummies. It may interest the viewer to compare the old-style topsails of this vessel with the double or split topsails of the *Warner* on the preceding page. The *Bethel,* in her broadside view, appears to be shortening sail under similar circumstances. Note that the upper topsails of the *Warner* are able to relax to leeward of the lower topsails, whereas the great deep topsails of the *Bethel* fall so as to chafe upon the forestays, a situation much more attractive in a picture than it would be to the foremasthands confronted by the task of coaxing them into gaskets.

"Recognizably American effects upon the world of sail" were remarked by foreign observers soon after the Revolution. A particular source of interest was the Baltimore clipper, such as this one encountered by the British Captain George Tobin in 1794 off the lighthouse of Cape Henry. Captain Tobin's sketch includes two Virginia pilot schooners—a form of craft which, to judge by the many pictures in British and French archives, was even more impressive to our visitors. The reason may have been that more of them were encountered, of necessity, ranging off the shoals between Capes Henlopen and Henry. Their cocky, rakish rig was like nothing else to be seen at sea in this early period.

America's CHARACTERISTIC CONTRIBUTION

t is Time that we should establish an American Character—Let that Character be a Love of Country and Jealousy of it's honor—This Idea comprehends every Thing that ought to be impressed upon the Minds of all our Citizens, but more especially of those Citizens who are also Seamen & Soldiers.

—Benjamin Stoddert to John Barry
11 July 1798

THIS STIRRING IF VAGUE PRESCRIPTION APPEARS IN A LETTER WHICH THE FIRST SECRETARY of the United States Navy wrote to its senior officer about three weeks after assuming the duties of a newly created post. Substantially the same exhortation recurs in his instructions to other officers as they put to sea. Secretary Stoddert was more sensitive than most to the problem of a new nation striving to create its own identity; yet he besought its citizens to display nothing more particularly characteristic than the orthodox conservative attitudes of patriotism. There was nothing significantly American in the qualities he specified for "an American character."

It is easier for an outsider to perceive what is new or different in a people. We take our shared qualities for granted. With allowances for bias, our own distinctive past can best be perceived through the eyes of foreigners who were more impressed by our differences from themselves: Alexis de Tocqueville and James Bryce are the classic interpreters of America to Americans, but there have been many others, and their most frequent chances to observe us occurred offshore. I have stressed the conservatism of sea practice because it offers a background against which America's achievements under sail appear with clarity. Conservatism, half the molding force of a strong society, is not a commitment to the past as a whole. That is reaction. Good conservatism guards the useful part of the past.

Mr. Stoddert had trouble with his definition because our colonial beginnings provided us with a past which was borrowed. Aspects of it were conserved in isolation, long after they had altered in their places of origin. It took us about a century to invent the beginnings of a usable past of our own. Recognizably American effects, upon the world of sail, began to be seen as soon as we stopped thinking of ourselves as colonials.

The early settlers did not lack ingenuity, or they would not have been colonists at all. For transportation they did the usual thing: they adapted existing types of craft to local conditions. New ideas came crowding before political independence could be asserted—obviously, for new ideas are what independence is made of. But it was only when seafaring America could confront the world with her destiny in her own full keeping that a characteristic creativity began to be noticed by others, in the design and use of our sailing vessels. The persistent conservatism of sea practice elsewhere provided both the need and the chance to be new.

This is a recurrent phenomenon. A similar upwelling of national character had taken place two centuries earlier, when the Sea Beggars of the Netherlands began a process which wrested a huge oriental empire from Spain and Portugal even while the Low Countries themselves were largely in the grip of Spanish troops. Our own early conquest of the oceans differed in that it was generally peaceful. Yet it began, like that of the Dutch, in a truculent impatience with the reactionary assumption that new generations should be bound forever by bad bargains forced upon their ancestors. That is the vice of conservatism, when its adherents wish to cherish even what has become evil from the past.

The waning eighteenth century, a time of revolution against inherited evil, actually confronted young America with two extreme forms of the usual conservatism that prevails at sea. These were monopoly in trade and orthodoxy in the management of navies. Our colonial trade, harshly limited by British law, had been well guarded by the British Navy. After the Revolution the surviving fragments of our Continental Navy were cheerfully sold. The American merchant marine confronted a shifting pattern of colonies bound to their possessors' rules of trade, which included entrenched monopolies such as the East India companies. Some of these at times could muster more political and military force than was available to most sovereign states. They monopolized not only the trade of subject peoples but also that of independent nations such as China. One of the quarreling powers might find the cargo of an American vessel useful, and provide a desirable return freight, or require it to accept an unwanted one. But the situation was ruinously uncertain. It was made focal by the depredations of the Barbary powers, beginning within a year or two of the dispersal of our Continental Navy, and became intolerable when spoliations of the French and British forced in 1798 the expansion of a small navy prepared only for the Barbary emergency.

America if she was to survive had left to her the two courses which nautical conservatism discourages: a wide-ranging experimentation in naval architecture and the employment of her ships in new sorts of ventures. The idea, usually credited to Joshua Humphreys, of creating a small fleet of oversize frigates, more heavily gunned than others in that category yet with frigate weatherliness for escaping from ships of the line, is the most notable instance of the sort of ingenuity that was called for. The huge fleets of the great powers were divided into offensive classes, to be employed under a developed tactical system. Those nations which had plenty of large vessels felt no need to create yet another confusing class, midway between fourth- and fifth-rate. But America needed an offensive force in a hurry. She could not afford to pit her six authorized frigates against the normal odds of sea conflict with scores of others of the same class.

Secretary Stoddert had his worries about the bold plan which produced "Old Ironsides" and her notable companions. Nine days before he sent off the letter quoted at the head of this chapter, he told a member of Congress that the largest British frigates, their 38s, "meas-

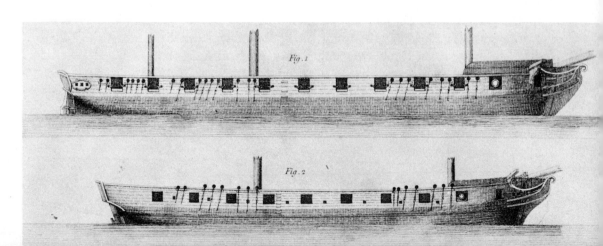

ure not exceeding 940 Tons," and noted that the *Constellation,* "carrying 38, measures upward of 1300 tons. It is still to be determined whether, a Ship carrying the same number of Guns, is better for being so much larger. . . ." The American frigates often carried a few more guns than the number for which they were nominally rated, and a higher proportion of guns of large caliber than were practicable in the fifth rates they were designed to overpower. The British historian William James devoted a large part of his irate study of the War of 1812 to the task of proving that the American frigates were in fact what they were designed to be: larger, stronger as to frame and bulwarks, capable of throwing a heavier broadside, than their probable opponents.

There was no incentive for a foreign shipowner to possess a speedy vessel. Merchantmen moved for the most part in convoys. The slowest vessel established the rate of progress for all the others. It made better sense to build vessels having a maximum of actual capacity for their rated tonnage measurement. Tonnage was determined with a ruler, not by a calculation of weight or even of displacement. Under the earlier tonnage laws length and breadth on deck dominated the formula, a fact that produced the kettle-bottoms of some merchantmen: vessels very narrow on deck, very broad below the waterline, cranky and dull sailers.

In the decade following the Revolution, American designers had the opposite incentive. With no navy in prospect, they had to develop vessels which could stay out of trouble by getting to windward of it; which could be handled smartly in difficult circumstances; which could fight their own battles when there was no other choice. The factor of speed probably

An Act of Congress of June 28, 1798, stipulated that "if a vessel of superior or equal force, shall be captured by a public-armed vessel of the United States" the prize money representing its value should be paid in full to its captors. Claims that American vessels in the War of 1812 had beaten vessels of equal force were based partly in a desire to compensate the victorious crews as an incentive to further exploits. Some of the claims aroused a justifiable indignation among Englishmen who had fought with an often reckless valor against force that was in fact superior, and had been planned to be superior. The illustrations at the left are from *Naval Occurrences of the Late War . . .* published in 1817 by William James, much of the material having previously been issued in a pamphlet while the war was still in progress. The larger of the two vessels seen in profile is the United States sloop of war *Frolic.* Below is a British brig of war of the *Epervier* class, several of which were taken in "equal combat" by the larger American ship-rigged "sloops." Both classes were rated by their own navies as of 18 guns, but James argued that in most cases the American vessels carried larger guns or more of them. The deck view is a comparison between the United States frigate *President* and a standard British frigate of the *Macedonian* class. James calls to particular notice the ring bolts for the breechings of four extra guns for each upper deck's broadside, with room provided on deck for their recoil—impossible in the more cramped deck structure of the British frigate. Both the *President* and the *Frolic* had been captured by the British, which made it possible for James to get their lines from the Admiralty. The *Frolic* was probably built by Josiah Barker at Boston, under the 1813 authorization for six 18-gun sloops of war. The weight of her metal remained in dispute because her guns were jettisoned in her attempt to escape from the frigate *Orpheus,* 36, and the schooner *Shelburne,* 12, which took her. This *Frolic* was named after a British brig captured early in the war and lost again two hours later (page 150).

Twenty-one-year-old Nat Palmer of Stonington, who had sailed a sloop of about 45 tons' measurement to the Antarctic Ocean, was looking for seal rookeries such as this one when he casually reported what some scholars have argued was the first sighting of the Antarctic continent.

has been overstressed. It was one of several objectives, and less important than the related capacity for weatherliness.

The great difference between sail and other propellants is its limited usefulness in going against the wind. A steersman looking downward at the compass card knows that twelve of the thirty-two marked points are unavailable to him. An old square-rigger could not sail closer than within six points of the wind. A larger ship could set the necessary press of sail to catch a smaller one. Pinched between these two standard factors, American designers recognized weatherliness as the most important quality to strive for. If one vessel could make progress within six and one-half points of the wind and another of the same speed could make progress within five and one-half points, the latter would get upwind by about one extra mile for every five miles sailed, the best way for a smaller vessel to escape from a larger and faster one.

Such considerations produced the Baltimore clipper schooner of the 1790s as a major climax in the long process of schooner development that began in Holland almost two centuries earlier. The concurrent refining of small pilot schooners, often in the same yards, followed a similar logic for opposite reasons. The impulse toward monopoly in the old world affected pilotage along with other enterprises: pilots generally waited in the likely spots and took their turns. It was more expressive of the American attitude that the pilot first alongside the incoming vessel should have the job. Virginia pilot boats, and their more northerly counterparts, were made swift and weatherly to reach the bigger ship in a hurry rather than to escape from it. America's characteristic contribution was reflected, in both classes, as individualistic:

Captain Stephen Decatur's victory in the frigate *United States* over Captain John Carden in the *Macedonian,* not far from Madeira, October 25, 1812. Casualties in the smaller British frigate were more than eight times as great as in her American adversary. Decatur maneuvered with a cold efficiency that outwitted Carden, but the fact that the *United States* could use her 24-pounders effectively at long range, when the *Macedonian*'s 18s were not even reaching her enemy, made the great difference.
From the oil painting by Thomas Birch.

ABOVE. A New York pilot schooner (probably the famous *Edward F. Williams*, built in 1863) preparing to put a pilot aboard a merchantman in distress in a freezing gale. From the beginnings of our nationality, pilotage developed in ways intensely expressive of America's enterprising individualism at sea. A contemporaneous woodcut from *Appleton's Journal*. BELOW. "Old Ironsides." The only survivor of six frigates, authorized in the Barbary emergency of 1794, that became the famous nucleus of the United States Navy. The *Constitution* has been extensively rebuilt four times.

The launch of the clipper *Great Republic* from the East Boston yard of Donald McKay, on October 4, 1853. Her original measurement, 4,555 tons, gave McKay for many years the distinction of having built by far the largest of wooden sailing ships in the world.

the vessel that could take care of itself amid enemies, the vessel that could outdistance its own compatriots.

Men who thought of themselves as free also undertook in their private capacities functions elsewhere understood to be in the province of governments. When Lieutenant Charles Wilkes at last made sail in 1838, commanding the first official United States Exploring Expedition, private American shipmasters had been nuzzling the far crannies of the map for half a century. One very young American skipper, Nathaniel B. Palmer of Stonington, is thought by some to have been first to sight a continent. He made inadequate note of it, if so, because he really was looking only for seals.

Thus the American characteristic contribution to the history of sail was more personal than national. The shipping community often regarded the government as the main enemy. The reluctantly accepted Naval Act of 1794, as it turned out, established our permanent Navy; but it was phrased to deal with a problem which the lawmakers viewed as transient.

Construction was to be halted if the Barbary States could be dealt with by tribute and other lures of diplomacy. William Eaton, American consul at Tunis, cried outrage in vain.

The early Navy itself was largely created by private persons. During the Quasi War with France at the close of the eighteenth century, funds were raised by subscription in the major ports to build frigates as a protection for shipowners' investments and a stimulant to local enterprise. Nothing comparable to the broad responsibility of the British Admiralty developed in the United States until after the decline of sail had begun. Here too it was the vigor of remarkable individuals—some officials, others acting privately in the public interest—that gradually forced the assumption of necessary functions by the government. Such men as Ferdinand Rudolph Hassler, who organized the Coast Survey; William C. Redfield, meteorologist; and Matthew Fontaine Maury, oceanographer, demonstrated ideas in action that could not be ignored. Appropriations became larger, but the sense of national responsibility for a healthy merchant marine has been oddly sporadic. Except for a few extraordinary years in the 1850s, when Lieutenant Maury exacted an enthusiastic tribute of factual information from the naval officers and merchant skippers of the world, a parsimonious indifference to the interests of deep-water carriers was to be expected of Congress throughout the definable era of sail.

A characteristically American era of sail certainly began with the confirmation of American independence, or soon afterward. When did it end? If the building of new sailing vessels as potentially profitable cargo carriers is the test, we might say that the era closed in 1921, with the collapse of an artificial demand for anything that would float, to replace tonnage sunk by submarines. The year 1922 might be taken as symbolic, because it was the last one in which the government's *List of Merchant Vessels of the United States* placed all the sailing vessels ahead of the steamers. Here and there, small craft still scrape a living. If we waste our oil fast enough, and if atomic energy proves intractable except for large vessels, the wind's ancient energy may again become competitive. Perhaps the era of American sail has not ended, and will persist as long as air moves over water.

The creative contribution of our country to the use of sail was first widely recognized in the War of 1812, and was confirmed in the following enterprise of the Yankee packet lines. The spectacular China clippers of the late forties and the California clippers of the early fifties were our most notable maritime advertisements, but a commercial panic in 1857 brought the

The *Benjamin F. Packard,* a representative, moderately successful Down-Easter. When launched at Bath, Maine, in 1883, she proved to have been shrewdly designed for the difficult years ahead. The marine historian William Armstrong Fairburn says of her, "The publicity in regard to this full-modeled ship's being a clipper is absolutely false." She made one 94-day passage from San Francisco to New York: several smaller clippers had made it in two weeks' less time. Her average for runs out to San Francisco was 148 days, for homeward runs, 126 days. But she was not built to be a racer. She measured 2,130 tons.

Captain Joshua Slocum was one of the "capable men faced by inevitable defeat" who occasionally have created out of the downfall of their calling an entirely personal triumph. Born a Nova Scotian, he was early naturalized in the United States. He first commanded a vessel at the age of twenty-five, in 1869. At thirty he built an 80-ton steamer in the Philippines, and in the same year took command of the *Northern Light*, which he considered "the finest American sailing vessel afloat." Fluctuations of fortune during the next twelve years led him, in 1886, to exercise a belief that a captain who owned his own vessel could best deal with the increasing uncertainties of a career in sail. He bought the *Aquidneck*, a 326-ton bark, not only as investment and command, but as his floating home. When she was wrecked on a Brazilian bar soon afterward he began his defiances of fate by building from the wreckage the 35-foot "canoe" *Liberdade*, which he sailed with his wife and two sons to New York. For six years, despite this notable feat of seamanship, he offered his services in vain. In 1893 he got the dubious job of taking Ericsson's *Destroyer* to the Brazilian revolutionaries. She was sunk, and he was never paid. Two years later, as a practical joke, he was given a "command" which proved to be a rotting little sloop in a cow pasture. He rebuilt her, put to sea, and rebuked the joker by becoming the first man to sail single-handed around the world. This courageous, philosophical expression, photographed in 1907 by Percy E. Budlong, seems to reflect the misadventures that had befallen his profession, and a triumph that was entirely personal. In 1909 Slocum sailed the little *Spray*, deliberately, into a wild southeast gale—and vanished.

LEFT. Getting in the blanket piece from a sperm whale, as painted in the 1870s by C. S. Raleigh of New Bedford. The American whale ship exemplifies both the durable tradition of the sea and the venturesome ingenuity of American seafaring. Most of the detailed procedures of whaling were well developed before the emergence of a little sandspit south of Cape Cod as the world's most eminent whaling port. The particular American genius was expressed largely in the co-ordination of these procedures with a co-operative system of shared investment and effort that made of the whale ship a small, independent town which often went adrift from the rest of the map for four years. Nantucketers built their whaling industry by developing an optimum sort of vessel and a principle of operation that could exist and accomplish the intended purpose anywhere in the world of water. It mastered competition by being able to reach as far beyond it as the occasion might require.

clipper-ship era to an abrupt close. Civil warfare obstructed what might have been a normal recovery; it caused the sale to foreigners of many famous American ships, and the sinking of most of the others that put to sea under American registry. Twenty years later, when Henry Hall was writing his remarkable report on shipping for the Tenth Census, the contest between sail and steam seemed to him to be far from settled. He thought a sound recovery possible. Several expedients were tried such as the multi-masted schooner. But this distinctive American design proved to be only transiently successful.

A curious, self-contained community of hunters and manufacturers, the whale ship recovered its world-ranging function again and again, after crushing disasters to the fleet in three wars and in the Arctic ice. It was the earliest general advertisement of the quality of American genius at sea. It succumbed at last, not to the motorized whale hunters, but to a competitive product from a spouter of another sort.

Many ventures of American sail disappeared with the ready availability of a once abundant product. The lumber trade of Maine moved east by north, dwindling. Fishing fleets made a gradual transition from sail to explosions as their source of power. With a brief bright spot here and there the story of commercial sail after 1857 was only a prolonged farewell.

Upon such considerations, my book has been framed as follows: The remarkable achievements which can be called characteristically American cluster almost wholly within a period of a little more than half a century, beginning in the 1790s, ending in the 1850s. That the quality of these achievements may be appreciated, the world of water in the colonial period is briefly presented, with a focal glance or two at adventures foretelling the special sort of ingenuity which later became attached to the name Yankee.

Some attention is given also to ingenuities of the later period when survival was problem enough. Optimism nags us with the dark-day hope that bad times will change, that enterprises upon which we have wagered our careers will again be highly valued. This spirit carried several masters in sail onward to their final retirement from the sea, but many went over to steam. A small number refused both alternatives, most notably Joshua Slocum.

Some of the great pages of history are concerned with the manner in which capable men have comported themselves in the face of inevitable defeat. Captain Slocum defied the inevitable defeat of his calling by choosing to use the last years of his great skill as a seaman to practice his art for its own sake. His career gathers up with a startling symbolism the forces that inexorably thrust sail aside for commercial uses and, in doing so, gave it to the inspired amateurs. For his indomitable, quiet pioneering, Slocum deserves the highest amateur rank—not in the loose sense of the term, but in its pure meaning: a commitment based in nothing whatever but love.

It may seem odd that a book chiefly concerned with commercial sail should put, near its close, a strong emphasis upon little craft that attempted great voyages for reasons which vary from the frivolous to the inexplicable. But my central concern is with the American contribution as such: an often extravagant pioneering, characteristically the work of free individuals. The very fact that this aspect of the national character was frustrated in the deep-water carrying trade under canvas adds interest to its emergence as the way to personal fulfillment for some few indomitable men and women.

Oyster dredges photographed in Delaware Bay about 1939 by Graham L. Schofield. Note the dredge lines aft and the heavy deckload of oysters. This, probably the last widespread use of sail by preference in a commercial operation, was justified by the argument that other sources of power might damage the oyster beds.

Captain Slocum is so central a symbol that his little sloop-yawl the *Spray* has received special study. Some have assumed that she must have come closer to perfection in her lines, for the purpose of meeting all weathers, than any other craft of record. But the only lines we have for her seem to have been taken off carelessly and are suspect. Knowledgeable opinion now favors the view that she was little more than a beamy, comfortable sea boat, managed with a trained assurance so masterly that it surpasses the comprehension of most seafarers.

Year for year, American sail as a world-ranging commercial enterprise dwindles to a close in tune with the mischances of Slocum, that curious reverser: professional turned amateur. His downfall, from master-owner one afternoon to seaman on the beach next morning, with years ahead of no job offered, epitomizes the downfall of his calling. A few more ingenious attempts were made, such as the calamitous use of frugal big schooners in the deep-water trades. In the special case of oyster dredging a positive advocacy of sail persisted: sailing craft would not damage the oyster beds by too vigorous dragging, or foul them with engine exhaust products. But even the Delaware oystermen capitulated, about two decades ago. That ended the use of sail as a profit-making source of power except in a few commercial adjuncts to yachting.

A subject in itself, and a joyous one, yachting is noticed in this book for its influence upon naval architecture generally and to bring into perspective our latter-day national attitude toward the sea. I have given Buttersworth's remarkable painting of the yacht *America* a promi-

The first of *Punch's* several comments on the *America's* victory. This is a close facsimile drawn for the New York *Illustrated Daily News* within five weeks of the race itself. Caption from *Punch*:

MASTER JOHN BULL IN TROUBLE
Mr. Punch.—"Why, Johnny, what's the matter?"
Johnny.—"If you please, sir, there's a nasty ugly American been beating me."

nent place, not because her lines had much positive effect upon the design of commercial vessels, but because her triumph over England's best yachts swept the dust from all shipyard drafting boards. The uproar following the great day at Cowes in 1851 certainly did no harm to the fortunes of William H. Webb and of Donald McKay, shipbuilders who received many orders soon afterward from foreign firms and governments.

And what of our seaward view, as a people? A century ago every little town on our coasts still was close neighbor to the antipodes: an offshore sail might be making its first land-fall since Java Head. Now the spiky canvas against a summer horizon bespeaks day sailers almost exclusively. The rough career of the private wreckers who once roamed the eastern seaboard in a half-magnanimous, half-rapacious way has been taken over by government. There are few wrecks of the old sort that drove ashore in every considerable storm. The remaining deep-water voyagers under sail are the most dedicated amateurs of all. The peculiar American shift to yachting does need to be reviewed in any study of the American character under sail. It has developed in two ways, both characteristic of our country.

Ordinary citizens abroad had neither the leisure nor the means to be yachtsmen. American yachting likewise was the preserve of eminent functionaries until George Crowninshield decided early in the nineteenth century to display in foreign ports the evidences of a democratic opulence. Wealthy yachtsmen, using immaculately upkept yachts as surrogates for the splendors of hereditary aristocracy, used to be content to exhibit their own persons in the capacity of owners. In this century some of them have taken a well-deserved pride in their personal skill as racing skippers.

Crowninshield took his *Cleopatra's Barge*, forerunner of the opulent yachts, to the Mediterranean in 1816. About twenty years later an opposite, rough-and-tough sort of yachtsmanship had developed among the bay pilots of New York and other groups who prided themselves in the ownership of speedy small craft for use in their regular occupations. These are more nearly the forerunners of the multitudinous owners of modest sailing craft today, since personal participation was from the beginning taken for granted among them. The designing of yachts and pilot boats became an ambivalent endeavor, each class profiting. George Steers had produced some excellent pilot schooners before he drew the lines of the *America*.

The New York Yacht Club, although not the earliest, has been the symbol of organized yachting ever since its founding in 1844 at a meeting aboard the schooner *Gimcrack*. Its members participated in the original amateur ocean race, of 1866, between three yachts having an average length of 106 feet. Taking somewhat different routes, all three arrived within a few hours of each other in fourteen days or less, in an elapsed time that had been equaled by only a few of the big clippers. The winner, indeed, was driven across by the famous Captain Samuel Samuels, formerly of the medium clipper *Dreadnought*. He also took part in the other two notable ocean races of the century, in 1870 and 1887.

A port side view of the *Cleopatra's Barge*, showing the odd herringbone pattern that identified her. The starboard side had a band comprised of several horizontal stripes of different colors. Originally named the *Car of Concordia*, she was the first large American yacht owned by a private citizen. Captain George Crowninshield, Jr., had her built in 1816 and took her on a European cruise in the following year. The astronomer Baron Franz Xavier von Zach was astonished by the demonstration that the yacht's cook, William Chapman, a Negro, could work lunar observations by three different methods. The *Cleopatra's Barge,* which measured 191 tons, later became the royal yacht of King Kamehameha II of Hawaii.

The start of the great ocean yacht race off Sandy Hook Lightship, December 11, 1866. James Gordon Bennett, Jr.'s *Henrietta*, G. & F. Osgood's *Fleetwing*, and Pierre Lorillard's *Vesta*. Bennett's schooner won: 13 days, 21 hours, 45 minutes to the Needles of the Isle of Wight. The other two arrived about 9 hours later. From the print by Charles Parsons for Currier & Ives.

As the country grew richer and more complacent, the aggressive spirit, which had put the qualities of our yachts on exhibition in foreign waters, relaxed. Regattas, particularly at Newport, became an adjunct to the domestic world of fashion. But another sort of amateur of deep water was emerging, even before the first great ocean race. Forerunners of Slocum, who put their own lives upon the wager, began to challenge the Atlantic in small craft that at times were ludicrous. Some candidly sought glory, others were reticent. They patched together something that would float, at least for a first offing, and set sail. Characteristically they were too impatient to bother even with a shakedown cruise. More information on these phenomenal midgets appears on later pages. Here is a summary.

Two men and a dog sailed for London from New York in 1864, aboard the one-ton brigantine *Vision*. This first of the recorded midget vessels went missing, but a second made the crossing successfully two years later, a few months in advance of the famous race of the three large schooner yachts *Henrietta, Fleetwing,* and *Vesta.* At least sixteen other west-to-east passages have been completed by Americans in vessels no larger than Slocum's *Spray*. There have been five such east-to-west crossings. A majority, in both directions, were made single-handed. The midget voyagers mostly lacked financial resources, and scraped their outfits together with difficulty. Some skippers took their wives along for crew. At least one connubial challenger of the Atlantic, Captain Thomas Crapo, had a solid background of experience at sea. Others had little or none. William Andrews, who began without any deep-water experience, made two successful Atlantic crossings out of four starts. He tried it a fifth time with his wife aboard, in a 20-foot dory fatefully named the *Flying Dutchman*. A week out of Atlantic City, headed for Spain, they spoke a westbound steamer but were never reported thereafter.

Would this headstrong seeking of the ultimate adversary, close to a love of death for its own sake, have emerged if merchant sail had continued in good health? I think so, but not for Slocum, probably not for Crapo—men thrust seaward by a need to demonstrate, at least to themselves, a high competence which the world undervalued. These were not the only two who had suffered commercial ruin before they threw their challenges at the Western Ocean. Whether consciously or not, they likewise tossed an Olympian rebuke to a nation so preoccupied with its fattening midriff that it had become indifferent to the source of its life, the sea.

When American square-riggers had gone past their creative phases, and when schooner experimentation had become more abortive than fruitful, a few individual voyagers still persisted in the heroic tradition of American sail. However tiny and absurd their vessels, they carried forward with purity an enterprise that in its great days had turned essentially upon the decisions of free individuals, acknowledging fate, but scorning otherwise to commend their destinies to external deciders.

The first small craft to challenge the Atlantic appears to have been the brigantine *Vision*, not quite 16 feet long or a yard deep. If the Currier & Ives artist who observed her departure from the Battery for Liverpool, June 26, 1864, was as accurate as usual, she probably was carrying too much canvas for her beam of 4' 6''. Her skipper-owner was Captain John C. Donovan, her crew a Rhode Islander named William Spencer, her passenger the dog Toby. The *Vision* put in at Boston, leaking badly. She made a second offing after repairs, and was never reported.

Theodore De Bry's reverse copy of Adrianus Collaert's engraving derived from Jan van der Straet's allegorical view of Columbus discovering the New World. The closely observed structural details of the vessels are more confusing than helpful, blending realism and absurdity. Published in Franktort in 1594.

THE SEA *of* MARVELS

THE EARLY EXPLORERS AND COLONIZERS OF AMERICA SAILED UPON A SEA OF MARVELS, FROM which we are not yet quite certain that the last sea serpent has departed. The world swung open on the turn of the fifteenth century, and a whole new geography had to be made for the better convenience of mariners. The mood of vast uncertainty persisted for about a hundred years. Then, almost as suddenly, the turn of another century brought the beginnings of a scientific attitude to sweep away, not all of the marvels, but most of the misconceptions. It is against this sixteenth century of enormous transition that the achievements of American sail at a later date need first to be considered. The American contribution, as I hope to show, was pragmatic, impetuous, scientific rather more by luck than by theory.

Some European stay-at-homes contributed remarkably to nautical science, but they had to work with the news brought back by seamen; and more seamen were turned toward the New World by a dispersal of pictorial as well as written evidence. Europe got its first widely distributed, detailed views of the Americas through engravings, chiefly those of Théodore de Bry, who did much of his work in England although he was a Fleming by birth. The plates

Adrianus Collaert's engraving of Jan van der Straet's allegorical view of the supposed discovery of South America by Amerigo Vespucci. Published by Philip Galle at Antwerp, about 1585, together with the original engraving of which the one at the left is a reverse copy. De Bry also made an unacknowledged copy of this plate.

shown above celebrate the two most famous persons associated with the early use of sail in American seas. I give them here, not as contemporaneous evidence (they were made about a century too late for that), but to indicate the state of mind from which scientific navigation had to take its departure. They serve also to call attention at outset to some of the problems of historical truth in pictures. The Columbus plate is from De Bry's *Collection of Voyages,* but De Bry copied it without acknowledgment from one of a series of four plates published about 1585 by Adrianus Collaert, who in turn had based his work upon drawings by Jan van der Straet. De Bry has been praised for the fine accuracy with which he observed the structure of shipping. In this case he observed, with a slavish accuracy, only the previous engraver's work, which itself was based in the conventionalized oddities of van der Straet. The engraving of Amerigo Vespucci is reproduced from Collaert's original series. All three artists were taking for granted the richly baroque symbolism that rioted on the waters as well as ashore in the last, restless phase of the Renaissance. Science had not yet been separated out from the emotional perceptions of the whole human being. It was still usual to personalize abstract ideas. Bounty was a goddess with a cornucopia.

At a quick glance, for example, it might seem that the Triton and his mermaid-lady under the bows of Vespucci's quaint vessel have each an arm too many. Perhaps so, for they are cannibals, gripping torn parts of a human body, and thus symbolizing an old danger of the sea that had become particularly notorious in reports from America. The oldest surviving illustration showing natives of America, made about eighty years earlier, was of a cannibal feast. Several of De Bry's later engravings stress the theme of cannibalism, with a gruesome exactitude here muted in allegory. (When De Bry pirated the Vespucci plate, he gave the Triton a leg to hold, in place of Collaert's arm.)

Van der Straet, in his originals, balanced Diana for Columbus against Minerva for Vespucci, stressing, I suppose, the role of the hunter seeking the unknown against that of the extender of knowledge. Historical scholarship had not yet exposed the element of falsity, perhaps the work of unscrupulous publishers, in Vespucci's writings.

Systematic colonization of inhospitable, remote coasts—a fair description of the Atlantic edge of territory that became the original thirteen states—could be accomplished in sailing vessels only after reliable devices of navigation had replaced trial and error in such a sea of marvels. The reasonably well-authenticated colonies of the Northmen all vanished. A pattern of vanishing persisted, with the French and English, at Roanoke and elsewhere, until

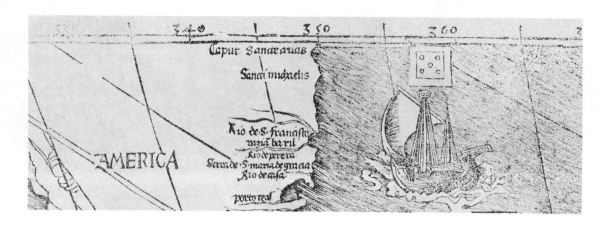

If American sail as a subject begins with the naming of America itself, then it carries from its origins the sort of problem which anyone concerned for the truth of pictorial evidence has to keep constantly in mind. In 1504 a Florentine, Amerigo Vespucci, sent to his former patrons the Medici an account of four voyages to lands beyond the Atlantic. His original account has disappeared, but condensations of it were translated. One of the translators was a German geographer, Martin Waldseemüller, who in 1507 or perhaps a bit earlier issued two maps upon which the name America first occurs. The map from which a small section is reproduced above was accompanied by verses in praise of Vespucci written by the Humanist poet Matthias Ringmann, along with a prose statement containing this passage: "a fourth part has been discovered by Americus Vespucius . . . wherefore I do not see what is rightly to hinder us from calling it Amerige or America." Until recently it has been assumed that Waldseemüller himself performed this most effective deliberate act of naming. However, in *Erkunde* for September 1959, Franz Laubenberger argued that Ringmann was the magical namer. Anyhow, Waldseemüller was responsible for placing the word on his own map and for the accompanying prose and verse, whoever may have written them. It seems clear that nobody, in 1507, had accumulated enough observations of the South American coast to judge such an account against other evidence. Vespucci's claim to have discovered the mainland of South America was not seriously disputed for more than three centuries. Most scholars nowadays believe that he did conduct extensive explorations in the later voyages, but that the first one, upon which the honor of having his name bestowed upon two continents depends, is mythical. Laubenberger implies that the mapmaker himself soon became aware of the alleged error into which he may have been led by his friend Ringmann. After Ringmann's death in 1511 Waldseemüller dropped the name America from his maps and never used it again. He was too late, however, to erase it from the usage of a world that liked it, right or wrong. The inference is that even carefully gathered contemporaneous evidence can lead a graphic artist astray. He may commit worse lapses of conventionality. The ship above is an inland mapmaker's ornament, a hundred years out of date when it was drawn.

The regions of the trade winds, between the tropics of "Cancri" and "Capricorni," had been mapped by 1507 with a rough idea of their real configuration. The inhospitable, remote coast north of Florida was still being guessed at. Japan was placed where it would have overlapped the western coast of Mexico, not yet visited by Europeans. This cartouche from Waldseemüller's large map (of which a portion appears on the opposite page) presents a contemporaneous portrait of Vespucci. Scholars dismiss the possibility that it was engraved from a likeness—but note the mole on the left cheek.

about a century after the permanent colonization of the temperate Caribbean. More southerly shores and islands, in the reliable trade-wind belts, could sustain life at all seasons without much foresight. They had that margin of advantage. Even hurricanes came in known months and were thus avoidable. The North Atlantic was swept by many of the same hurricanes and by savage winter storms as well. Summer brought sou'easters and perilous fogs. Voyagers often found themselves out in their reckoning by hundreds of miles, on a coast that included the shoals of Hatteras and of Nantucket among its many dangers.

Lawrence C. Wroth, in his essay *The Way of a Ship,* calls this approximate period the "Century of Error." Many schemes were brought forward to improve navigation, but most of them were based in a misconception of the physical world. It is a pleasant curiosity in the history of conceptual thought that a deliberate distortion of reality, propounded in 1569 by Gerardus Mercator, provided the chief device through which the average seaman could plot his course with accuracy and "keep track" as he went along; but this possible application of Mercator's projection, for sea charts, was not brought to the point of use until the end of the century. A summary of existing knowledge of navigation and shipbuilding was written and published in Mexico City fifty-two years before the first press was established in what is now the United States. In applied nautical theory, as in so many other matters, no significant contribution was made by the more northerly areas until the thirteen colonies had confirmed their independence. From Diego García de Palacio's Mexican treatise of 1587 I have included one of the four illustrations accompanying his "rules of thumb." Such concepts of measurement, involving the human body, persisted through the century of error—and long afterward in popular usage.

23

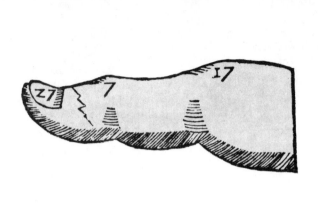

LEFT. The Mexican navigator García de Palacio's first rule of thumb for calculating an astronomical cycle. García lived with confidence in an extendable present. He evidently assumed that his book would still be in use in A.D. 2500, to which date his four rules of thumb carry the formula. CENTER. The naturalist Rondelet said he received this drawing and the attendant description of a sea monk from that "tresillustre dame Marguerite de Valois," Queen of Navarre. Gesner included it without question in his *Historiae Animalium* of 1588, from which this reversed woodcut, almost identical with Rondelet's, is taken. RIGHT. Rondelet's sea bishop. A specimen was introduced to the King of Poland in 1531, but it indicated by signs that it preferred the underwater life. Taken back to the shore, it immediately plunged from view. A reversed woodcut from Gesner's compendium of animals. The naturalist Rondelet saw letters in Rome which convinced him of the truth of this account.

In 1599 Edward Wright issued one of the few books that have absolute importance in their effects upon the history of the Western world. The author is not included among the six Wrights given special articles in the *Encyclopædia Britannica,* nor even among the twenty or more Wrights in other encyclopedias. Yet his book, just at the century's end, is one of the great pivots upon which applied science has turned toward clarity and order: *Certaine Errors in Nauigation, Arising either of the ordinarie erroneous making or vsing of the Sea Chart, Compasse, Crosse staffe, and Tables of declination of the Sunne, and fixed Starres detected and corrected.* For an adequate realization of the contribution one should glance over it side by side with other scientific works of about the same time: The "Century of Error" witnessed, for example, a gradual development of the old bestiaries into orderly scientific descriptions of fishes and other animals. I have before me the *Libri de Piscibus Marinis* of Guilielmus Rondeletius, which is full of woodcuts of fishes rendered in the 1550s with such precision that they are instantly recognizable as species in the European fish markets of today. Mixed right in with the others are the two sea creatures reproduced on this page, described with a similar care, accounted for by citation of the places and dates of their observation. Rondeletius's book, incorporated into Konrad von Gesner's *Historia Animalium,* was the basic treatise on fishes until the eighteenth century. It was not so much gullibility, perhaps, that carried the mythology of the sea into recent times as it was a reluctance to reject the well attested. Seamen have always brought home strange tales, sometimes with tongue in cheek, sometimes colored by hallucinations of thirst or disease, sometimes preposterous fact later verified. It is only the attribution of semihuman qualities to these sea creatures that makes them any more remarkable than, say, that incredible creature the giant squid—or even that commonplace improbability the whale.

The sea of marvels persisted long after the austere separation of nautical science from rule of thumb. It is the more astonishing that Edward Wright was able, in this context of myth and symbol, to perceive a sort of crystal cylinder embracing the sidereal globe, as a

LEFT. The sixteenth century mermaid was sometimes surprising. Early voyagers to Newfoundland were troubled by a particularly nasty one with blue hair. This noticeably female but unenticing "Monstrum Marinum" appears in Gesner's history of animals, along with the whale, dolphin, and starfish. RIGHT. Gesner's Hydra must have been sired by Cerberus, if the facial expressions are indicative. The two marine creatures on this page do not appear in the earlier separate work of Rondelet, who contributed most of the fishes and marine mammals to the comprehensive work of Gesner.

means to the construction of a sea chart upon which curving voyages would become straight lines of constant compass direction. Wright, like Nathaniel Bowditch, the great American contributor to practical navigation who was to emerge almost exactly two centuries later, was a mathematician first of all, with experience at sea additional. It is likely that on a voyage to the Azores, Wright discussed problems of navigation with Captain John Davis. Perhaps not, because Davis was in a different ship of the fleet. At any rate, these two members of a single expedition made the two great basic advances in navigational equipment that turned rule-of-thumb into precise science. Wright worked out the mathematical principles of the Mercator projection and showed how it could be used to make sea charts in which planned distortion led to a precise result. Davis invented, first the backstaff, then its more accurate form, the quadrant.

Many others were at work on such problems in the 1590s. Hariot developed a Mercator chart independently, for the secret advantage of a few. It is the book that counts, making knowledge widely available. Wright did not publish his own manuscript until stolen portions of it—like the actors' copies of Shakespeare's play—began to appear. He was particularly annoyed when the Flemish mapmaker Judocus Hondius, to whom he had described in confidence his adaptation of Mercator's projection, published charts of the sort without even an acknowledgment. Displaying a modesty not always to be counted on in those times, Wright wrote in 1610, "So far as I can yet learn I first published to the world the exact way to make the parts of the meridians and parallels keep the correct proportions."

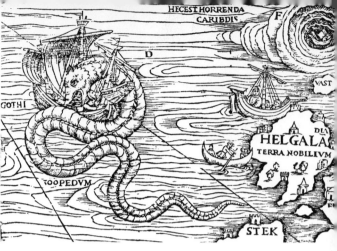

ABOVE, RIGHT. The sea serpent from the 1539 marine chart of Olaus Magnus is described with some detail in the good bishop's *History of the Northern People*: not a type but a particular individual, 200 feet long and 20 feet thick, who lived at a known point from which he ranged the coast of Norway. "He hath commonly hair hanging from his neck a Cubit long, and sharp Scales, and is black, and he hath flaming shining eyes. This snake disquiets the Shippers, and he puts up his head on high like a pillar, and catcheth away men, and he devours them." Gesner, recognizing it as a beast that swims all waters traversed by sailors, copied it by reversed woodcut for his *Historiae Animalium*—accurately enough, but with the tail disposed for better economy of space in the text. Such continuance of information from book to book frequently involved distortions, deliberate or careless. Gesner, if incautious about some reports he accepted, had the scrupulous scientific attitude, which rules out capricious changes in data. Commenting upon the map made by Bishop Olaus, the marine scholar E. G. R. Taylor has said, ". . . the title of Carta Marina is a misnomer, for certainly no mariner could have made use of it: the errors in the western sea area are grotesque. . . . In the matter of sea-monsters the map has, indeed, no rival . . ."

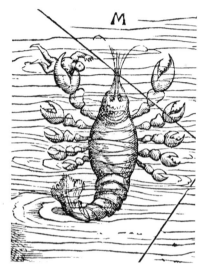

The Carta Gotha Marina, prepared in 1539 by Olaus Magnus, Bishop of Uppsala, presents an unrestrained view of the dangers of seafaring, as the three samples of its many cautionary embellishments will suggest.

About thirty years later, the mood was shifting toward the satirical. The *Theatrum Orbis Terrarum* of Ortelius, first of the widely distributed true world atlases, poked fun in 1570 at the tales of ferocious beasts of the sea of marvels.

26

The sons of Hondius, nineteen years after his death, thought it only fair to honor Mercator by placing him on a par with their father in the huge title-page engraving of the atlas which they issued in 1630. The artist allowed for the comparative ages of the two subjects: Mercator was fifty-one years older than Hondius, and lived to be eighty-two. The contribution of Wright is still nowhere acknowledged, unless he is the little dog by the armillary sphere. Here, in contrast with the animate symbolism of Van der Straet, the baroque impulse has stiffened from gods and mythic beasties into stilted, ornate furniture. The old, wild intermingling of flesh and instrument is gone. Maps issued from the firm of Hondius, by comparison with those of their predecessors, announce that the sea of marvels is conquered, at least for the learned. The surviving beasts have become conventionalized decorations. Permanent colonization of the American coast north of the Caribbean—thanks to Wright, Davis, and the unknown contriver of the mariner's compass—has been accomplished. The era of native American sail can have its hesitant beginnings.

To proceed from Olaus to Ortelius, a third of a century across the sea of marvels, is to leave the grim and gloomy north for a world of grace and light. It is hard to understand why anyone would have wanted to go voyaging with the Bishop of Uppsala for a mentor. The maps and charts of Abraham Ortel of Antwerp invited the seafarer to the voyage, and counseled him not to worry. Even if his gear aloft should give way before the tempest, the sea beasts that might come to investigate were more curious than malign: a cask or two thrown overboard would divert them. His mermaids re-established the species of classical times, the unattainable but seductive muddle of Atergatis, the fish-tailed Semitic goddess, and Aphrodite rising from the sea. This northeast corner of the Indiae Orientalis shows America still leaning close to Japan, which is oddly contoured but perhaps is intended only to express reports of the southerly minor island of Kyushu. If so, it is fairly well related to the adjacent China coast, which is in surprisingly good shape.

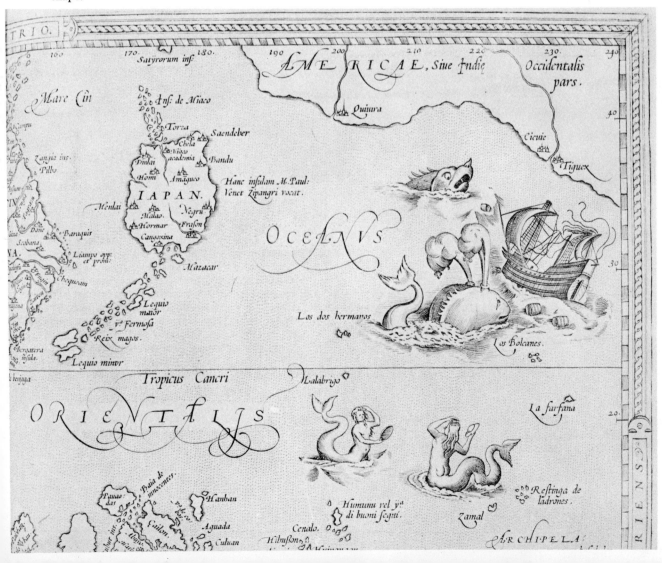

ABOVE. The pictorial pretitle page of the great Mercator-Hondius atlas of 1630 seems to announce that able men have achieved order out of distant report. There is nothing mythic or perilous about the last beast in evidence, a docile tapestry retriever, subordinate to the armillary sphere. The chart is given, of course, the place of first honor—but a pair of cross-staffs, favored by most seamen long after better instruments were available, completes the scene. LEFT. Milford Haven, on a chart by Hondius. "The best and most commodious harbor in Britain for the trade with America" has been little used because of the difficulties, for navigators, in its approaches. The sea beasts have become as conventionalized as the vessel.

COLONIAL VENTURERS: 1

"IT IS SINGULARLY EXASPERATING THAT THERE IS SO LITTLE AUTHENTIC INFORMATION IN existence regarding the ships and boats that have figured in some of the most dramatic scenes of American history. Human nature seems to demand pictures of such episodes whether facts are available or not, and the landing of the Pilgrims at Plymouth has led to paintings and engravings no less absurd than Mrs. Hemans' too frequently quoted verses."

So commences the leading editorial in the *American Neptune* for January 1950, which goes on to say, "It is equally exasperating when artists engaged in historical reconstruction insist upon evolving improbable craft out of their heads." One finds references to "the best model" of the *Mayflower,* made by the first-rate scholar R. C. Anderson. Yet Anderson claimed only to have produced an assemblage of authentic contemporary details of other vessels. In spite of that, the phrase "best model" is used as if it meant the most faithful to a known original—when no details of the original *Mayflower* are known.

Improbable craft contrived out of the artist's imagination have a less objectionable counterpart in the well-observed structure that happens to be an anachronism. The picture reproduced on this page is from Peter Parley's charming school history of 1832. It is meant to portray the three vessels that carried the first settlers to Jamestown in 1607. Instead it presents two topsail schooners and a sloop of the sort common in the year of the book's preparation. The artist has at least looked at his history, because the sizes roughly reflect recorded measurements: 100 tons, 40 tons, and 20 tons. We know nothing of the rig of the two larger vessels. The third was a "pinnesse," a name given to a variety of small sailing craft of three hundred or four hundred years ago, and also to ships' boats of medium size over a much longer period.

A forthright anachronism. Vessels of "Peter Parley's" own period used to illustrate an account of the Jamestown landing 225 years earlier.

Fishermen, trying their luck far offshore, were the first routine transatlantic voyagers. Their practical developing of small carriers that would consistently come home again must have influenced the explorers' choice of the Vlieboot, or flyboat, as a shallow-water auxiliary to explore the coast lines and inlets. This fisherman is enlarged from one of Theodore De Bry's plates showing a typical European harbor, and is probably a coastal craft. The standard Vlieboot, as used on the river Vlie itself, was much larger, but the rig was similar. Intermediate sizes were safer than large Vlieboots in heavy weather.

The largest of the Jamestown vessels is recorded as the *Sarah* (or *Susan*) *Constant* (or *Content*), and the middling one as the *Goodspeed* (or *Godspeed*). The smallest was unambiguously the *Discovery*. A scrupulous artist has these names and tonnages to go on, and nothing else. The issue of the *American Neptune* from which I have taken my opening quotation carries a discussion by Griffith Baily Coale of the sources he studied for his fine but supposititious murals of the Jamestown landing. "There is little data," he admits, "on small English merchantmen at the dawn of the seventeenth century and there is no information as to the previous history or origin of any of the three vessels concerned."

I have tried, in selecting pictures for this book, not to be tempted by even such persuasive synthetic productions as those of Commander Coale.

Jamestown was not the first English settlement in southern Virginia. Sir Walter Raleigh's lost colony of Roanoke preceded it. Raleigh's efforts to relieve his colonial venturers were hindered by the sputtering war with Spain, but also by difficulties of navigation. Rescuers who arrived nearly three years late found only the mysterious word CROATOAN carved on a tree for romancers to speculate upon.

The coast from Florida to Labrador had been frequently visited, and mapped as well as most, in the middle part of the sixteenth century. The problem was to come twice to the same coastal intricacy, on schedule. The popular concept of an empty Atlantic, with a vessel or two braving the unknown, is incorrect for the period. The Western Ocean teemed with shipping, but much of it was punitive or piratical, or engaged in the fisheries.

French and Basque vessels were fishing in large numbers off the Newfoundland coast soon after its official "discovery" by Giovanni Caboto in 1497. The ancient secretiveness of fishermen cloaked a widespread earlier voyaging to the Grand Banks. Sixty French vessels were counted off Newfoundland in 1541. The same number set out from French ports in mid-winter of 1544, within a two-month period. Captain Edward Haies, on the expedition that proved fatal to Sir Humphrey Gilbert, reported seeing "sometimes an hundred or more sailes of ships. . . . During the time of fishing, a man shall know without sounding when he is vpon the banke, by the incredible multitude of sea foule houering ouer the same, to pray vpon the offalles & garbish of fish throwen out by fishermen." That was shortly before the Spanish Armada involved in its own ruin the Basque Newfoundland fleet of more than two hundred sail. Craft of modest size, that could regularly cross the most dangerous part of the North Atlantic in winter for the spring fishing, had obviously been perfected before the Elizabethan age of exploration began. The next step—permanent colonization of undeveloped coasts, peopled by nomads with no surplus wealth—awaited the opening of the seventeenth century, when the coast lines traced by Richard Hakluyt's voyagers could be transferred by Wright's mathematics to charts on the Mercator projection.

The story of local American sail begins in the region where it had its longest successful survival—in the northeasterly part of Virginia, as it then was called, later the Province, County, or District, and after 1820 the State, of Maine. Monhegan Island, already a fisher-man's rendezvous, was the meeting place in August 1607, of the *Mary and John* and the *Gift of God*. With the prudence of most early expeditions, this one sponsored by Chief Justice Sir John Popham consisted of a sizable transport and a "flyboat" to explore the shallow inlets. The light-draft flyboat *Gift of God* was blown far to leeward, but the competent navigation of Captain George Popham brought her to the agreed rendezvous. "One Digby of London," a master shipwright, was a member of the expedition.

When the colonists had established themselves on the west bank of the Kennebec, Captain Robert Davies returned to England in the *Mary and John* to bring out supplies "betymes the next yeare." The colonists "fully finished the fort, trencht and fortified yt with twelve pieces of ordnance, and built fifty howses therein, besides a church and a storehouse; and the carpenters framed a pretty Pynnace of about some thirty tonne, which they called the *Virginia.*"

The Maine tradition of shipbuilding began very well indeed. Chief Shipwright Digby built from green wood a vessel that had a valiant career. The *Virginia* of Sagadahoc, as she has come to be called to distinguish her from many other *Virginia*s, made several transatlantic passages and continued in service for twenty years. Her size was about that of Slocum's *Spray,* and 50 per cent larger than the *Discovery* of the fleet which in the same year had sailed to Jamestown from England. For comparison it is worth noting that the two surviving vessels in which Sir Humphrey Gilbert's 1583 expedition sailed for home, the *Golden Hind* and the *Squirrel,* measured 40 and 10 tons, respectively.

Espionage is not often appreciated by those against whom it is practiced, but it can be a wonderful boon to historians. It was an act of espionage that preserved for us what has been thought by some to be a close portrait of the *Virginia* of Sagadahoc. One of the Popham colonists, John Hunt, prepared a draft of St. George's Fort which he dated 8 October 1607 (18 October by the corrected calendar). This draft was taken back to England where it passed somehow into the possession of Don Pedro de Zuñiga, the Spanish ambassador in

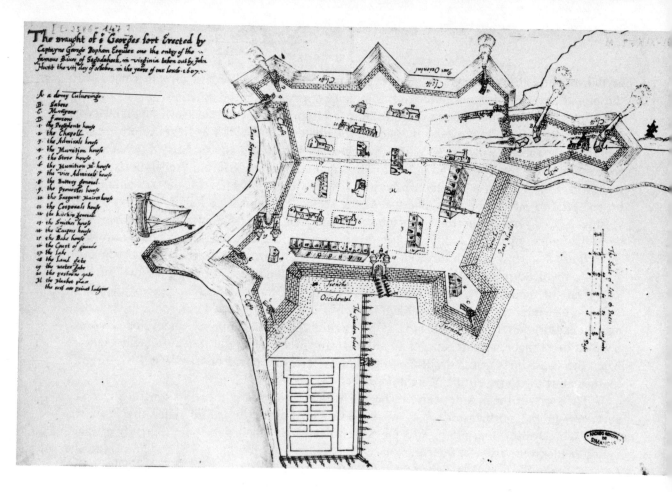

This 1607 "draught of Sᵗ Georges fort" is probably the earliest drawing, made on the North American coast, that presents a dated view of a fore-and-aft rigged vessel. Lift this leaf to compare the enlargement on page 33 with the similar European fisherman on page 30.

London. Don Pedro had been instructed to keep a careful eye on the activities of the English colonizing companies. Consequently he sent Hunt's draft of the Popham colony's fort off to Philip III in September of 1608, together with a map and a report of Virginia "given me by a person who has been there."

These documents are still preserved at Simancas in Spain, where a hand-drawn copy of Hunt's plan of the fort was made about seventy years ago for inclusion in Alexander Brown's documentary collection *The Genesis of the United States.* A small vessel appears on the margin. It has been reproduced before, from the line cut in Brown's book, as a probable picture of the *Virginia* of Sagadahoc. If this were true, it would extend backward by more than a century the pictorial history of specific American sailing vessels. It seemed advisable in such circumstances to go to the source, and I have consequently secured, through the kindness of Señor Ricardo Magdaleno, director of the Archivo General de Simancas, a photographic copy here reproduced. An enlargement proves that the "facsimile" was drawn with some care. Details become clearer. There is no doubt that a spritsail is intended, whereas the hand-drawn copy (certainly not the work of a sailor) might be thought to portray a drooping pair of peak lines. The state of things forward of the mast is puzzling in the "facsimile." A headsail furled to the forestay might seem to be intended. In the photocopy the sail obviously is set and drawing.

Did a spy make a contemporaneous, hand-drawn copy of Hunt's American draft? Señor

Magdaleno thinks that the plan now at Simancas is the actual original. The handwriting is typically English of the period.

Assuming that it is at least a careful espionage copy, what sort of case can be made for the further assumption that the little vessel is the *Virginia?* She is not well placed for merely decorative effect. The stone-buttressed structure adjacent is a jetty. It seems more likely that she is shown under sail near it to emphasize the location of the landing place, down to which a ramp leads from the "water gate." The artist has rendered with care the differing structures of the houses, and has distinguished by size between the four sorts of artillery, from the single culverin to the three light falcons. The bakehouse looks like a bakehouse. All details are crude, but with a sort of scrupulous crudity. I assume that the same rough care of observation is involved in the drawing of a vessel actually present off the jetty.

But is she the *Virginia?* I doubt it because there would hardly have been time or reason to build her in the period of less than two months between the landing, on August 19th, when work was commenced on the fort, and the making of the draft dated "the viii day of october." What we know of the enterprise is derived chiefly from William Strachey's *The First decade of The Histoirie of Travaile into Virginia Britannia,* published five years later. Strachey is not the most orderly of historians, but his sequence of events puts the framing of the "pretty Pynnace" last. The odd placing of the vessel on the draft does suggest one other possibility. It was not until the 15th of December (Christmas day by the revised calendar) that the supply vessel with the plan aboard sailed for England. Although the plan of the fort is dated in early October, the little vessel may have been awkwardly crowded in just before the dispatch of documents, to bring this one up to date.

So much for the fascinations of pure guesswork. What matters is the portrayal, on a plan probably made in America in 1607, of a fore-and-after very similar in rig to vessels frequently appearing at a somewhat later date in pictures of European harbors. Turn back to page 30. Here is an enlarged detail from De Bry's engraving of the traveler Girolamo Benzoni's arrival, on his way to America, at San Lucar, the port from which Columbus also sailed for the New World. The engraver admits that his shore establishments are imaginary. He had no picture of San Lucar de Barrameda to copy. But the closely observed shipping resembles other harbor scenes of his which survive critical comparison with independent contemporary sources. His little fisherman probably was drawn from life. She is of a type developed in the Low Countries, used widely in the seventeenth century, and affords the only precisely dated example I have happened to notice of what looks like a spritsail-headsail combination earlier than the spritsail and headsail seen off the jetty of the Popham colony. The rig thus seems to have been based in at least thirteen years of prior European experience.

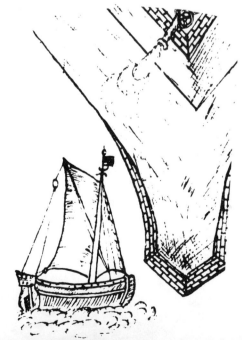

". . . having in the time of their abode there (notwithstanding the coldness of the season, and the small help they had), built a pretty bark of their own, which served them to good purpose, as easing them in their returning." This phrase from *A briefe Relation of the Discovery and Plantation of New England,* 1622, possibly refers to the vessel in this picture, drawn at the Popham colony on the Kennebec in the fall of 1607. It is more probably the flyboat which brought out some of the colonists under the command of Captain George Popham. The English name seems to have come from the Dutch Vlieboot, and the Flemish engraver De Bry shows a Vlieboot almost identical with this one in his 1594 engraving (page 30) of Benzoni's arrival at San Lucar de Barrameda. The earliest published account of the Popham colony calls the vessel built there a pinnace. The only precise references to the rig of pinnaces in American waters imply that they had two masts.

Human beings, in early delineations of sailing vessels, are often enlarged out of scale. Allowance should be made for this conventional practice when judging the intended size of De Bry's fishing vessel. I think from her fittings that she was meant to be a coastal fisherman, a smaller version of the modest vessels employed on the Grand Banks. A rig and hull long tested in this service would be a logical choice for the mutually inconsistent functions of crossing the unpredictable Western Ocean in safety and exploring shallow inlets upon arrival.

If the vessel on the draft of St. George's Fort is meant to be a portrait, she thus is more probably the flyboat *Gift of God* than the *Virginia*. This photocopy should at least settle some arguments over the date at which fore-and-aft sail, particularly the headsail, came into use in America. L. G. Carr Laughton, in a recent number of the *Mariner's Mirror,* says that but for one doubtful representation "the jib is not known to have been used before 1600." It appears to have been in use on De Bry's fisherman of 1594, and certainly had migrated to America at least by 1607.

Four of John White's water colors, made between 1585 and 1587 in or near the region still called Virginia, include high-pooped three-masters of the period, carrying square sail except for a lateen mizzen. A few small craft are included, at perspective distances that make the intent of the brush strokes uncertain, but they seem to be carrying each a single square sail. The common assertion that the *Virginia* of Sagadahoc was the first sailing vessel built on the coasts north of the Caribbean should perhaps be qualified. One of John White's water colors carries the notation: "The XIth of Maie the General in the Tyger arriued at St. John's Iland where he fortified in this manner, toke in fresh water and buylt a Pynnes, And then departed from thence the XXIIIth of the same month. 1585." The sketch includes a boat with oars, in the river, and a simultaneous representation of the same craft, inverted, just after caulking, on the beach. Pinnace is an ambiguous descriptive noun. "Buylt" probably means "assembled." The craft called a Pynnes was probably a rowboat. In the highly crowded conditions of transatlantic travel, it was an early practice to carry small boats taken apart. These then were assembled upon arrival, without a need for hand-fashioning and fairing. Here, as in the case of the Popham colony, it seems unlikely that a sizable vessel could have been completed so quickly while a fort was being built as well—in this case in the total period of twelve days.

The claim that the *Virginia* of Sagadahoc was the first sailing product of North American shipbuilding thus seems reasonable, despite White's report of Sir Richard Grenville's "Pynnes." Since there is no evidence that the latter was a sailing vessel, I have not included White's picture, which can be found on page [185] of Stefan Lorant's *The New World.*

RIGHT. An Eskimo *umiak,* or skin boat, possibly a survival, with a minimum of structural change, from Irish and Viking influences of the pre-Columbian period. I can find no convincing evidence that sail was used by American aborigines. The earliest reports of native sail all are dated a few years after foreigners had entered the regions in question, with sailing craft that the natives probably imitated. Fanciful illustrators have confused the record. The picture at the left is from the 1855 edition of Gonzalo Fernández de Oviedo y Valdés's *Historia General* . . . , written early in the sixteenth century. The use of double canoes to transport horses is described in the text as a notable invention, but Oviedo nowhere hints that they carried any kind of sail. This queer rig, with no provision for its management, would have been a seaman's nightmare.

If, as seems likely, the *Virginia* of Sagadahoc was the first specifically identifiable sailing vessel built on the Atlantic coast of North America, a more basic question remains. Western historians have had a smug way of assuming that history began, everywhere, when the first European turned up. What sort of sailing craft were made in America before the usurpers arrived? I have found no credible evidence that the American aborigines were sailors. Some on the Pacific coast of South America may possibly have been, but the recorded early observations of sail in use by native Americans seem always to have been made after the art could have been acquired from the conquerors themselves. The sort of "scholar" who can reconstruct his apish ancestor, all complete, out of a splinter of jawbone, can as confidently trace upon the pre-Balboan South Sea a pattern of trade routes of balsa sailing rafts. Girolamo Benzoni saw rafts under sail on the coast of Peru when the Spaniards had been numerous in these waters for two or three decades. His *History of the New World,* first published in 1565, contains a woodcut of one. Great importance has been put by some writers upon an engraving in J. van Spilbergen's *Miroir Oost & West Indical,* Leiden, 1619, of a two-masted Peruvian fore-and-aft rigged raft—but Spilbergen had observed it a full century after the first European sailors reached this coast. There are other references, all so late and abbreviated that they have no authority comparable to that of reports from early voyagers to Polynesia who saw native sail on the day of arrival.

Similar, perhaps greater, uncertainties confront us in the case of the Eskimos. Hans Egede, who tried in 1721 to make contact with the lost Greenland colonies of Norsemen, reported native sailing craft. He also reported a huge sea serpent. Sir Martin Frobisher, a century and a half earlier, seems to have encountered nothing but kayaks, an excessively sporty craft too unstable to sustain a sail in any event. Male Eskimos reserved the kayak exclusively for themselves. The larger umiak, the women's boat, has frequently been observed under sail, but many features of its structure support the assumption that the hull may have been derived from the seafaring skin boats of Ireland and the rig from the Norsemen. Nobody really knows. Dr. Vilhjalmur Stefansson, by whose kindness I am able to use the photograph on page 35, suggests that the sailing umiak may be a direct and continuous descendant of influences originating about a thousand years ago, in the times of Eric the Red. If this is so, Eskimos are probably the earliest and longest users of strictly American sail.

COLONIAL VENTURERS: 2

SHIPBUILDING WAS THE INEVITABLE MAJOR INDUSTRY OF EARLY COLONIAL AMERICA. THE investment required was much more of energy than of wealth. Any firm and gently sloping bit of shore line was the factory. Materials could be had for the cutting, a few feet away. It was possible to build seaworthy vessels almost entirely of wood, with wooden fastenings, to bring in the hemp and iron not available locally.

What record we have of the first century of intense activity is statistical rather than pictorial. The growing importance of native American shipping is revealed in the Navigation Acts of 1660 and 1663. Their aim was to operate the commerce of the colonies to the advantage of Great Britain rather than to that of the colonies themselves. Sir Josiah Child, generally regarded as a liberal economist, warned in 1668, "in my poor opinion there is nothing more prejudicial and in prospect more dangerous to any mother kingdom than the increase in shipping in her colonies."

The acts were again stiffened, in 1673 and 1696, to prevent both the exportation and the importation, by the colonies, of any goods or manufactures except by way of Great Britain. Coming or going, all cargoes had to be unloaded at a British port for taxation. The laws of supply and demand thus operated only within boundaries set by legal monopoly. The American shipper might accept an offer for his cargo while it was on shore in England, to save the expense of getting it aboard again and discharging it a second time. But this incentive, foreseen in drafting the Navigation Acts, resulted in a continuous depression in the net prices received by American exporters amounting to no less than the tax exacted in transit to a third country. Special permission had to be secured for re-exportation of many products. There appears to have been a deliberate policy of delay in granting these licenses, which further pressed the American shipmaster to accept the best British offer he could get.

Trade between adjacent colonies, except in vessels owned in Great Britain, was also hindered. The northern colonies and the Caribbean islands each produced basic materials which the other region lacked or found it too costly to exploit. The basic traffic was in salt

The headpiece of this chapter is a reproduction of the cartouche of the Extrema Americæ map in Blaeu's atlas of 1662, emphasizing the colonial economy based upon fish.

fish to feed slaves who produced sugar and rum which could be exchanged for all the necessaries of fishermen. The logic of this fundamental economy fostered shipbuilding and the rearing up of seamen, both to secure the product and to deliver it to the consumer. Yet there was a constant British effort, for more than a century prior to the Revolution provoked by that policy, to protect shipbuilding and the rearing of seamen at home by hampering both activities in the colonies.

Letters of instruction, from owners to shipmasters, often were candid on the question of evading the Navigation Acts in any possible way. Such a system of privilege fosters its own downfall, encouraging routine corruption in minor officials. They amiably changed the registry of New England vessels in the Caribbean to cloak an illegal trade between the British islands and the colonies of other countries. The duties would have gone home to England. The bribes remained in the tax collector's pocket. It is surprising that so much documentary evidence of illegal practices survives when other meaningful records of marine activity are scanty or lacking. The candid claim of virtue, for frustrating bad law, was to mount to the level of proud public violence some years in advance of the military phase of our Revolution. The Boston Tea Party, the most famous occasion, was only one of many.

In spite of the calculated hampering of maritime enterprise in the colonies, it grew steadily. The dramatic achievements at sea that followed American independence proceeded from long practice in the means of checkmating arbitrary power. Full freedom was needed to bring full innovation into play. The earlier efforts were hampered by their own conspiratorial aspects: it was meritorious to frustrate a tyrannical statute, but the accomplishment should not be openly advertised. An unusually swift and handy vessel was suspect for these very qualities, before 1783.

A British report, exactly one hundred years prior to the Declaration of Independence, noted that Massachusetts had become a surplus producer of grain and meat as well as of the first staple, fish. Manufactured lumber, including barrel staves, clapboards, and shingles, in addition to masts and spars, was being produced abundantly for export. Timber that could not be readily transported down the inland waterways was being burned for potash and charcoal, two of the three ingredients of gunpowder. Most of the potash was exported. The Massachusetts Bay Colony, in this year 1676, owned "430 ships of from 30 to 250 tons that

Almost continuous warfare, with its captures and recaptures, mixed the seventeenth century merchant fleets of most countries and helped to standardize hull and tophamper. The universal small merchantman of the period is well represented in this one, gracing a Mercator-Hondius map of 1630. I have found no reliable pictures of particular vessels designed and built in America prior to the *Fancy*, Colonel Lewis Morris's sloop yacht (page 51) which is exactly identified in the 1717 Burgis view of New York. Several earlier prints show typical vessels in the same waters, which may or may not have been built locally. One such appears on the next page.

The Bass

have been built in and belong to the jurisdiction." English laws were being flouted. "Massachusetts has sent ships to Egypt, to the slave markets of West Africa, and even to the pirate headquarters of Madagascar. . . . Boston may be esteemed the market town of the West Indies." The total of vessels built in New England by the end of the seventeenth century had probably gone beyond the thousand mark. One test of the quality of the product may be noted in the career of the 54-gun ship *Falkland,* built in Portsmouth, New Hampshire, in 1690 for the Royal Navy. She remained in service for seventy-eight years.

There was a persistent opposition in Great Britain to the employment of American shipbuilders for naval vessels. A few more were built—the last of any considerable size in 1749—and in times of emergency American vessels were purchased afloat by the Admiralty for coastal defense of the colonies. But an apprehension prevailed that mechanics trained to such an occupation might use their skill against their benevolent overlords. This, coupled with a steady pressure from the British shipyards to protect their own monopoly, upheld the ancient realization that Britain's strength in times of crisis lay chiefly in her own ability to produce on short notice the means of maintaining complete control of the surrounding seas.

Yet English practice in shipbuilding was crosshatched with absurdities fostered by this very monopoly. An example was the "ship's husband" who had a right, sometimes hereditary, to supply at stipulated intervals a new ship in place of the former one which he had "husbanded" for the East India Company. If one of the Honourable John Company's ships did not wear out fast enough, it still had to be retired on schedule so that the husband could produce a new one. The company did not own its ships. It rented them from the husbands, who were the mainstays of the shipbuilders. Ownership would have decreased the costs, but the John Company was egregiously opulent, at the expense of India. An interlacing system of privilege distributed the wealth widely enough to sustain a solid, conservative, interdependent mercantile class that could buy enough seats in Parliament to manage England in the continuing interest of the chief devices of its own monopoly—most importantly, the East India Company.

This situation should be in mind when American shipbuilding and ship employment are compared, before and after the fact of full political freedom. Men and resources that had been badly integrated into a world system of monopoly suddenly found themselves disintegrated, in the opposite system of relatively free competition. The new government sought to impose its own regulations and taxes, of the kind which Americans had for generations been bred up to oppose. But off soundings the individual enterprise of owner, builder, and master was pitted against laxities of the structure of privilege. There were flaws in abundance, which the monopolists acknowledged by placing between them and the adventurer a barrier of naval might.

Vessels built for the Royal Navy in America had been designed in England. Colonial merchantmen had differed but little from their prototypes abroad. The schooner, in which American builders took a relatively late but intensive interest, had developed slowly. Nearly all schooners for which pre-Revolutionary drafts survive were chubby on the load water line.

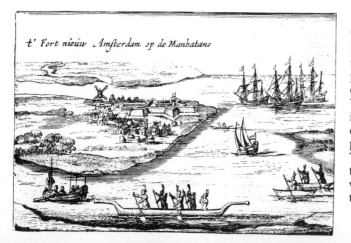

t' Fort nieuw Amsterdam op de Manhatans

The well-known Hartgers view of New Amsterdam. First issued in 1651, it purports to show the town about twenty-five years earlier. The geography is reversed, perhaps an indication that the engraver worked directly on the metal from a drawing sent from America. Whether the shipping represents the earlier or later date is doubtful. In many instances when both drawing and engraving exist, engravers can be shown to have "improved" the scene with vessels from another source. There are difficulties with this, and with other seventeenth century pictures of American marine scenes, which preclude their being presented here as valid contemporaneous views.

They wore square topsails before these had become common elsewhere. American ships also had rid themselves of the awkward lateen mizzen decades before it was retired by the Royal Navy. But in its more fundamentally structural aspects the real American revolution in ship design, coincident with that in politics, awaited the year of the Declaration of Independence.

The nature of a coast line and the products of the region are strong influences upon the design of the vessels that serve it. Plantation country, around Chesapeake Bay, probably produced the first distinctively American types of sailing craft: carriers handy enough to work far up the estuaries and rivers to the landing stages which in this map from the John Speed atlas of 1676 can be seen dotting the banks of the James and the Potomac a hundred miles and more from Chesapeake Bay. The shoals between the Virginia Capes also encouraged weatherliness in trading vessels. Shipbuilders of the New England coast had a different problem, which may be inferred from a companion map of that region on page 50. The practice of "orienting" the east edge of all maps did not become standard until a later period.

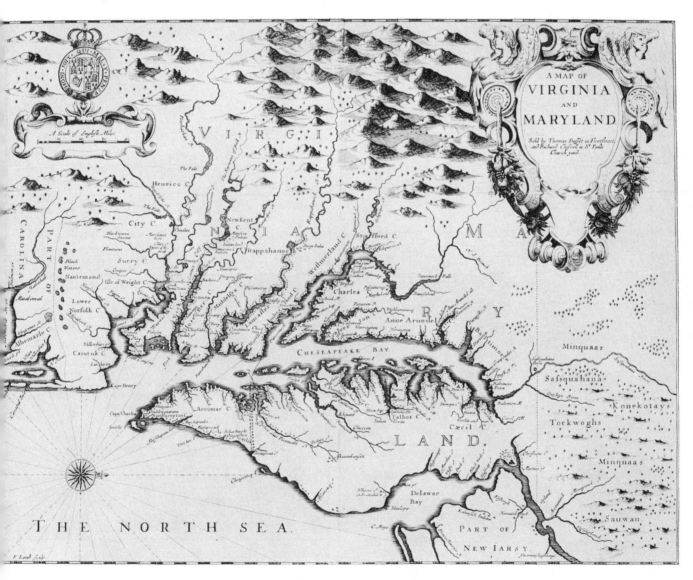

Some individual men arrive at newness far ahead of fashion. They are rare among colonials, who tend to cling to what they regard as the virtues of the countries which they have abandoned in their personal discontent. While a few men and women in the colonies were developing the coming character of American freedom, there were so many who sought to impart doctrinaire virtues to their children that doctrine itself, in the second generation, tightened into vicious bigotry. The most scandalous instance involved two men very prominent in the world of shipping. When the witchcraft frenzy swept over New England and became focal near Salem, the port's most enterprising shipowner was caught in its glare, and the colony's most famous and adventurous seaman, prototype of the new American man, took it upon himself to put an abrupt end to the lurid nonsense.

Sixteenth century navigators added lurid embellishments to the demonology that Europe took for granted. Colonists headed for New England, when they consulted the standard source of information, De Bry's *Voyages,* could not miss the inference that the Devil and his fiends were in charge of the New World. Devilish brutalities of the conquistadores, in the name of Christ, begin to be comprehensible on that assumption. Europe was passionately obsessed with the hunting down of a few witches in a Christian community, whereas the conquistadores thought of themselves as a few God-sent Christians among a people wholly in the grip of witches. Somewhat later, the same mood reached a distracted New England.

The New
AMERICAN MAN

IF THE FATES HAD BEEN PUT ON NOTICE TO PRODUCE A MAN WHO WOULD BEST SYMBOLIZE the emergent, distinctive qualities of American enterprise, they could have tinkered together no better example than William Phips. Cotton Mather, something of a snob, began his biography of Phips with a bracing foray into metaphysics to steady him in the rashness of the attempt, and proceeded:

"So *obscure* was the *Original* of that Memorable Person, whose *Actions* I am going to relate, that I must, in a way of Writing, like that of *Plutarch,* prepare my Reader for the intended Relation, by first searching the *Archives* of Antiquity for a *Parallel.* . . . a Person's being *Obscure* in his *Original,* is not always a Just Prejudice to an Expectation of *Considerable Matters* from him. . . . our PHIPS was born *Feb.* 2. *A. Dom.* 1650. at a despicable Plantation on the River of *Kennebeck,* and almost the furthest Village of the Eastern Settlement of *New-England."*

Up to the age of eighteen the boy was a shepherd. Then he was apprenticed to a ship carpenter. At twenty-two, having moved to Boston, he learned to read and write, soon married a reputable widow, and headed back to the Kennebec to build a ship. She had been launched, and a lading of lumber was on shore, when fiends of the forest descended upon the small community which "had no Refuge from the Infidels, but the *Ship* now finishing in the Harbour." Mather notes that Phips's first action "after he was his own Man, was to save his Father's House, with the rest of the Neighbourhood, from Ruin,"—this at the serious financial loss of abandoning his cargo of lumber. He carried the refugees free of cost to Boston, and there proceeded with other enterprises. "But his disposition for *Business* was of the *Dutch* Mould. . . . He would *prudently* contrive a weighty Undertaking, and then patiently pursue it unto the End . . . cutting rather like a *Hatchet,* than like a *Razor* . . . Being thus of the *True Temper,* for doing of *Great Things,* he betakes himself to the *Sea,* the Right *Scene* for such Things; and upon the Advice of a *Spanish Wreck* about the *Bahama's,* he took a Voyage thither."

He was thirty-two. His first speculative adventure might have discouraged a less dynamic character. In the great waste of shoals he found the sunken vessel to which rumor had directed him, but if the Bahaman wreck had ever contained the reputed treasure, someone else had carried nearly all of it away. His divers brought up a modest number of pieces of eight, probably of the cob type shown in the illustration on the following page, and their efforts convinced him that his equipment was too primitive.

Phips, by necessarily secretive processes of the treasure hunter's trade, got wind among his disappointments of a much more promising wreck. It is at this point in his impetuously careful career that his personal quality of enterprise responded to a comparative failure. Another equally ambitious man might well have sailed for home to organize a new expedition.

Phips, well aware that treasure hunting had become a competitive and quarrelsome business from Bermuda to Hispaniola, decided to go straight to King Charles II. Under English law all treasure-trove belonged to the king, who customarily granted patents permitting his subjects the right to exploit certain areas for a percentage of the trove.

Cotton Mather tells anecdotes of Phips's early boasting that he would some day command a king's ship. He would "frequently tell the Gentlewoman his Wife . . . That he should come to have the Command of better Men than he was now accounted himself; and, That he should be the Owner of a *Fair Brick-House* in the *Green-Lane* of *North-Boston*." Such prophetic gossip is easily invented after the accomplishment. In the case of Phips it is believable because the largeness of his intention turned him again and again, without hesitation, toward the higher and more dramatic choice. Instead of returning to Boston, he sailed directly for England to seek both a royal patent and the command of a king's ship.

There must have been a bluff magic in his personality. The shipwright-shepherd of ten or fifteen years ago presented his arguments to favorably placed officials surrounding a gay monarch, who had a small surplus of ships and a large absence of ready money. William Phips sailed away as captain of a king's "Frigot," the *Algier-Rose* in Mather's account, the *Rose of Argier* as listed by the Admiralty. He had made, with his crew of turbulent scoundrels, a bold, unworkable compact. It was a forerunner of the articles of agreement in American whalers, although it gave a surprisingly low proportion of the expected profits to the commander himself. With a few exceptions, all were to share alike after the king's portion had been deducted. Boys were to get half-shares, the mate only one-eighth more than a foremasthand, and Phips three times a foremasthand's share, one of his three captain's shares being intended as reimbursement for his personal purchases of apparatus. The crew had to find their own food, arms, and ammunition. It seems clear enough that Phips's shoestring was showing: he could not have provisioned his "Frigot" in any other fashion. The hands did agree that if the commander could secure a majority vote he might cut the size of a crew member's share for misbehavior, the cut portion to be given to a meritorious seaman. The Admiralty's orders were explicit that the *Rose of Argier* was a ship on His Majesty's private adventure. She had no status as a naval vessel. A hapless, diligent soul named Knepp was put aboard to protect the king's interest.

Details of the voyage to Boston, beginning September 5, 1683, are a bit more mad than one might foresee under even such a compact. The seamen plundered a farm on the Irish

"Pirate Money." A piece of eight, cob type, minted in the reign of Philip IV, prior to 1665.

America, in the primary age of colonization, spelled treasure to the European mind. It was still her mineral wealth that most impressed the younger Blaeu when he designed a frontispiece for the huge *American Atlas* of 1662. The theme of a diagonal half of the engraving is mining, both shaft and surface operations, with baskets of ore and the eventual ingots laid at the feet of the original cigar-store Indian princess. A baroque symbolism persists amid a greater realism, seventy years after De Bry began to publish his *Voyages*. The aboriginal spirit seems still to dominate, one foot resting upon a symbol of the cost of conquest. In her hands she holds hints of the additional cost to come. The uninhibited demons of De Bry are here gathered into the single figure of Blaeu's falling Lucifer, struck down by the plumed cavalier of the queen of heaven, who by this time is receiving the worship of the Indians themselves. Caribbean gold and silver, the sterile symbols of real wealth, haunted the imaginations of frugal New Englanders—and so did Lucifer. William Phips of Maine, prototype of the new American man, became deeply involved with both symbols.

43

coast. They stole Knepp's stores and liquor, got wildly drunk, were even caught burning brandy and smoking in the powder magazine. Somehow, after fifty-two days, the ship reached Boston unexploded. Knepp wrote an outraged protest to England that Captain Phips had disciplined no-one, saying that "men that paid for their own victualls and receive noe wages will not be corrected for every Small fault."

The stay in Boston was one elastic calamity, stretching over three months. Drunken riots ashore brought Phips and his crew repeatedly into court. Knepp, suspected of being what he was—an informer—was attacked and almost murdered. Phips insisted that the *Rose of Argier* was a naval vessel—to be saluted by every passing craft. Whenever one failed to do so, he put a shot across her bows and then charged the bewildered infringer of etiquette for the cost of powder and ball. Claiming the naval rank he did not have, the treasure hunter refused to answer in court for the crimes of his crew, who put a finishing touch to their record, as they sailed at last for the Bahamas, by landing on an offshore island to plunder one more farm and rape the farmer's wife. Such details, cherished up in documentary archives, are not to be found in Mather's glowing biography.

It is hardly surprising that Knepp remained in Boston, nor that the turbulent crew soon tired of fruitless treasure hunting. About ninety signed a round robin of mutiny, with an intent to regularize their piratical predilections. On shore at the time, on a desolate island, they needed to make sure of an essential crew member: the carpenter. He was in the ship, and managed when approached to get word to the captain. While the mutineers continued their plotting, out of sight in the woods, Phips and eight faithful men charged the ship's guns and drew the charges from those that were set up ashore to guard a tentful of provisions. The mutineers, discovering that they were outwitted, begged for mercy. Phips had intended to maroon them, the fate they had plotted for him. His personal force and daring are shown by the fact that he finally took them aboard again and dumped them ashore in Jamaica.

Having recruited a new crew, "he fished out of a very old *Spaniard*, (or *Portuguese*) a little Advice about the true Spot where lay the *Wreck*" north of Hispaniola. Reliance upon such information seems nowadays a bit too credulous, but Phips was dealing with possible survivors of the last great calamities that befell the plate ships. One of the richest was known to have gone down near enough to Cape Cabrón to permit the bringing ashore of some of her treasure before she foundered. The very old Spaniard (or Portuguese) seems in the upshot actually to have been a survivor of the event. Ten thousand such tales have been told for a glass of rum. Phips somehow managed to listen to a true one that convinced him. He searched the indicated waters carefully, found nothing, and continued to believe the story of his ancient

The first wreck, fished with little success by Captain William Phips, on the Bahama Bank, is indicated by the arrow. The engraved words within the circle read: "Here Sir William Phips took up a vast Quantity of Silver from a Spanish wreck, in 1685." This is a portion of Herman Moll's map of the West Indies, in a series issued between 1708 and 1720. The date given on the map is that of the first expedition. It should be 1687.

mariner. With a more knowledgeable idea of the necessary equipment, and aware that his smallpox-stricken crew should be replaced, he pointed rashly back for an England where Knepp's reports of misbehavior must have preceded him. They had. Orders were out to seize the *Rose of Argier* in the king's name.

The very frankness of Phips's return, with little to show for his endeavor, probably startled the officials into taking a lenient view of his derelictions. The Navy Board's survey indicated a net loss for the adventure of about £230. Something far worse had doubtless been anticipated. These were the ambiguous days of Captain Kidd, when men were judged for the same acts as loyal servants of the king today and as pirates tomorrow. Phips might well have regarded himself as lucky to be out of jail. Instead, he went looking for another set of backers.

A new king, James II, proved more solicitous for his ships than his predecessor had been, but the second Duke of Albemarle was impressed by the blunt American. A stock company was organized; two ships were purchased. Late in November 1686, Phips was back upon his fishing grounds between Puerto Rico and Hispaniola. He personally spent most of two methodical months trading for hides, as a hedge against complete ruin, while his mate Francis Rogers searched for the wreck. On February 7, 1687, Rogers returned from yet another combing of the reefs. As Cotton Mather tells the story, Rogers and some of his men "went back unto their Captain whom for some while they distressed with nothing but such *Bad News,* as they formerly thought they must have carried him." After a while they placed an *"Odd Thing"* under the table. "At last he *saw* it; seeing it, he cried out with some Agony, *Why? What is this? Whence comes this?* And then, with changed Countenances, they told him *how,* and *where* they got it: *Then, said he, Thanks be to God! We are made;* and so away they went, all hands to Work . . . in a little while they had, without the loss of any Man's Life, brought up *Thirty Two Tuns* of Silver; for it was now come to measuring of Silver by *Tuns."* Later "they knockt out whole Bushels of rusty Pieces of Eight . . . there were vast Riches of *Gold,* and *Pearls,* and *Jewels,* which they also lit upon."

Mather claims that Phips arrived in London with nearly £300,000 aboard. The official accounts check reasonably well with his figures, of weight and value. It is one commentary upon the self-discipline, in great matters, of a man often unruly in small ones, that Phips left about as much treasure in the wreck on the Ambrosia bank as he took away. His provisions were short, the weather was threatening, and the Spaniards at Porto Plata had reported a French privateer in the offing. The new American man did what a winning gambler can seldom bring himself to do: he stopped in time, while the luck was running strongly in his favor, and silver was still to be had at the rate of a ton a day. Albemarle and his friends, even so, realized the unusual profit of almost 10,000 per cent on their investment. Phips became the hero of a nation of seafarers. The inevitable court intriguers tried to prove that he had defrauded the king, and even issued a warrant for his arrest, but the king himself recalled it and knighted the former shepherd on the 28th of June, 1688. It may be that the most suspicious aspect, to courtiers who measured the motives of others by their own, was the fact that Phips contented himself with £12,000, about one-twentieth of the sum he brought to England. It was a large fortune for the times, and provided the first forthright instance of the rags-to-riches tradition of American promotional business.

Phips, native-born in what was to become the most durably maritime state of the still-distant Union, had a contemporary named Philip English, one year younger, whose career exhibits another recurring aspect of the American pattern of success without privilege: that of the penniless immigrant boy whose achievement of eminence may be explained in part by his very lack of the encouragements available to the members of a settled society. English landed in Salem at about the same date when Phips became an apprentice shipwright. William Bentley's diary states that the newcomer, like Phips, partly offset a lack of formal education by marriage to a woman of some intellectual attainment and much spirit.

Philip English had no Cotton Mather to be his biographer, although he was fated to collide with the influential young zealot in a grim public way. Like many of his successors in Salem, English appears to have learned the intricacies of foreign trade on the quarter-deck in his twenties before turning to the management of a growing fleet of vessels from his counting-house ashore. Salem as yet had no customhouse. Her merchants could cheerfully ignore the Navigation Acts, and continued to do so even after the arrival of Governor Andros in 1686 to assert arbitrary royal authority.

Philip English sent his sailing vessels to a wide periphery: the Channel Islands of his origin, France, Spain, the West Indies. Among Puritan-Congregationalists, whose faith was hardening into formal decadence, he persisted an Episcopalian. Cotton Mather was observing the behavior of a deranged girl, taking careful notes for his *Memorable Providences Relating to Witchcrafts and Possessions*. His father, Increase Mather, might have brought wisdom and experience to moderate the intense young scholar's preoccupation. But Increase was in London, trying to wheedle King James II into restoring the Charter of Massachusetts, which had been withdrawn in 1684 largely because of the colony's defiance of the Navigation Acts.

The elder Mather, when that project failed, encouraged Phips to seek the office of provost marshal general, or sheriff, of New England. Another knight, with a royal office, might ameliorate the tyrannical behavior of Sir Edmund Andros. All New England estates had been technically forfeited to the crown. Sir Edmund had left the owners in possession, exacting as much as a quarter of the estates' value for confirming grants under the new order.

Phips received the appointment, but he had intermediate business to attend to. After quitting the Ambrosia bank wreck, he had wanted to return promptly with better equipment. This time there was no difficulty in securing the means. Sir John Narbrough, Commissioner of the Royal Navy, wished to head an expedition. But with the dynamic American in a subordinate capacity, processes of a majestic orderliness made a ruin of the most important element: time. He sailed from the Thames in command of the *Goodluck and a Boy* on August 31, 1687, with a fleet that had been ready seven weeks earlier but had been held up by the illness of an official and by the insistence that the vessels sail in convoy. Phips had been away from the wreck eleven months when he sighted its location again, easily, by the fact that eight ships and twenty-four smaller vessels were at anchor, merrily putting over their Indian divers, with rakes and tubs. The wreck had been gleaned to the ribs.

Phips strove ingeniously to break up a coral formation which might conceal the plate room of the ship. He experimented with underwater blasting, and with grapnels and chains, but nothing more of consequence was ever recovered from the Hispaniola wreck, except four copper cannon and a little silver. It is a comment upon the rate at which technical change was occurring that the guns under water for almost half a century were promptly mounted in other ships.

Phips, the individual enterpriser, had wanted to dash back quickly to the Ambrosia bank. His backers, accustomed to the mesh of formalities in naval administration, had dribbled his timely luck away. He sailed for New England on May 8, 1688, leaving Narbrough to organize the return of the other ships to England. Sir John was spared the personal humiliation of reporting the sad failure for which the pace of his organization was largely responsible. He died of fever on the Ambrosia bank.

The new American man. William Phips, born on the Kennebec, shepherd, ship carpenter, shipbuilder, shipmaster, merchant, treasure hunter, inventor, commander of military and naval operations—a rough, dynamic genius who could not read or write until he was twenty, who, when knighted and appointed governor of Massachusetts, hobnobbed with shipwrights and hinted that he would like to take up the broadax again: fabulously lucky, yet a man who earned his luck, who went in person to fight when because of his responsible office he could properly have ordered others to do so. He broke the heads of officials with his cane when they displeased him. By three sudden, arbitrary orders he cleansed New England of the long mania of witch hunting, within a day or two.

Andros, who had worn the collar of his kings long enough to resent the intrusion of the upstart knight, used all the obfuscations of legal process to delay confirmation of the new high sheriff. Phips built his brick house in the Green Lane. Still the tangle of legalities, to cope with which he had no special training, frustrated his efforts to relieve the people from Andros's tyranny. Someone tried to murder Phips on his own doorstep. On July 16th, in one of his abrupt decisions, he sailed for England to seek redress. King James II was in exile—but an agent of the deposed monarch offered Phips the governorship of New England for his assistance in a counter-revolution. He refused, and joined Increase Mather in renewed efforts for a legal restoration of the charter. Hearing that the Bostonians had imprisoned Andros, and that King William approved the provisional government under Bradstreet, Phips returned to Boston. He formally joined the congregation of Cotton Mather, who at twenty-six was the most influential clergyman in a society that looked to the church for its authority in politics.

When Mather writes of "Devils in the *Shape* of *Good Men*," "*Daemons* hideously scattering *Fire* about the Country," "Rage of the *Diabolical Indians*," it is not always immediately clear whether he is talking about aborigines or expeditionary forces spewed up from a fire-and-brimstone Hell. Phips had to deal with both. An Indian raid on Salmon Falls convinced the New Englanders that they must shut off the supplies reaching their tormenters by way of French Canada. On March 22, 1690, Phips was sworn in as major general—because he was the colony's most famous seaman!—to lead an attack on Port Royal. There was no money in the public till. Public subscription was resorted to, in the expectation that the investors would make a profit from plunder.

The fleet sailed on the 28th of April to an easy victory over a small garrison. Phips was criticized for having ignored the politer rules of war in his seizures of personal property. Yet he had been chosen because he was the kind of man who could turn a profit, who knew how "to make a voyage," as the contemporary shipowners put it.

Later that summer, in the rising port of New York, agents of several colonies met to concert a more ambitious attack upon the French: an army to be sent up the Hudson, while a naval expedition converged upon Quebec by way of the St. Lawrence. Phips was given command of the latter.

This time his luck ran low. The land expedition failed to find the expected transport on Lake Champlain. Its Indian allies deserted. It turned back. Phips had great trouble in navigating the St. Lawrence without pilots. For once his sense of timing failed him. Before Quebec he was at first too cautious, then too rash in a frontal assault which left some of his ground forces unsupported. The French, aware of the failure of the land expedition, had had just enough time to concentrate their troops and armament. Some military historians believe that an assault a day or two earlier would have succeeded easily, but the whole record suggests that Phips, as the leader of a complex expedition, was unable to make use of his own forthright qualities.

A view of New York by Peter Schenk, published in the year 1690 when the colonial commissioners met in the city to set in motion the first notable military and naval operation involving a measure of united action between the colonies, against a foreign power. Sir William Phips was confirmed in his command of all naval forces for the attack on Quebec by way of the St. Lawrence. New York's governor went out of his way, two years later, to give shelter to the Salem shipowner Philip English, when he escaped the witch hunters. This view, published in Holland sixteen years after the city ceased to be New Amsterdam, is retrospective. The buildings and wharves are close copies of the "Restitutio" view which celebrated the retaking of New York by the Dutch in 1673. The shipping is supplied by the copier. Note the spritsail topmast. Of the four small craft, two are lateeners and two have square sail, possibly a distinction beween shallops and pinnaces of the period.

Weather confirmed the failure. A fierce storm caused the fleet to run for sea room outside the river. There the calamity increased in violent gales. One ship disappeared, one burned, one was wrecked. The rest reached Boston over a period of six weeks. Cotton Mather's account of the wreck emphasizes the nearness of cannibalism in the life of the seafarer.

The unquenchable Phips sailed for England to tell the king that a modest expedition could expel the French from Canada completely. He was probably right, but the job that took a great deal more doing in the second phase of the French and Indian Wars, about half a century later, seemed remote to a sovereign whose roots were in a distracted Europe. Yet if Phips failed in his precise intent, he worked hard with Increase Mather for the restoration of the Massachusetts charter. Although they could not win royal assent to the right of the people to choose their own governor, King William relaxed in practice and allowed Mather to nominate the man. Sir William Phips sailed home as captain general and governor in chief of the Province of Massachusetts Bay.

Arriving in May of 1692, the new governor found the interchangeable fiends of Cotton Mather raging not only in the forests of the Kennebec but also inside some of the most influential New Englanders. The impromptu jails of Salem were bulging with persons arrested upon suspicion of having had commerce with the Devil. One was Mary English, whose husband owned fourteen buildings, twenty-one vessels, a wharf, and a warehouse. The frenzy was no longer confining itself, for victims, to the superstitious, defenseless poor.

A public clamor against the indicted was renewed in the excitement of Phips's arrival. Urged to confine them in chains, he acted decisively—twice. In public he ordered them put into irons, and in private instructed the jailors to strike the shackles off again, immediately.

A few days later, the wealthy shipowner Philip English was thrust into jail with his wife. One might think it evidence of a special influence that the Englishes were taken from Salem to Boston, soon after the arrival of Sir William. The fate of others in the same group makes it at least dubious. The impromptu Salem jails were jammed.

Phips's appointment of a court of laymen to try the witchcraft cases has been criticized, but the new governor appears to have chosen the most eminent men he knew—probably expecting of such a court something very different from what he got.

But before he sailed to do battle with the other set of alleged devils, the Indians, Mr. and Mrs. English were mysteriously freed to turn up a few days later in New York. There is testimony that the new governor was willing in their case to have it happen. Four of those who had been transferred to Boston with the shipowner and his wife were hanged, protesting their innocence. A fifth, indomitable octogenarian Giles Cory, chose to be pressed to death rather than answer anything at all to an evil charge. He was three days dying. When his tongue bulged out of his mouth, an official pushed it back in again with his cane. The Indians against whom Sir William had taken the field kept matters at a nice balance by torturing another New England prisoner to death, in their somewhat different but quicker fashion.

In July Captain John Alden, son of a signer of the *Mayflower* Compact, was the victim of the informers. He had been second in command to Phips on the Port Royal foray. Alden's escape into hiding in Duxbury probably was "contrived."

Sir William Phips was one of the early American yachtsmen. He used his "frigot" for important journeys, but also had at least two yachts. In the early fall of 1692 he returned from the last of that season's forays against the Indians to confront the work of his special tribunal: nineteen persons hanged, one pressed to death, and the jails as full as ever. He dissolved the court, freed some prisoners on bail, and insisted that living conditions for the others be made tolerable.

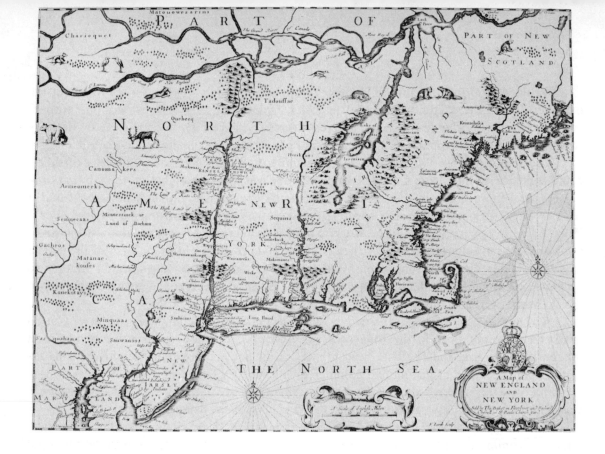

ABOVE. If land forces in support of the naval assault of Sir William Phips upon Quebec were following such maps of the period as this one from the Speed atlas of 1676, it is no wonder that they turned back. Lake Champlain, here probably confused with Lake Winnepesaukee, lies east instead of west of the Connecticut, and approximately south of Niagara Falls. The two "Grand Rivers," of Canada and of New England, approximate the Ottawa and the St. Lawrence, but where is the eastern end of Lake Ontario, which should be shown due north of Chesapeake Bay? This map actually is either a copy of one from which the "Restitutio" view of New Amsterdam (page 48) also was lifted, or both were made from a common earlier source. Men on the spot had better information. Note the high degree of accuracy of the northeastern coastal region, by comparison with the wild errors that begin a short distance inland. It emphasizes the great contrast between the offshore economy of New England and the onshore economy of Virginia, as revealed in the companion map on page 39. Different types of sailing vessels were developed for the different primary uses of securing their cargoes up a river, in one case, and on the Grand Banks in the other. BELOW. The first permanent lighthouse on the shore of North America was erected in 1716 on an island called the Little Brewster near the entrance to Boston harbor. In this view, made by William Burgis about a year later, we have what appears to be a reliably explicit representation of an armed sloop of the period. Captain Arthur H. Clark identified her as the lighthouse tender, but gave no evidence for the assumption, which seems dubious. In those less than affluent times a sizable armed vessel would hardly have been needed to supply a structure so close to the wharves. She is more probably a typical modest trader, armed primarily against piracy which flourished early in the century. Vessels of about the tonnage of this one were owned by Philip English, the most celebrated early merchant of Salem.

ABOVE. The sloop *Fancy* (in forewater), Colonel Lewis Morris's yacht. Detail from the Burgis view of New York, 1717. This is supposed to be the earliest named vessel specifically identified in a contemporaneous American picture. BELOW. The Roberts view of Charleston, South Carolina, shortly before 1739. The intervening leaves may be lifted for a comparison with much of the Cooke-Bennett view, which puts the observer close to the same spot a century later (page x). For most of the early views that include shipping in American waters, we have only the print from which to judge fidelity to observed detail. In this case the original Roberts drawing survives to show that the engraver took no serious liberties. Note the similarity, but for a topsail yard added, of the sloop under the church steeple to that of the Burgis mezzotint on the opposite page.

A short period of stock taking followed, in which Samuel Sewall, the diarist, reports having had the honor of driving a treenail, on November 19th, into the governor's yacht: a brigantine. In January a new court dismissed eighteen witchcraft cases. Three more persons were sentenced to death. In May Governor Phips abruptly pardoned these three and freed the 150 who were waiting trial. The terror was over. Cotton Mather repented in a roundabout, allusive way. Sewall was the only judge who had the stamina to stand up in church to say that he had been wrong. Phips, the blunt man of action, seems to have handled an outbreak of savage, metaphysical lunacy about as well as anyone could hope to do, having come upon it when it was fully developed and with an Indian war to fight at the same time.

Political tensions began to take more usual forms. Phips beat the captain of one of His Majesty's frigates over the head with a cane (breaking said head), similarly chastised His Majesty's collector of customs, and ended by being summoned to London, where he died in 1695.

The nobility of Salem's first notable self-made shipping merchant emerges in his behavior toward those who had turned with such savagery upon himself and his wife. Learning that the hard winter of 1692–1693 had brought starvation to a community too agitated to attend properly to its crops, Philip English, a few weeks after reaching asylum in New York, shipped off a hundred barrels of flour for the poor of Salem, and later in the year returned to take up his affairs as if nothing had happened. Mary, his valiant wife, sickened and died as a result of the brutal stupidities to which she had been subjected.

Treasure hunting and witch hunting have both been recurrent since then, in American life, but without the emphatic coincidence which in this case marked their part in defining the character of the new American man, who for a long while was to be, most characteristically, a man concerned with American sail.

TOWARD A REVOLUTION:
The Spirit of New England

THE KIND OF SELF-CONFIDENT ENTERPRISE THAT HAD A SPECTACULAR EMERGENCE IN William Phips spread rapidly in the northeastern colonies. It recurred in another native of Maine who, as if to fill the loss, was born about a year after Phips's death. Enterprise cannot in William Pepperrell's case be explained by the thorns of poverty. His father of the same name was a shipowner. The son was a soldier of a sort, rather than a seaman, but his most notable achievement was the amphibious Louisbourg expedition in which he had command over a fleet of more than a hundred small vessels and three or four ships.

The Pepperrells at times held the principal shares in more than thirty vessels. An account of one voyage of their pink *Bonetta,* in 1718 (contributed to the *American Neptune* for April 1949 by Byron Fairchild), reveals hazards of the West Indies trade of the period. The pink, just before the voyage, had been mauled by a pirate; she fetched up in London, not according to plan, and there was sold.

Letterbooks and logs discourage a popular notion that New Englanders developed fast-sailing vessels early in the eighteenth century. Normal sailing time, from Massachusetts to the nearer ports of the Caribbean, was more than a month. Improvement in speed was not general until after 1750.

The Louisbourg expedition, like the two Canadian forays of Phips, began as a domestic American affair. Benjamin Franklin, the wise man of the colonies in most matters, discouraged it. "Some seem to think," he wrote, "that forts are as easy taken as snuff." But the impetuous quality of the New England spirit, which was to mount in the next three decades to an unquenchable flame, had become general by 1745. The ardent governor of Massachusetts flattered the pompous one of New Hampshire into a reluctant participation. Rhode Island contributed the public sloop *Tartar* of 14 guns, Connecticut two sloops and about 500 men. The situation was almost like that of half a century earlier. Louisbourg, on an island commanding the entrance to the St. Lawrence, protected the line of supply from France to the Indian warriors of the interior. In the hands of New Englanders it could cut that supply line.

Parkman's comment on the choice of a commander still seems just: "Pepperrell joined to an unusual popularity as little military incompetency as anybody else who could be had." The great difference between this expedition and that of Phips against Quebec, significant for the future of America, was in the altered spirit of the populace. No draft was needed. John Storer raised in one day a volunteer company of 61 men, aged 16 to 60, in the small Maine town of Wells. The story was similar elsewhere. New Hampshire contributed her entire navy, a 14-gun sloop. All the vessels probably were locally built. For a flagship, Captain Edward Tyng, Pepperrell's naval commander, spotted a likely brig almost ready for launching and had her converted into a 24-gun frigate, the *Massachusetts.* There were three vessels of 20 guns, four of 16, two of 14, one of 12, and two of 8, in the fleet of thirteen fighting sail, to protect a flotilla of about ninety fishing vessels as transports.

Details of the expedition are as close to comic as anything is likely to come that involves the suffering of even an amateur military operation. Historians differ over the importance of a belated supporting fleet under the British Commodore Peter Warren. Capture of the 64-gun French ship *Vigilant,* which approached Louisbourg unaware that the place was under siege, would have been unlikely if the large British ships had not been on hand. She carried supplies which the besiegers found invaluable, and which probably would have stiffened the defenders enough to survive the siege. Here luck favored Pepperrell.

The story of the siege, ashore, is well told by Parkman in *A Half Century of Conflict*. It involved prodigious flanking operations in which heavy guns were dragged through swamps believed by the defenders to be impassable: an early instance of the same ignoring of orthodox military considerations which during the Revolution gave the ill-equipped Continental forces tactical advantages not supposed to be available to them.

The only contemporary painting of the Louisbourg operation is inaccurate. It appears to have been made in England when William Pepperrell was knighted, for his services, as the first native American Baronet. Captain Rous of the *Shirley,* who had captured a number of armed French merchantmen, was recognized by being given a command in the Royal Navy. And the British ministry, in a move not calculated exactly to delight the enterprising American colonies, a few years later gave Louisbourg back to the French: "in exchange," as Smollett noted, with a sense more of coincidence than of balance, "for a petty factory in the East Indies." The French did give up Madras as a part of the pattern of restorations at the Peace of Aix-la-Chapelle, when the British gave up Cape Breton Island, but there was much more to the trade than that.

The revolution in mapmaking that provided a means of sailing at a steady angle to the meridians did not eliminate all mapmakers' quirks. Seamen were unaffected by the slowness with which standard orientation was adopted: their training had not yet led them to expect an invariable eastern right edge. But the oddity at the lower edge of this map of the Windward Lesser Antilles might have been calamitous to an unwary voyager. Grenada, the southernmost island, here has simply been pivoted on its northernmost cape and swung upside down to bring it inside a badly calculated border. Guillaume de L'Isle, in whose *Atlas Nouveau* of 1741 it appears, might at least have given warning by inverting the place names too. A more usual Caribbean complication is suggested by the three pieces of eight which were placed upon the map when it was photographed: examples of cob money of the early eighteenth century; Mexico City coinage of 1789; and Potosí, Peru, issue of 1808. These "Spanish dollars" were roughly reflected in the original United States unit, but American traders, both before and after the Revolution, were confronted by a multitude of currencies, good, bad, and fraudulent. Weight and fineness, rather than stamped denomination, determined the value of all of them.

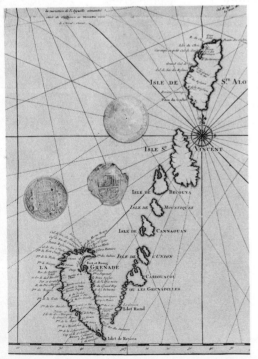

Mapmakers' Sad Tricks

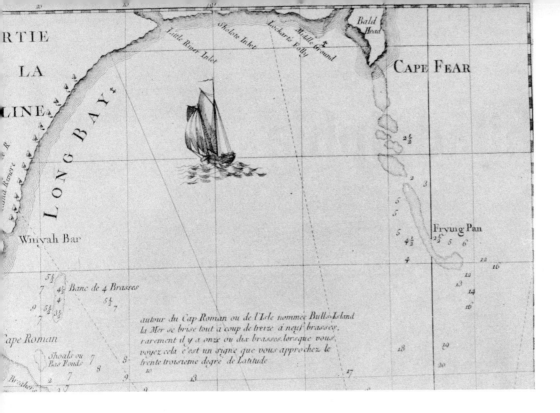

An uncommon formation of shoals extends seaward off Cape Fear. In the days of sail, when safety in the westerlies depended upon an ability to claw to windward, the Frying Pan was a major hazard. It provided one of many reasons for sailing the long way to the Florida Strait, on two sides of a triangle, far out into the Atlantic, by preference to a straight course down from New England past Hatteras and Cape Fear. The major marine atlases, such as the 1777 French revision of Jefferys' *American Atlas* (from which the above detail of a large chart is taken), began around the middle of the century to delineate important shoals with care. But there were few masters of the multitudinous sloops and schooners who could afford to own such splendid productions. They were lucky to have Speer's more modest *West India Pilot,* first issued in 1766. Its astonishing treatment of the Frying Pan Shoal, reproduced below, persisted into the edition of 1774. The fine script reads, *The Frying Pan Shoal runs off due N & S from Cape Fear, & is reduced to a small Scale & placed E & W for the Conveniency of bringing it into the Plate.* The careful skipper undoubtedly would have read it before bearing up to the coast—but in an emergency, foul weather, poor light . . . ?

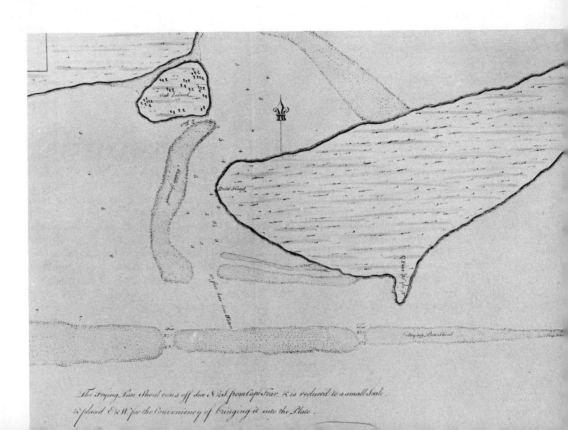

Philadelphia

AN EAST PROSPECT OF THE CITY OF PHILADELPHIA: taken by GEORGE HEAP from

The Battery

A DESCRIPTION OF THE SITUATION, HARBOUR &c. OF THE CITY AND PORT OF PHILADELPHIA

To the Honourable Thomas Penn and Richard Penn,
and Counties of NEWCASTLE, KENT and SUSSEX on DELA

This, in four panels dated 1754, is the largest view of Philadelphia, and one of the best for a study of contemporary sailing vessels. A test of the artist's observation is his care in depicting the effect of wind on various sails in the same scene. The flags and pennants in this case all are behaving consistently. The ship just above the word "Pennsylvania," on the right-hand page, appears to be coming to an anchor (her starboard bower), which accounts for the relaxing of her sails when others are full. Among the many details of interest to the student of nautical history, the following should be noticed. The ship and brigantine in the forewater of the right half of the print show why the adoption of the spanker, in place of a lateen sail on the mizzen, caused the abandonment of flagstaffs at sea in the nineteenth century. Here the brigantine's large fore-and-aft mainsail (corresponding in position to a spanker on a three-master) has a boom which would require the unshipping of the staff whenever the vessel came about. Another aspect of interest is the variety of rigs of the smaller craft: spritsails, fore-and-aft mainsails with long, short, and no gaffs, all apparently loose-footed; some with, some without headsails.

This is known as the Heap view. George Heap, the artist, worked under the direction of Nicholas Scull (his name is spelled with a "k" on the first issue of the print, and corrected on this, the second) who was

America's Principal Seaport in the 18th Century

SEY SHORE, under the Direction of NICHOLAS SCULL Surveyor General of the PROVINCE of PENNSYLVANIA.

and absolute Proprietors of the Province of PENNSYLVANIA: this Perspective View is humbly Dedicated by Nicholas Scull.

THE DESCRIPTION CONTINUED   REFERENC

appointed surveyor general of the province of Pennsylvania in 1748. He dedicated the production to its proprietors, Thomas and William Penn, and in these circumstances would probably have quelled any tendency toward inventiveness in the artist. Such factors, which have a bearing upon the veracity of the contemporaneous view, need to be considered when we search for intimate detail in the shapes of ships. The drawing by Heap was sent to England to be engraved and printed, which probably accounts for the misspelling of Scull's own name in the first printing. It is possible that details of the vessels were determined by Gerard Vandergucht, the engraver. The little sloop at the extreme right is a veritable Dutchman; the larger vessel over the name "Thomas Penn" is flying the striped flag of the East India Company; and the leeboarder to starboard of her is a shallow-water Dutch type. But most engravers copied slavishly what was before them. In the international confraternity of the sea, all of these vessels might have had a reason for being in the river off Philadelphia. All but the leebounder might possibly have been built there. Prototypes of the jib-headed bugeye rig are in evidence, and these are as thoroughly local to the region as anything we have record of. The *Groete Baer,* a leeboarder very similar in size to the one above, crossed the Atlantic a few years ago, and one like it appears in a painting of New York harbor probably done on the spot in 1647.

RIGHT. New York as it appeared from the northwest, shortly before the Revolution. Early engravings made in America by Paul Revere and others seem crude when compared with the delicate assurance of such aquatints as this one, prepared about 1773 for J. F. W. Des Barres who included it in the *Atlantic Neptune*. But crudity often has historical advantages. The more skillful work of art in this case tells us much less about the structure and rig of small vessels in the distance. LEFT. The earliest reliable general source for structural details of specific vessels built in America is the illustrated logbook. A professional seaman, drawing his own vessel, is dealing with a mechanism that he himself knows well. The typical logbook illustration shows evidence of having been sketched in pencil, then carefully inked with a pen. This well-known early example is of the schooner *Baltick* of Salem, with more sail set than she would have been likely to carry all at once. Note that the course has not only a row of reef points for shortening sail in heavy weather, but also a laced-on bonnet at the foot. The drawing is dated 1765, when the schooner was registered as of 80 tons. Its authenticity is discussed by E. P. Morris, on pages 187–189 of *The Fore-and-Aft Rig in America*.

BELOW. This is the famous Paul Revere engraving of British troops debarking in 1768 to keep order in Boston. The eight larger vessels comprise the British fleet, but a close look hints at a standardization of rig on the sloops and schooners. The moderately long gaff has become universal. The troops are assembling on the Long Wharf. Hancock's Wharf is at the right. The establishment of engraving as a domestic artifice in America enlarged our opportunity for a reliable view of shipping in American waters.

REVOLUTION
The Navy of Trials & Errors

EVEN BEFORE THE DAYS OF DE BRY THERE WAS A BRISK PUBLIC DEMAND THROUGHOUT THE Old World for prints that celebrated great occasions, including the calamitous. Organized armed services encouraged specializing artists to respond promptly to notable encounters. The makers of our Revolution were too busy fighting it to worry about an adequate pictorial record of its swift events. Colonies long dependent upon militia, with a sloop or two as a naval force, had no sustaining employment for military and marine artists. Those who became skillful at portraiture were tempted toward Europe, both for study and for patronage.

The name of Paul Revere, synonymous with rebel patriotism, first appears on a historical print with the dedication, *To the Earl of Hillsborough, His Majest^s Sec^y of State for America. This View of the only well Plan'd Expedition formed for supporting ye dignity of Britain & chastising ye insolence of America, is hum'ly Inscribed.* That was in 1768. Two years later a print of *The Bloody Massacre perpetrated in King Street* was boldly signed, *Engrav'd Printed & Sold by Paul Revere Boston,* and the choosing up of sides was under way.

In 1772 the *Gaspee* incident emphasized the maritime origins of the coming struggle which was to be settled on shore. John Brown of Providence—a man consistently muddled in his ethics—led a longboat expedition down Narragansett Bay to burn the stranded British armed cruiser *Gaspee* which had been interfering with his smuggling operations. The unanimity of opposition to the system of duties and taxes is revealed in the fact that no-one tried to collect a heavy reward offered for information. Brown had engaged in the slave trade when it was legal. He later tried to turn an infamous dollar at it after it had been outlawed.

During the first two years of the Revolution our Navy consisted almost wholly of purchased vessels, with an average armament of less than eleven small-caliber guns. Two exceptions, the ships *Alfred,* 24, and *Columbus,* 20, had modest successes, but in 1778 the former was captured and the latter chased ashore and burned. All but two of the others had been eliminated earlier. Eight were destroyed by their own crews to prevent capture. Two

An inland lake probably was the key to the outcome of both the American Revolution and the War of 1812. Lying as a part of the most feasible supply route from Canada to New York City, Lake Champlain was twice the scene of battles between relatively small naval craft that had the effect of frustrating armies of invasion. In October 1776, the still loyal commander of the American Revolutionary fleet was Benedict Arnold. Of his service at this point Commander Dudley W. Knox has written, "It held up the projected British invasion from Canada until the season was too far advanced for that purpose. On that account Howe in the south abandoned his campaign against Washington east of the Hudson." And from that time onward it became possible to win the Revolution.

were surrendered in 1777, one in 1778. Another was condemned after grounding on a ledge. One, the *Reprisal* brig, 16, foundered. She was the first naval vessel of the independent United States to visit Europe. Fortunately the accident occurred on her homeward journey: she had carried as her outward passenger the invaluable Benjamin Franklin.

Most, perhaps all, original vessels of the Continental Navy were converted merchantmen. The largest measured less than 500 tons. But more than six months prior to the Declaration of Independence, the Continental Congress had moved to establish a professional fleet. It was in one sense a forerunner of the largely successful frigate Navy of 1812, since the best talents were concentrated upon the problem of design. Politics as usual dictated the locations of the yards to receive public money, with some unfortunate results.

Thirteen frigates were authorized on the 13th of December, 1775. Five were to carry 32 guns, five 28, and three 24. The delegates had a fine confidence in the shipbuilding industry; they expected all the frigates to be ready for sea in three months. Two of them, still incomplete, were burned in the Hudson on October 6, 1777, to prevent their capture. Two more, complete except for their guns, were burned by enemy action a few months later. Of the nine that were finished, five had been put out of action by the close of 1778.

The final reckoning—eight captured and the rest destroyed—is not a fair reflection of the service rendered by a group of well-designed vessels, some of which were also well built. Mahan's considerations of the effect of a fleet in being apply somewhat to a fleet coming into being. The enemy's naval force had to be disposed so as to deal with vessels known to be under construction in seven different ports. To prevent the frigates from getting to sea, enemy squadrons which might have swept the coast were kept concentrated off Chesapeake Bay, Delaware Bay, and New York. Only one of the seven built in these places ever got to sea at all.

The general orders of the Marine Committee in 1776 were strategically well conceived: "The Navy is in its infancy and a few brilliant strokes at this Era would give it a Credit and importance that would induce seamen from all parts to seek the employ, for nothing is more evident than that America has the means and must in time become the first Maritime power in the world." The difficulty was tactical. Not enough of the frigates could be shaken loose in time to force the enemy to divide up his concentrations of power, with which no single frigate could cope.

The *Randolph,* 32, the one Philadelphia frigate that slipped to sea, took four prizes off Charleston on September 4, 1777. She was then ordered to France, but the French policy at the time was pacific. Discouragements appear to have been put upon her joining the American privateers that were doing very well in British waters. She was ordered back to Charleston, and sailed again with four vessels of the South Carolina Navy. The fleet took one prize, then encountered the *Yarmouth,* 64. Captain Biddle of the *Randolph* fired the first broadside. Accounts by observers in the other American ships, while partisan, are fairly well borne out by Captain Vincent's report from the *Yarmouth.* Despite the great difference in armament it appears to have been a brisk, mutually disabling fight for fifteen minutes, when the *Randolph*'s magazine exploded.

"Immediately on her blowing up," Vincent wrote, "the other four dispersed different ways. We chased a little while two that stood to the southward and afterwards another that bore away right before the wind, but they were soon out of sight, our sails being torn all to pieces in a most surprising manner."

Eight days later Vincent was astonished to come upon some floating wreckage that bore four uninjured survivors of the explosion. The episode provided one of the few pictures of naval actions of the American Revolution that were made no great while after the events themselves: in this instance, eleven years.

The end of the beginning. The *Randolph* was the first frigate, designed and built for the Navy of the United States, that actually got to sea. Six months and three days later, during a brisk action with the *Yarmouth* which was rated at twice as many guns, the *Randolph* blew up. Her capable young commander, Captain Nicholas Biddle, died in the explosion with all but four of her people. This primitive woodcut focuses attention upon her survivors, who were not known to have survived until the *Yarmouth,* returning five days later into the same waters, came upon them. Her captain reported that they "had nothing to subsist on from that time but by sucking the rain water that fell on a piece of blanket which they luckily had picked up." William James, a truculent British historian, implies that the condition of the *Yarmouth* after the engagement ("our sails being all torn to pieces in a surprising manner") resulted from the explosion of her adversary rather than from Captain Biddle's gunnery in an unequal contest, as the American public had been quick to assume. The picture is from a British history of North America, published in 1789.

Congress authorized the purchase and construction of other vessels. Not counting those listed as gondolas, a total of about thirty saw action. In most cases a first encounter put them out of the war. The *Alliance* frigate and the *Providence* brig fought four actions apiece, the *Andrew Doria* brig three. Two apiece were fought by the sloops *Hornet* and *Sachem,* and by the schooners *Fly* and *Wasp.* In some of these actions the enemy was a fort.

Three ships of the line were authorized by Congress. The only one actually built, the *America,* was begun in 1777 at Portsmouth, New Hampshire, and launched late in 1782. John Paul Jones had overseen the latter stages of her construction and had been appointed her commander. When ready for sea, to the understandable annoyance of Jones, she was given to the king of France to replace one of his ships lost in Boston harbor. Mistaking this vessel for a successor of the same name in the French Navy, one historian has given her a distinguished career and a long life. She actually was condemned as rotten after four years of service. It seems probable that, with the French at last supplying an adequate naval arm in the final phase of the struggle, the congressmen were glad to be rid of the maintenance cost of their only major ship.

The nature of the naval conflict explains in part the lack of pictures to celebrate it. The British were not elated over the capture of sloops and schooners by their 64s. Ships were seldom brought to action in the "proper" way: broadside to broadside. The fleet actions were largely fought by small craft: no spirited focus. Sketches sent home by eyewitnesses produced few prints from foreign artists; in these, meaningful views of American-built vessels are rare. The best known, here reproduced, shows an early attempt made in the Hudson to burn H.M.S. *Phoenix,* 44, and *Rose,* 24. In this case we have all of the elements of good authority for a nautical print. It is identified as originating in a sketch made by James Wallace, commander of the *Rose,* who was made an admiral twenty-five years later. It was engraved by Dominic Serres, a well-known nautical specialist, and published less than two years after the event by J. F. W. Des Barres in a compilation of views and maps prepared specifically for the benefit of British naval officers in American waters.

This compilation, the *American Neptune,* is the finest of the great marine atlases covering the western Atlantic coasts. Its authority as a historical source is strengthened by the fact that no two copies are alike. Des Barres revised the charts and added new ones as rapidly as information came to hand. Each major ship, when sailing for American station, was supplied

Two of the thirteen original frigates authorized by the Continental Congress, the *Congress,* 28, and the *Montgomery,* 24, were built at Poughkeepsie. It was a consequent objective of British policy to control the Hudson and destroy the frigates before they could be used. The *Phoenix,* 44, and the *Rose,* 24, were assigned to clear the river, which was guarded by a few small armed vessels, including the galleys *Lady Washington, Spitfire,* and *Washington.* Of these vessels there is no reliable record except their shadowy appearance in this picture and an inference that the first had one bow gun and the third two. On August 3, 1776, they fought the *Phoenix* and the *Rose* for two hours. A participant reported upon the weight of metal: "the lower tier of one side of the *Phoenix* was equal to that of all gallies." On August 16th, by marine time, two fire ships were sent up the Hudson. An officer of the *Phoenix* reported, ". . . she boarded us upon the Starboard Bow, at which time the Rebels set fire to the Train and left her. Set the Fore Topsail and Headsails, which fortunately cast the ship and disengaged her from the Fire Ship, after having been Twenty Minutes with her Jibb Boom over the Gun whale." This view, looking southward in the Hudson at flood tide, with little wind, seems in close accord with the separate description: the fire sloop's boom across the *Phoenix*'s starboard gunwale; the fore-topsail partly visible in the smoke from a smaller vessel astern of the sloop, the tender of the *Rose,* previously ignited by another fire ship. At a close inspection, two men can be made out in the waist of the 44, staving off the perilous visitor, which has only just been ignited by the "train," since her sails are still in evidence. About a year after this action the two Continental frigates were destroyed in the Hudson by their own people to prevent capture.

with a quickly bound-up collection of the latest sheets. None of the inclusions was frivolous or decorative. The scenes of harbors, headlands, and military installations were all "views" in the nautical sense—intended to help the navigator to get his bearings on objects ashore for the avoidance of those under water. Such productions, offered for the critical inspection and explicit use of seamen, are as reliable in detail as any products of human judgment, guiding the human hand, are likely ever to be.

The *Phoenix* and *Rose* picture concentrates attention upon these two vessels and one of the two fireships, an orthodox sloop. It is noteworthy, however, that the small vessels in the middle background all are crossing lateen yards. There is a flickering specialists' argument over the extent and persistence of the lateen rig in the smaller American fighting craft.

This picture has been identified as the earliest that shows vessels of the United States in action. Most other English contemporary prints are fanciful.

The more skillful contemporaneous Revolutionary prints were made by professionals who seldom had trustworthy information. British engravers understandably stressed British vessels in the few naval prints that were made. An example is the fine view of the battle which began on October 11, 1776, on Lake Champlain. It was published with surprising speed, about ten weeks after the event.

A summary British view of naval operations in "the American war" is reflected in a biographical sketch of Admiral Wallace by his countryman, Professor J. K. Laughton: ". . . during 1775 and the first part of 1776 he was actively engaged in those desultory operations against the coast towns which were calculated to produce the greatest possible

irritation with the least possible advantage." The little port of Stonington has exulted for nearly two centuries over the repulse, by its militia, of a raiding party sent ashore by Wallace to seize some cattle for the *Rose;* but there was no glory for English artists to celebrate in the ensuing reprisal that filled an unfortified village with cannon balls for souvenir hunters of the future, killed no-one, and exasperated a lonely Quaker into dashing down to the shore for a try at winging the *Rose* with a musket.

There is another side to the story of American sail in the Revolution that has been both overglorified and undervalued, depending upon the disposition of the historian. When the official fleet was suffering humiliations and disasters, many privateers were doing excellently well. When frigates were blockaded in the major ports, bizarre idiots went to sea from minor ones with nothing aboard but muskets and cutlasses, intending to capture the necessary cannon by boarding the enemy. Lines of communication and supply were kept open throughout the war; but the ancient notion that it was the job of the Navy to protect commerce had to be ignored. The few naval vessels that slipped to sea spent most of their time behaving like privateers, seizing enemy merchantmen. It can even be argued that the swarm of American privateers in the waters off the British Isles made it possible for a few ships of the Navy to get to France and back on diplomatic missions. Many British fifth- and sixth-rates were busy close to home, hunting down the impudent semiprivate marauders, when they might have kept a tight blockade of the French or the American coast.

The bite of the argument over privateering is chiefly felt in the contention that this activity gravely damaged the efficiency of the Navy itself. Naval commanders who had a desperate struggle to recruit their crews appealed to the central authorities to embargo the sailings of privateers, but the merchants of the Marine Committee were hesitant. Some of them owned shares in privateers; prizes came in almost daily, laden with supplies for the building Navy as well as for the armies and the populace.

Nothing the British could do stopped the splash of a thousand privateer launchings while the Marine Committee was struggling to get a few naval vessels finished. James Hackett laid down the *America,* 74, in May of 1777. In the Navy Department's new *Dictionary of American Fighting Ships* the terse explanation is made, "shortages of money and skilled workmen delayed her launching until 5 November 1782." Skilled workmen were available—where the money was supposed to be, in privateering. Salem had a privateer at sea more heavily gunned than any of the original fourteen vessels of the United States Navy. She had twenty-five others that were more heavily gunned than all except two of the first fourteen.

Discussing the question about fifty years ago, Gardner W. Allen came to the conclusion that if half of the privateering effort had been diverted to the regular Navy, it would have been "able to act offensively against the British Navy to some purpose. The other half, devoted to privateering, would have been able to accomplish more in destroying commerce than all the privateers actually did, and would have suffered fewer losses, because of the protection afforded by a strong, regular navy."

Scholars who add up the privateers of the American Revolution come out with widely different answers. Many vessels were captured and recaptured, commissioned and recommissioned. The name of what is obviously the same vessel is spelled in different ways: a warning against assurance in cases when the identity is less obvious, and the names still vary in the spelling. Is the *Betsy* of Salem the same as the *Betsey* of Salem? When the number of guns differs, after the same name, is it a mistake, or has her armament changed, or are we dealing with different vessels?

A frequently used estimate is "upward of two thousand" American privateers, after deductions for duplication in the lists. This estimate appears to add all vessels used as privateers after capture but to subtract no losses. Some definite statements can be made: 1,699 vessels were bonded by the Continental Congress. Paine's list of Salem privateers includes 196 vessels mounting an average of ten guns apiece. Morison reports that of the letters of marque issued by the Continental Congress, 626 went to Massachusetts vessels.

COMMODORE HOPKINS,
COMMANDER in CHIEF of the AMERICAN FLEET.

Contemporaneous fraud. This mezzotint, frequently published as if it were a real portrait of Esek Hopkins, was published in London nine months after his appointment as commander in chief of the first fleet gathered together by the Continental Congress. The man of the picture might be in his Madeira-soaked thirties. Hopkins in 1776 was an old privateersman of 57, a former slaver and, briefly, a brigadier general in the Continental Army. He was born in Rhode Island. A similar French print, undated, was said to be based upon a painting "par Wilckenson a Boston." As this latter print carries the statement that it is sold in London "chez. Thom. Hart," who was the proprietor of the one here reproduced, it is not certain which was the original fraud. The lettering on the flag at the right seems integral. That on the left-hand flag looks like an applied afterthought. The flags in the French print carry their legends in both French and English. Samuel Eliot Morison, the naval historian, calls both flags fantastic. The spars and sails are not the work of a seaman. Hart published other prints of prominent American rebels, all suspiciously similar. There was much sympathy for the Revolution in England itself, which may help to explain the market for such "portraits." A London friend of William Hickey, the raffish diarist, named his yacht the *Congress* and used to sail her to a French port now and then to toast the rebels.

The
PRIVATEERS' WAR

THE CONFUSED RELATIONSHIP BETWEEN PRIVATEERS AND NATIONAL SHIPS WHICH BEHAVED as if they were privateers emerges grievously in the case of Gustavus Conyngham. Like many citizens of a young United States (which allowed decades to drift by before its legislators began to define citizenship), Conyngham was an Irishman by birth and thus an enemy of his king by osmosis. George III in turn called Conyngham a pirate. Through a bizarre twist of documentation—or the lack of it—the true status of this remarkable officer was in doubt for a century and a quarter.

When Benjamin Franklin was beginning to draw the French cabinet "deeper and deeper," as Trevelyan put it, "into a policy which was the salvation of America, but which, in the end, brought utter ruin upon the French monarchy," he was seeking ships in French ports and people to man them. On May 1, 1777, he sent to sea from Dunkirk the lugger *Surprise*, Captain Conyngham, disguised as an honest smuggler making a benign voyage that only the master of a revenue cutter would want to interrupt. England was horrified a few days later when the brash young man became the third person in all history to presume to seize a packet carrying His Majesty's royal mail across the Channel: the *Prince of Orange*. She and a brig, the *Joseph*, were brought safely into Dunkirk, where pressures from the British ministry upon the French caused the release of the two prizes and the imprisonment of their captor. Conyngham claimed that his commission as an officer had been submitted to the French authorities on this occasion and never returned. The English later contended that the commission had never existed and that his seizure of the packet and brig had been piracy.

Conyngham when released got to sea again on the 16th of July in the *Revenge,* a cutter of ten guns—this time with an indisputable commission, but with written instructions to attack only if previously fired upon: a condition quickly met. The *Revenge* was fired upon by "several british frigatts, sloops of War & Cutters," but eluded them. For eighteen months thereafter Conyngham crosshatched the English Channel, the Irish Sea, the Atlantic coasts of France and Spain, like an all too solid ghost. He sent 33 English vessels to the bottom, and 27 more into port as prizes.

He was not the first officer of the United States Navy to ravage Britain's own waters. The *Reprisal* brig, which had brought Franklin to outwit the shrewdest diplomats of Europe, had tarried before her fatal returning to pick up several prizes off the French coast; and Lord Stormont had to admit that it would be "next to impossible for our Frigates alone to get the better of the numberless small American vessels with which the seas swarmed." But Conyngham displayed the touch of bizarre genius that makes a sea raider, that brings him repeatedly to the quarry and sends him scurrying in time from a heavily armed antagonist. He was our most continuously effective naval officer of the war, and his country practically disowned him. If he had been a mere privateer he would have tried to save many vessels he sank or burned. Instead, he balanced the two functions of a raider in war: aid to his own side and injury to

The most continuously successful commissioned officer in the early Navy of the United States, Gustavus Conyngham fought his own private war with his former king, completely in a privateersman's fashion. The artist puts him in the attire of a French freebooter, while giving him the title of "Commodore." His commissions designated him as "Commander." Evidence is abundant that he was, as the title announces, "the terror of the English." Note, by his left foot, the tomahawk, a weapon that appears frequently on the armaments lists of our early naval vessels and privateers.

the enemy. The rich prizes he sent into Spain financed a substantial part of Franklin's invaluable diplomatic maneuvering; yet when the *Revenge* got safely to Philadelphia, the Marine Committee which had charge of the war at sea could think of nothing better to do with her than to unload the cargo of munitions Conyngham had taken out of prizes and put her up at auction.

The Executive Council of Philadelphia had more enterprise. They chartered the vessel from her new owners to protect commerce of the port, with the stipulation that her former commander should continue at his post, but Conyngham grew impatient. He later attested: "I applied to the Marine board if the Commission I held was or was not sufficient to entitle me as expressed an officer in the AM Navy, should I continue in the comd. of said cutter, & they, and different members of Congress assured me it was. In consequence went on a cruize under sd. AM commss.—" His luck failed him at last. The *Revenge* was taken by H.M.S. *Galatea* on April 27, 1779. In a letter to Franklin, Conyngham reported upon his treatment: "a pair of criminal irons put on my legs, weight 50 pounds; at the door put into the hangman's cart,—all in form as if bound to the gallows." That was prior to the voyage to England, in which the captain of the packet had orders to keep him in the coal hole but refused to do so. The captive continues, "In those irons I was brought to Pendennis Castle. Then not contented, they manacled my hands with a new fashioned pair of ruffels fitted very tite. In this

First step in a legend. This earliest elaborate response of the printmakers to the capture of the *Serapis,* centered upon a rumored incident of the great sea fight that seemed to express both John Paul Jones' indomitable will and his ruthlessness. A week after the battle, the *London Evening Post* had published an affidavit made by British seamen who had taken service under Jones to escape captivity in France, and who had got ashore at night when the wounded were being taken out of the *Bon Homme Richard.* A news report quoted them as adding, what they did not say in the affidavit, "that during the engagement Paul Jones (who was dressed in a short jacket and long trousers, with about 12 charged pistols slung in a belt around his middle, and a cutlass in his hand) shot seven of his men for deserting their quarters; and to his nephew, whom he thought a little dastardly, he said, 'That d—n his eyes he would not blow his brains out, but he would pepper his shins,' and actually had the barbarity to shoot at the lad's legs, who is a lieutenant in his ship." From this point the lurid stories spread, mixed with some exactitudes. A letter from Amsterdam, in the same paper for October 19th, described Jones as having turned up "in the American uniform, with a scotch bonnet edged with gold."

condition I was kept there 15 or 16 days, then brought to Plymouth and lodged in the black hole for eight days, before they would do me the honour of committing me on suspicion of high treason on his majesties high seas; then put into Mill prison, where we committed treason through his earth and made our escape."

The harsh treatment of American prisoners at this period may have been related to the success in English waters of the *Ranger,* a raider which had begun in the preceding year about where the *Revenge* had left off. Another born subject of George III, a Scot who called himself Jones, had even had the impudence to take the *Ranger* into the British harbor of Whitehaven, spike the guns of the battery, and burn some of the shipping. Conyngham had first encroached upon His Majesty's own preserve in seizing a packet carrying the mails. Jones had gone an audacious step further by capturing a vessel of His Majesty's Navy, the *Drake,* somewhat superior in armament to his own ship. These activities, punctuating his seizures of merchantmen, had got him the same designation that Conyngham had acquired: pirate, which was not helpful to a "pirate" already in captivity. The worst blow to the pride of the Royal Navy had fallen on the 23rd of September 1779: defeat and capture of the *Serapis* within sight of her home coast. The few British naval losses hitherto had been sixth rates. The *Serapis* was a fifth rate, a new and powerful ship within that classification. Her opponent had been a patched-up old French merchantman, plus John Paul Jones.

The legend narrowed itself from "seven shot and one peppered" to the durable nonsense that Jones had shot a sailor (later it became his lieutenant) for trying to haul down the flag. In his own report to Franklin, Jones said that his gunner, when told that the ship was sinking, had "run aft on the poop, without my knowledge, to strike the colors. Fortunately for me, a cannon ball had done that before by carrying away the ensign staff." John Collet, artist of the original print at the left, used a number of supposed facts with care. Thereafter his picture produced its own weird offspring. The one shown at the right was offered for sale thirty days later. It is significant that the scene is reversed, and that no painter is identified. The engraver may have worked directly on the metal, taking hints from the prototype before him, a standard practice. When prints were pulled, the scene reversed itself. The features of Jones in both pictures bear a slight resemblance to the later Moreau portrait, making it possible that the engravers already had some sketch taken from life.

The undated print at the right is one of a number, almost identical, issued within a few months of the tremendous fight off Flamborough Head. Another is dated February 7, 1780. That they represent an objective if crude attempt at true portraiture may be inferred from their resemblance to the authoritative Moreau portrait (page 80) and the Houdon bust. Jones liked the latter well enough to have several copies made for friends, and for influential statesmen. In this picture we can really see the man who surprised Abigail Adams into writing, "I expected to have seen a rough, stout, warlike Roman—instead of that I should sooner think of wrapping him up in cotton wool, and putting him in my pocket, than sending him to contend with cannon-balls. He is small of stature, well proportioned, soft in his speech, easy in his address, polite in his manners, vastly civil, understands all the etiquette of a lady's toilette as perfectly as he does the masts, sails and rigging of his ship."

"...The Most EXTRAORDINARY of all Naval Engagements."

OFF FLAMBOROUGH HEAD, MIDWAY UP THE NORTH SEA COAST OF ENGLAND, A BATTLE BEGAN in the evening of September 23, 1779, which enthusiasts have called the greatest sea fight in history. Some, with a touch of restraint, have said it was the greatest of single-ship actions. As it began in a contest between fleets, and as three ships were engaged at the climax, it certainly was not the latter. To call this action, centering between the *Bon Homme Richard* and the *Serapis,* the former is to ignore the usual test of a great military accomplishment, its decisive character in turning the balance of a wider conflict toward final victory. Americans had fought such a battle two years earlier, at Saratoga. It is a quirk of such assessments that the importance of the engagement itself depends upon outside and later factors. If the Continental Navy had been so organized as to permit John Paul Jones to follow up his victory as he wished to do, the course of history might have been changed by it. But Britain had more than a hundred major fighting ships in commission; the United States had four of any consequence, the best of them under the command of a demented Frenchman.

Jones's stunning victory gave the Americans confidence and pride; but there was hardly anything afloat except privateers to further the expression of these qualities. The conduct of the naval war had been ceded to France, which had power but not much enterprise. Count d'Estaing, commander of French ships in American waters, was a brave and forceful admiral who had the glum luck, at the best moment for achievement, to encounter that as yet misunderstood phenomenon, a New England mid-August hurricane.

The four restive French captains who sailed under Jones from l'Orient on June 19, 1779, to harass the British in their private seas, included only one—Denis Cottineau—who could be trusted to follow his orders. Pierre Landais, the irrational captain of the American-built *Alliance,* was repeatedly insubordinate. He sent prizes to Norway, against explicit orders, where they were surrendered to the English. Having the fastest and best ship, he could range as he pleased. The flagship was a superannuated Indiaman. Jones had asked for 18-pounders, but she was not strong enough to sustain them. He received a main battery of 12s, old and pitted, including some that had been condemned. His crew included only 79 Americans. A larger number were British. He carried 137 French soldiers to act as marines.

The intricate story of the great fight with the *Serapis* should be read in the original accounts of Jones, Richard Dale, and Nathaniel Fanning. Melville called it "the most extraordinary of all naval engagements." For grandeur in the telling, his adaptation stands out wonderfully in a piece of hack-work, *Israel Potter.* Samuel Eliot Morison's recent retelling, in the definitive biography that Jones so long has lacked, provides a judicious treatment of conflicting testimony—without a loss of liveliness. The impress of Jones's achievement is evident in the multitude of its retellings. Having pointed out what it surely was not, I should like to note a few details in the large outline of the fight to support an estimate of the phenomenal achievement which it was.

Jones, in his own reports to Franklin and others, reveals himself as one who countenanced war as most great military leaders of modern times have done: thinking it a brutal, hideous activity, justified only as a temporary measure to redress a longer-lasting state of affairs that would be even worse. For one who takes the responsibility of command, such a view probably has become the only alternative to the earlier idiocies of viewing war as a chivalric exercise, or a religious duty, or a system of unavoidable revenge. Jones had an excess of true chivalry for the times, when the bad manners of the duelist flourished as chivalry's last corruption. Some British writers vilified him for refusing a "man of honor's challenge." He went into action viewing war with disapproval. But like many others, he had emotions that did not always accommodate themselves to theory. He was a quick-tempered and violent man who, after committing homicide in peacetime, had been persuaded to escape the jurisdiction rather than stand trial.

These are aspects of the complicated character of a self-made American, commanding a turbulent, international force of five vessels that contained, along with their other problems, several hundred prisoners of war. An attempt was made on September 22nd to decoy a fleet of merchantmen out of the Humber. A change of weather frustrated this, but on the 23rd Jones saw them—41 sail—off Flamborough Head on the sea road to Russia. Two of his own fleet had wandered away. He made the signal for line of battle to the other two. The insubordinate Captain Landais, in the *Alliance,* ignored it. Since she was the only American-built ship in the first famous victory of the United States Navy, the manner of her use particularly concerns us.

The convoy fled. Its two protectors stood out from shore. The larger, the *Serapis,* a two-decker of 50 guns, hailed. "We answered him," Jones wrote, "with a full broadside." It was

These are the two earliest carefully made engravings of the sea fight off Flamborough Head that centrally involved the *Bon Homme Richard* and the *Serapis*. A description of the action will be found in the accompanying chapter. The extent to which these pictures reflect it is discussed on pages 76–77. The scene above was painted by Richard Paton, a poor boy whom Admiral Knowles helped to a career at sea that later gave authority to his many fine marines. His print was issued January 1, 1781, about fifteen months after the battle. The one at the right, a little over two years in preparation and more accurate in some details, is the work of Robert Dodd. Note that the latter, generally abler artist, although he reconceived the main scene, made an almost literal reverse copy of the American frigate *Pallas* in the distance.

after 7:00 P.M. The two ships maneuvered to rake, exchanging broadsides. Noting that the *Serapis* was the handier, Jones knew he must close to prevent too much raking fire. He wished to get across her stern, but damaged rigging slowed the *Bon Homme Richard* at the critical instant. The vessels closed alongside each other, bow to stern. Jones swung a grapple and cried, either, "Well done, my brave lads, we have got her now!"—or, "I've got the son of a whore!"—depending upon which informant the reader elects to credit. According to Lieutenant Dale of the *Bon Homme Richard*, the ships then were bound together with a hawser. Captain Pearson of the *Serapis* reported that they were held by his anchor hooking his opponent's quarter. Both agree that they lay with the gun muzzles of each touching the topsides of the other while a weird fight raged for more than two hours, aloft and alow. Jones's 12-pounders quickly became unserviceable. He had six old 18s on his lower gun deck. Of the first three to be fired, two exploded, killing their crews. No effort was made, after that, to get the three portside 18s across the deck. Some soldiers on the poop ran for cover. The rest abandoned it in good order.

Pearson had anchored in an attempt to shake the *Bon Homme Richard* off, and remained at anchor throughout the action. Soon after the ships closed, Jones found that he had only two cannon that had not been silenced, both 9-pounders on the quarterdeck. The commander of these guns having been wounded, Jones took his place, and got a third 9-pounder across from the lee side. Protected by fire from his men aloft in the tops, Jones reports, he "directed the fire of one of the three cannon against the main-mast with double-headed shot, while the other two were exceedingly well served with grape and canister-shot to silence the enemy's musketry and clear her decks, which was at last effected."

The disputed episode of the famous phrase, "I have not yet begun to fight," came soon afterward. Jones did not use it in his written reports. When three subordinates "by cowardice or treachery" called out to the enemy, Captain Pearson asked if a cease-fire was being requested. "I having answered him in the most determined negative," Jones wrote, "they renewed the battle with double fury."

The Americans kept the decks of the *Serapis* clear, but Pearson replied with his lower battery of 18s, knocking the lighter *Bon Homme Richard* almost to pieces. "Both ships were set on fire in various places and the scene was dreadful beyond the reach of language."

In the meanwhile Captain Cottineau in the *Pallas* had forced the other British vessel, the *Countess of Scarborough*, to strike. The American-built frigate *Alliance*, which so far had done nothing, approached suddenly—when it seemed evident that the *Bon Homme Rich-*

ard was sinking—and began to sail around the locked ships throwing broadsides into the smoke. This is the kinder account, based partly in Captain Pearson's statement. The preponderant testimony in a later inquiry was that Captain Landais was careful to fire only into the *Bon Homme Richard*. The ships being anchored, in bright moonlight, with the smoke drifting all one way, it would hardly have been possible for a responsible seaman to mistake them. The British ship was newly painted yellow; the American was black.

There are two usual explanations. Landais was already mad (his subordinate officers deposed him from his command as mad, in mid-Atlantic, some months later), or in his hatred for Jones he had waited for the two ships to batter each other so badly that the older one would sink and he could easily sink the other. Both theories may be true, since each makes the other more plausible. In such appalling circumstances, the passionate Jones may not have maintained the highest level of rational behavior himself.

A strange feature of the fight had been occurring aloft. As the decks of the *Serapis* were cleared by two of Jones's 9-pounders, the *Bon Homme Richard*'s topmen crossed on the interlocking spars into the tops of the enemy, where they were well protected from below. According to Midshipman Fanning of the maintop, "we transported . . . hand granadoes, &c, which we threw in among the enemy." One grenade exploded some loose powder which in turn touched off cartridges that killed more than a score and ripped the clothing from others. Pearson stated in his report to the Admiralty that the disaster "blew up the whole of the people and officers that were quartered abaft the main-mast, from which unfortunate circumstance all those guns were rendered useless for the remainder of the action." After the misunderstanding over a supposed surrender, Pearson tried to board and was repulsed. But the *Bon Homme Richard* was sinking. "My treacherous master-at-arms," wrote Jones, "let loose all my prisoners without my knowledge and my prospects became gloomy indeed." To keep them from reinforcing the enemy he put them to work at the pumps. A captive British captain slipped through the ports and informed Pearson of the release of the prisoners, but Pearson ignored him, stating that it was a final broadside of the *Alliance,* raking him from astern at 10:30 P.M., that caused him to strike.

After the usual punctilio between commanders, Jones found his ship to be "mangled

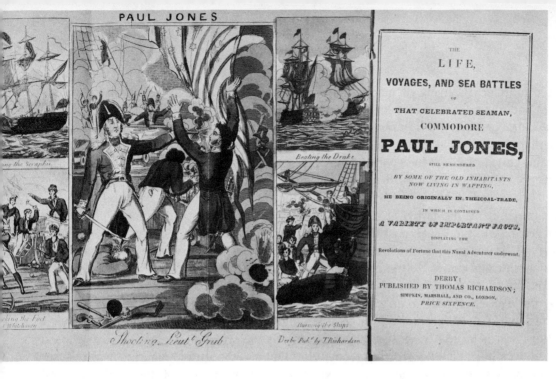

Shooting Lieut.ᵗ Grub

Beating the Drake

Burning the Ships

Derby Pub.ᵈ by T.Richardson

THE
LIFE,
VOYAGES, AND SEA BATTLES
OF
THAT CELEBRATED SEAMAN,
COMMODORE
PAUL JONES,
STILL REMEMBERED
BY SOME OF THE OLD INHABITANTS
NOW LIVING IN WAPPING,
HE BEING ORIGINALLY IN THE COAL-TRADE,
IN WHICH IS CONTAINED
A VARIETY OF IMPORTANT FACTS,
DISPLAYING THE
Revolutions of Fortune that this Naval Adventurer underwent.

DERBY:
PUBLISHED BY THOMAS RICHARDSON;
SIMPKIN, MARSHALL, AND CO., LONDON.
PRICE SIXPENCE.

beyond my power of description." There was hardly anything left to support the upper deck. "A person must have been an eyewitness to form a just idea of the tremendous scene of carnage, wreck and ruin that everywhere appeared. Humanity cannot but recoil from the prospect of such finished horror and lament that war should produce such fatal consequences."

And there we have the mystery: Jones's dislike of war and his solicitude for the ship's people appear often in his writing. A man of these sensibilities, a small man, "soft in his speech . . . vastly civil," not only permitted a desperate, seemingly doomed encounter to continue; but upon at least three occasions when his full duty surely had been done, personally insisted that it continue.

Within war's unconscionable framework, a great commander spends the lives of other men with a fearful prudence to attain an objective. Jones seems never to have wavered in this spending. He did what the captains of fighting sail generally did: exposed his person to the whole of the action, asked no greater risk of a subordinate than he was willing to take himself. He personally directed, in response to a broadside of more than twenty 18-pounders, his preposterous remaining battery of three 9s. From this seemingly foredoomed, small focus he carried what had become almost a one-man war upon the water to victory, against even the mad treachery of the strongest ship still engaged.

With so many involved, there is never truly a one-man victory. The loyal Cottineau and his crew in the *Pallas* kept the *Countess of Scarborough* from an interference that would have been decisive. The topmen of the *Bon Homme Richard* made their fine courage effective through their ingenuity. And still the special greatness of this fight emerges as the accomplishment of one ill-equipped, indomitable genius. I avoid the word "glory." The glory that once appeared as present in war is gone, now and in retrospect—and a good thing too. The madman on the fringe of this action, who by the account of each captain fired into his ship alone, looms as a sort of circling, symbolic judgment upon the madness of the whole performance, in

The later American offspring of the British prints became positively jolly. Versions of this woodcut appeared in a number of popular American song-books. This one is from the *Pearl Songster,* New York, 1849.

which the most nearly living of man-made contrivances were used to test the last extremes of human endurance, locked in a long agony of mutual destruction of the beautiful.

The battle between the *Bon Homme Richard* and the *Serapis,* and of the *Alliance* against both, perhaps was decisive in an inverse fashion. The Royal Navy had fallen into easygoing ways again, gutted of virtue by a corrupt bureaucracy. The loss of so fine a ship as the *Serapis,* to an enemy still diligently described as a pirate in official correspondence after the event, produced an uproar of anger in England. When the pirate was allowed to spend more than five days rerigging his dismasted prize a short distance off the coast, and then was able to take his fleet in safety to the Texel, past the Channel Fleet dispatched to stop him—the anger became fury. It was not long afterward that the great roster of individualistic captains who fought alongside and under Nelson began to emerge, despite the Admiralty's mismanagement. Jones's quality of personal enterprise, of using inadequate means to do more than could be done by the well equipped, soon was in the ascendant again in His Majesty's vessels. The huge climaxes at Copenhagen, the Nile, and Trafalgar were built upon a long series of single-ship actions in which the British were almost uniformly victorious.

There was in England a growing recognition that a stubborn bureaucracy was misusing a powerful navy so foolishly that a distant small war was being lost on the land even while British power still technically dominated the oceans. The fight off Flamborough Head quickened this discontent in a vast literature of controversy. Much of it was spiteful or scurrilous, but even the many "Notorious Pirate" chapbooks glitter with admiration between the lines; the majority of accounts published in England are generous to the hero foeman, exhorting Englishmen to do as well once more.

Prints from two paintings of the action by Richard Paton and Robert Dodd, reproduced on pages 72 and 73, are representative of the sort of pictures the public in England expected to be offered it after any notable sea fight. Both artists were eminent in their specializing profession. There had been the usual rush to get something lurid on the market, but men like Paton and Dodd worked with care, consulting participants and inviting corrections of their sketches.

The print engraved by Daniel Lerpinière from Paton's painting came out fifteen months after the action. Dodd's, engraved by John Peltro, corrected a number of technical faults in the earlier one, which evidently had been called to notice by the knowledgeable. Morison says it is the "least inaccurate" because the *Bon Homme Richard* heads downwind, as she would have had to do when made fast to the anchored *Serapis.* He also notes that the bearing of Flamborough Head is more nearly correct, but objects that the action in the backsea at the left is out of timing because the *Countess of Scarborough* had struck before the *Alliance* joined the central battle. I suggest that Dodd was following an artist's convention, which persisted long after this date, of showing two differently timed events as separated portions of the same scape. (I have included other prints and pictures so conceived, both earlier and later.)

Both prints give us a contemporaneous view of the first thoroughly successful American-built frigate, but neither is a convincing representation of the swift and weatherly *Alliance.* It is not likely that either artist had as good information about this ship as could be secured for the *Serapis,* which in both prints is dominant. The *"Alliance"* of these pictures is more probably a competently drawn typical British frigate. The figureheads differ. Paton's appears to be a man, Dodd's a woman. Dodd evidently intended to show the climax of the action as described by Pearson, with the *Alliance* raking the *Serapis* from astern. Paton's intention in the earlier print is less certain. The mainmast of the *Serapis* has fallen. Most accounts say it occurred just after the act of surrender. Neither picture indicates that the *Serapis* was anchored. The disposition of the sails and pendants in Paton's view would have been possible only if the *Bon Homme Richard* had been the one at anchor. Captain Pearson claimed that the anchor on his starboard bow had fouled his adversary. It would consequently have had to be the larboard anchor that he let go, but in both prints the larboard anchor appears to be at the cathead.

These errors, made by two of the most careful experts of the period, do not add up to a total disparagement of their pictures. They are worth noting because, if we are to look truly at the past in the surviving evidence of what other men thought they saw, it is important to understand the conditions that produced the evidence as well as the conventions of the day that helped to form it. Some future inquirer, wishing to look truly at the twentieth century, would do well to examine the later work of Picasso—but not for photographic, objective representations. Similarly, in viewing these prints we should discriminate between the unlikely, the possible, and the probable. The printmakers must have wanted to sell copies to the survivors of the *Serapis* and their friends: critical purchasers. She probably is correctly shown. Details of the action emerged in discussion: the second print is truer to official reports than the first, but not entirely true. And we should have in mind the standard device of showing different moments of time together in the same scene; otherwise we may be unfairly critical. There is no likelihood that these artists would have had access to exact information about the *Alliance*. It is pointless to expect a good portrait of her.

These are matters of organization and detail. If we are to look meaningfully into past times through the eyes of the contemporaneous viewer, we have to concern ourselves with the general spirit of the times. The public has always maintained with the artist a mutual interchange of expectation and fulfillment. Paul Jones the savage pirate, Paul Jones the abominable traitor, Paul Jones the valiant enemy, Paul Jones the soft-spoken—which did the print-buying public want him to be? From a wide range of portraits we learn more of the times that demanded them than of the man himself. Melville had something of the sort in contemplation when he wrote, "—intrepid, unprincipled, reckless, predatory, with boundless ambition, civilized in externals but a savage at heart, America is, or may yet be, the Paul Jones of nations." Writing in 1854, long before the wicked falsifications of Jones's behavior were exposed, Melville may have characterized the United States, sliding toward civil war, more truly than he did the man in whom he saw mirrored her image.

It was to join Jones, behind the dikes of the Texel, that Gustavus Conyngham made his way after emerging on November 3rd from His Majesty's earth. He had had little trouble in finding friends and money in London—a reminder that the division between Rebels and Tories existed on both sides of the Atlantic. The swapping of populations between sovereigns, in wars and alliances, left the question of allegiance in an uncertain condition in many areas. As late as in the War of 1812 the British ministry was alarmed over the large proportion of Englishmen who willingly entered the ships of the United States Navy to fight against their own.

The rest of Conyngham's career is anticlimax. He made one cruise in the *Alliance* under Jones. It is noteworthy that both of these officers, who had taken their allegiance by choice, proved on occasion stubbornly loyal. Orders arrived that all vessels of Jones's squadron, including his prizes, be taken into the French service while at the Texel, to avoid a diplomatic crisis with Holland when England demanded their surrender. Jones alone rejected a French commission for himself and refused to permit the *Alliance* to be commissioned in the French

Navy. Although his reasons were more personal and basic, his decision made it possible for one last American-built frigate to be flying her own flag at the war's end. The *Alliance* was not one of the first thirteen. Of these, only the *Boston, Providence,* and *Trumbull* were still in service at the end of 1779. All three were soon to be lost to the enemy, largely because the policy of dispersal, in building and in use of the new American fighting ships, procured a temporary possible advantage at the cost of an almost certain eventual encounter with a greatly superior force. Two fine frigates, the *Alliance* and the *Confederacy,* had been laid down a year after the original group. The latter, despite her remarkable sharpness and speed, was as unlucky as most of her predecessors. Her lines, taken off by the British Admiralty after her capture, are a clear proof of the impact of freedom and necessity upon American ship design during the conflict. The earlier frigates were sound and up-to-date in structure, if we may judge by the *Randolph*'s plan, preserved in the National Archives, and by the three captured frigates, the lines of which were taken off by the Admiralty. The *Confederacy* had a remarkable berth-deck length-to-breadth ratio of more than four to one, was fairly shallow, had sweep ports for the emergency use of oars—all obvious responses to difficulties encountered by the first vessels to be commissioned.

No detailed information about the *Alliance* has survived, but her performance suggests that she was as unorthodox. When Jones took her out of the Texel, alone, he worked promptly to windward of the blockading squadron. It would have been prudent for a single frigate to head for the unfrequented waters north of Scotland. Jones took the *Alliance* storming down the English Channel. He ran past the Straits of Dover within view of the British fleet, and two days later reached the Atlantic, "having passed by windward in sight of several of the enemy's large two-decked cruising ships." He took one prize and then called at a Spanish port where Conyngham, in poor health from the harshness of his imprisonment, sailed for home as a passenger. He would have done well to stay with Jones. The vessel was captured, and another year in a British jail was the consequence. This time the "pirate" was eventually released as an exchanged prisoner of war. Franklin was about to send him to sea again in command of a 24-gun ship when peace was concluded.

Year after year Conyngham petitioned Congress for recognition of his commissioned status, upon which his claims rested for a portion of the value of his many prizes. It was finally ruled that the blank commissions which had been sent to France in the early days of the war had not been intended "to give rank in the Navy" but only to authorize "temporary

expeditions" at the discretion of Franklin and other American agents. The petitioner had been dead for almost a century when the vanished commission validating his first cruise turned up in a batch of old documents in a Paris auction room.

Conyngham's troubles were inherent in the improvisations of the early Navy. Prior to the blockade-frustrated building program, we had no ships that could withstand action against British vessels of equivalent rate. True equality of force called for scantlings in both vessels equally capable of absorbing a broadside, and guns not only in the same number but also of the same calibers and lengths. Our naval ships that got to sea in the first two years of the war were at best good privateers, commanded by men whose fighting experience had almost all been confined to actions against private armed vessels. The few ships of the built-to-purpose Navy that survived their first encounters were used largely to carry diplomats. Between whiles, they too fought a privateers' war. It would have been ruinous for them to seek battle with the blockading squadrons. The United States frigates consequently became commerce raiders too.

Privateering has always represented a sordid complex of motives. Since our Revolutionary Navy followed a privateer strategy, it is not hard to comprehend the British attitude toward ravagers of the Channel and the Irish Sea. They began as traitors, were grudgingly called rebels, and behaved like pirates. Northern writers, with exactly the same logic, had the same things to say of Confederate commerce raiders during the Civil War. The original commissions, in both instances, came from a "government" that had no legal existence in the view of its opponent. With such a British attitude toward privateersmen who had been born in America, an even more truculent detestation of the born Irishman Conyngham and the born Scot who called himself "Jones" followed inevitably.

Arthur Lee, one of the American commissioners in France, presented a batch of complaints concerning the behavior of Conyngham, who was of course accused of the standard privateersman's mistake: seizure of vessels that really were neutral. Many officers in a tense time—including Conyngham—sailed with different documents for different sets of eyes, and with spoken instructions varying from the written ones. An accounting was difficult when the evidence had been burned at sea. The French ministry, before Franklin's diplomacy drew France into the conflict, had made protests for the record while privately conniving at anything that would harass England.

We shall probably never know whether Arthur Lee's opposition to Conyngham's claims originated more in apprehension or in malice. Conyngham certainly regarded Lee as the malicious contriver of his frustrations. While in Europe, Lee spent much of his time undercutting Franklin's structure of diplomacy, which does nothing to encourage a generous view of the motives for his other undercuttings.

The standard measure of Conyngham's achievement is the insurance rate at Lloyd's Coffee House: while he was at sea it reached a level higher than in the recent periods of general warfare around Europe. Another measure appears in the fact that, second only to John Paul Jones, he was a printseller's delight. The caricature reproduced on page 67 is one of several done at various times and places. The wide differences between their styles serves only to stress the agreement on features and expression. A prominent nose, a long chin, full lips, a piercing eye are common to all of them. One bears the legend "Engraved from the Original Sketch which was taken by an Artist of Eminence and stuck up in the English Coffee House at Dunkirk." Other sketches doubtless were circulating: unlike those of Jones, it is quite evident that none of the Conyngham prints was pirated from another and that all had some basis in direct observation of the subject.

Dutch prints were made of the taking of the Harwich packet. Her appearance is so

JOHN PAUL JONES: probability toward perversion of the image. The French print at the left seems to have been done from life, or from a life sketch. The proportion of head and body shows a small man, which Jones was. Compare the features with the accurate Moreau print on page 80. Seemingly an honest picture, not well drawn. The middle print is one of the "grudging respect" variety done in England. The third, an early nineteenth century caricature, was made after all reality had faded from the legend. The artist, with no particular malice, was merely slandering a dead man for a few Grub Street shillings.

During one month John Paul Jones was treated both fairly and well by the artists. The bust by Jean Antoine Houdon and the portrait by Jean Michel Moreau le Jeune both were made in May of 1780, when their subject had had half a year to mature his spirit after winning the "most extraordinary" of naval actions. The great men of France had done him honor. The most charming of women had invited the conqueror to extend his conquests. One of them, also probably in the month of May, painted him in miniature —rather less successfully than Moreau, who did the preliminary work himself on the plate from which the above print was pulled. It is our good fortune, amid all the malicious and nonsensical misrepresentation, to have two well-timed portraits in both two and three dimensions from artists otherwise noted for their refusal to flatter the sitter. Moreau and Houdon obviously saw the same man in slightly different moods. There is a little more of humor in Houdon's Jones, a little more of contemplation in Moreau's. But each supports the other in assuring us that this was the man himself, the best sea fighter of the age, and by no means its worst composer of verses.

closely similar in these renderings that the artists obviously also knew her well, but their representations of Conyngham's vessel vary extremely. One shows her as a brig larger than the packet, another as a much smaller lugger. The latter is probably nearer the truth. She was British built.

One late episode of the privateers' war produced that rarity, a skillful British artist's authoritative view of an American-built Revolutionary privateer. To see her, however, one must not be misled by the flags flying from the spanker gaff halliards of the two vessels. The action of May 29, 1782, off the harbor of Halifax, was fought between "His Majesty's brig *Observer,* commanded by Lieutenant John Crymes (to whom this Print is Inscribed)" and the Salem privateer *Jack,* John Ropes commander. The latter has been identified as "possibly the same *Jack* captured from the British by *Perouse,* in the previous year, off Louisbourg." The former, without any question, began life as the Massachusetts-built privateer *Amsterdam.* It is consequently to the British brig of the picture that we should look for an example of American design. The *Jack* may also have been a product of an American yard. The only piece of evidence I have come upon raises a doubt.

The engagement between the *Observer* and the *Jack* had a prelude as confused as the question of their origins. The crew of H.M. frigate *Blonde,* cast away on Seal Island near Nova Scotia, was rescued by the American privateers *Lively* and *Scammel.* The castaway Britons held at the time the crew of a third American private vessel, the letter of marque *Lion.* Safe conducts were exchanged, for what they might be worth. Captain Edward Thornbrough, late of the *Blonde,* requested that British blockaders allow the *Lion*'s people to enter Boston unmolested: the American captains Adams and Stoddart asked other privateersmen not to molest the Britons on their way from Cape Race to Halifax. The former might have been binding, between officers of the same Navy. The latter could have been at best persuasive.

The captured *Amsterdam,* being made ready for sea at Halifax under her new name, *Observer,* needed men. The crew of the wrecked *Blonde* arrived just in time to make up her complement under the command of Lieutenant Crymes. Returning from a first short mission,

The luck did not last. In September, 1781, a print was issued "from a design by C. J. Notté" who obviously was influenced by Moreau. The orientation of the head is nearly the same. The expression has been changed enough to comport with the surroundings. The sashful of pistols was picked up from British prints of the preceding year. Reproduced without comment, the Notté print has been a favorite of naval historians. It represented a quick shift back toward the lurid deck scenes that were to persist until other wars, with their own heroes and scoundrels, diverted the illustrators. Jones has been similarly unlucky with his biographers. The two-volume work by Buell, issued and reissued by a respectable publisher early in this century, is a mishmash of truth and deliberate fraud, which still regurgitates in the writings of the unwary. Three notable attempts have been made in the last two decades to bring objective order out of the mess. The latest biography, and in most ways the best, is by Samuel Eliot Morison.

she encountered the *Jack,* lurking outside the harbor of Halifax. Both vessels probably mounted 12 guns, but the *Observer*'s crew may have been three times as large as the *Jack*'s. In the action, which began at 9:00 P.M., the American captain, John Ropes, was mortally wounded by the first broadside. His also wounded mate, William Gray, directed the fight thereafter. The tactical problem was to keep the more numerous crew from boarding. For two hours Gray was successful. Then there was a lull while the crews of both vessels repaired their chopped-up rigging. The larger crew here had the advantage. The *Observer* regained her ability to maneuver before the *Jack* was ready. As the ships closed, the American flag came down.

Such interlacing of punctilio and humanitarianism with orthodox hard hammering often marked semiprivate warfare at sea. Exchange of prisoners between the regular armed forces was a routine matter, after Franklin secured British recognition that rebels should be recognized by such exchanges, but privateersmen could not secure the persons of large numbers of captives. They sent their less useful captured vessels to a neutral port to put prisoners ashore, or simply plundered them down to the ceiling and let them go. But it seems not to have occurred to two captains of the Age of Reason that the primary objective of their commissions—injury to the enemy—would have been advanced by leaving a trained frigate's crew to take their chances on a desolate island. It would have been quite proper to chop them all to bits with gunfire, if the castaways had had something to respond with in kind. But, rather than abandon them to the risk of starvation, the Americans transported them back into the fight and even provisioned their further journey. Result: more American deaths and the loss of a fine ship under the American flag.

In this action, as in most, the reports of opponents differ. The print itself lists the *Observer*'s force as twelve 6-pounders and 60 men, the *Jack*'s as sixteen 9-pounders and 65 men. American reports give the *Jack* 60 men, the *Observer* 175, and mention twelve guns apiece with an implication that the larger ones were in the enemy. The print probably lists the *Observer*'s regular complement, without adding the extra hands she had just picked up from another wrecked British fighting ship.

The authority of the print rests upon two principal factors. The painting and engraving both were done by the specialist Robert Dodd, who in the interval since the *Bon Homme Richard* fight had begun to make his own plates; and the print was inscribed to the victorious captain, whose patronage would have been important in assuring a good sale. Dodd seems to have had time to consult with Captain Crymes over details, because his print was published twenty-seven months after the action, and a year after the signing of the peace treaty. Thus it is likely that the *Observer* (originally the *Amsterdam*) is an accurate representation of an American-built privateer brig of the latter Revolutionary period, and that the *Jack* is at least a representative privateer ship. It may be noted, by comparison with Dodd's picture of the Flamborough Head action (page 73) that flagstaffs have disappeared in favor of the more manageable gaff halliards. The situation of the *Jack*'s main and mizzen square sails is a bit puzzling. Perhaps, with her bowsprit afoul of the main shrouds of the brig, she is being rotated by the way of her opponent, causing these sails still to be held aback in a small private whirlwind set up by the staysails.

The fight had an ironic postscript, in a British hand. One week later a letter from Captain Thornbrough of the wrecked *Blonde* appeared in the Nova Scotia *Gazette,* thanking his American rescuers publicly "In justice to humanity . . ." The letter included this passage: "For the relief and comfort they so kindly affoarded us in our common Sufferings and Dis-

H.M. brig *Observer* engaging the American privateer ship *Jack* off Halifax, May 29, 1782. The *Observer* began her service as the American privateer *Amsterdam,* built in Massachusetts.

tress, we most arduantly hope that if any of their Privateers should happen to fall into the hands of our Ships of War, that they will treat them with the utmost lenity, and give them every endulgance in their Power . . ."

The *Jack* had fifteen men killed and nine wounded. The *Observer* reported three killed, with her commander and seven others wounded.

As the sea war dwindled to a close, Americans had one notable naval personage to be thankful for. The marvelously inept and willful Earl of Sandwich had been retained in his office as First Lord of the Admiralty—for no apparent reason except class solidarity in a society of privilege—until Lord North's entire ministry toppled, earlier in the same year as the battle between the *Observer* and the *Jack*. The earl's preposterous mismanagement of the Royal Navy throughout the war has to be reviewed point by point to be credited—and then it still seems incredible, not so much that a corrupt Tory could behave with such consistent folly, as that abler if equally obstinate Tories would permit it for so long. It is a real question whether the Revolution could have succeeded if a run-of-the-fleet sea officer had been in charge at the Admiralty. America showed scant gratitude to the Irish and Scottish heroes who joined her cause. She should at least have gone out of her way to thank one wayward English earl.

What it meant for a ship to be on her beam ends.

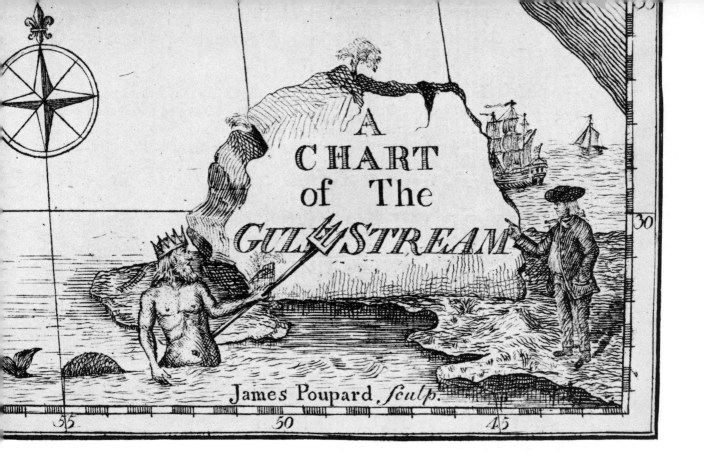

A CHART of The GULF STREAM

James Poupard, *sculp.*

AMERICA'S GENIUS

THE WAGGISH CARTOUCHE HIDDEN IN THE CORNER OF JAMES POUPARD'S CHART OF THE Gulf Stream deserves enlargement if we are to appreciate the reproving forefinger and expression of Benjamin Franklin, and the abashed attitude of a hitherto unchastised Neptune. Franklin was America's Baconian, universal genius. His mind reached upward for the meaning of lightning, downward for that of a warm river flowing within strict but elusive shores of colder water. He set up in 1731 the model from which American libraries developed their distinctive form, and furthered the ordering of knowledge as prime mover in the founding of a university. In 1747 he persuaded the merchants of Philadelphia to send a ship to seek the Northwest Passage. Many inventions popped from his teeming mind, among them the efficient Franklin stove. His aphorisms did as much as anything to create the American character. He was probably the cleverest statesman of the age, in any country, yet never lost his homely humanity. When he manned American fighting ships with exchanged prisoners, he cautioned their commanders against the vengeance such men might practice upon British prisoners, who would not have been responsible for the evil conditions in England's jails.

Franklin had been postmaster of Philadelphia at the age of thirty-one, and later became Postmaster General of the Colonies. This experience, and the problems of transatlantic communication during his diplomatic missions in England and France, stimulated his scientific interest in the behavior of air and water. Seamen long had been aware of the Gulf Stream's existence, but Franklin appears to have been the first to subject it to scientific inquiry. In 1769 he sent to Anthony Todd, Secretary of the British Post Office, the prototype of the

Poupard chart here reproduced, with instructions for shortening the voyages of westbound packets by staying out of the Gulf Stream, and for speeding eastbound passages by making use of its current. The bureaucrats were not interested. Returning from England in 1775, Franklin kept his thermometer busy, sampling the ocean's temperature from two to four times a day. Soon after his arrival he wrote to his friend Joseph Priestley that the results formed "a valuable philosophical discovery" which he would send along when he got "a little time."

His attention for the moment was occupied by the battle at Lexington, consequences of which intensified daily until he sailed for France in the *Reprisal,* with the expectation of being hanged separately if captured. Again he had the opportunity to take the temperature daily of air and water, but no time for an adequate study of the results. In the ten crowded years of his diplomatic exile, the chance to organize his findings never arrived. But when he sailed for home at last, with the great work of statesmanship completed for others to mangle, he had leisure for a return to his old interest in natural philosophy. Aided by his grandnephew Jonathan Williams, he extended his sampling of temperatures, dunking his thermometer as deep as twenty fathoms. The long-impeded flow of ideas started, and would not stop. ". . . the garrulity of an old man has got hold of me," he confessed, "and, as I may never have another occasion of writing on this subject, I think I may as well now, once and for all, empty my nautical budget."

And so he did, with a great spill of suggestions, most of which proved useful in a practical way at a much later date. The one upon which he had been working longest established the basis for studies that culminated about sixty or seventy years afterward in the remarkable publications of another pragmatic American, Matthew Fontaine Maury. It is a happy comment upon the stretch of Franklin's intellect through time that the American Philosophical Society, which published his "nautical budget" in 1786, had been organized by Franklin himself forty-two years earlier, when he thus extended to wider membership a group which he had brought together sixteen years before that. Franklin had been the society's absent president for a long time when he contributed the leading article and three others to the second volume of its *Transactions:*

> . . . *on the Causes and Cure of Smokey Chimneys,*
> . . . *proposing a slowly sensible Hygrometer for certain purposes,*
> *Description of a new Stove for burning Pitcoal, and consuming all it's Smoke,* and finally
> . . . *sundry maritime Observations.* . . .

The first, third, and fourth were written during his homeward voyage in 1785, in the *London Packet,* commanded by Thomas Truxton, one of the most successful privateering skippers of the Revolution. It was a notable voyage, not only in returning to his own country her universal genius but also in bringing together in the same vessel three contributors to the suddenly growing American literature of nautical inquiry. Truxton was to publish in 1794 a work on the variation of the compass, and Williams *The Use of the Thermometer in Navigation,* in 1799. Science feeds itself. What are the chances that either of these books would have emerged if their authors had not been shipmates with the mellow exponent of Try-It-and-See?

Displaying the directness that characterizes a whole mind amid partial ones, Franklin begins his maritime observations with a homely statement of the complete problem: "Those mathematicians who have endeavoured to improve the swiftness of vessels, by calculating to

Colonial Postmaster Benjamin Franklin's proposal for shortening the sailing time between America and England. A first step toward the physical geography of the sea.

find the form of least resistance, seem to have considered a ship as a body moving through one fluid only, the water; and to have given little attention to the circumstance of her moving through another fluid, the air."

His mechanical drawings analyze some of the difficulties with conventional rigs. He then proposes the replacing of a square sail by seven separately manageable triangular sails on the same yards. ". . . more or less sail may be made at pleasure . . . the advantage of swiftness would be very considerable; besides the vessel would lie nearer the wind." I have found no evidence that his idea was tried at the time; but his concept, with a different system of spars, appeared a hundred years later in the big four-, five-, and six-masted coasting schooners. A four-master, with three headsails, produced approximately the effect and the advantages that Franklin was arguing for.

What Benjamin Franklin, writing in his eightieth year, called his "nautical budget." Following a practice of the times, he put his ideas into a letter to a friend which then was published in the *Transactions* of the American Philosophical Society. His budget includes observations on the causes of instability in ships, the efficiency of paddle wheels and jet propulsion, the management of sails, the strengthening of ships' frames, and the best means of preserving sea biscuits. There is even an advance hint of Ericsson's screw propeller.

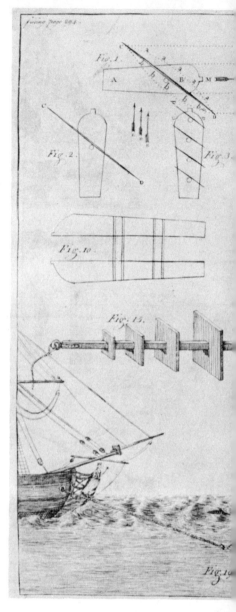

Along the way he reminds his countrymen of the Chinese practice of dividing the hold into several well-caulked compartments, and of experiments with paddle wheels. Two drawings at the right show methods of jet propulsion. One, which he had seen in France, pumps water in at the bow and out at the stern. He suggests, as a method involving less friction loss, the direct pumping of a jet of air.

Franklin's contrivances are cheerfully presented as improvements upon existing ones, and not as inventions out of the blue. The big timber at the left, fitted with four squares of planking, is a sea anchor proposed by someone he knew. He points out that it would float at the surface, and would thus be washed along by the motions of the waves. What is needed is something to sink into the quiet area below the surface disturbance: something collapsible and less cumbersome to store. Many impromptu objects, and several prepared forms of sea anchors, were used to check a ship's sternway in heavy weather and keep her head to the violence of the waves. But the form suggested by Franklin is the ancestor of what became the

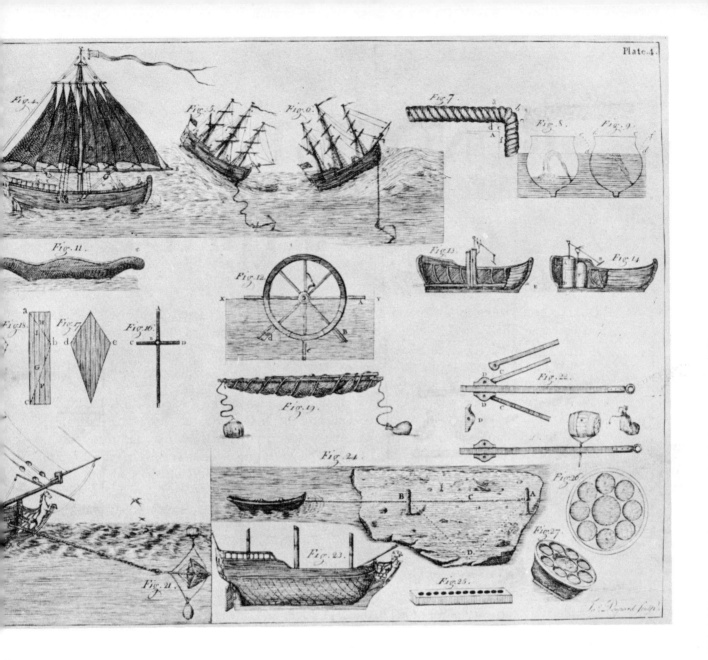

standard drogue. A simpler form of the drogue was used by whalers at least as early as 1725, not to anchor the vessel, but to help tire out the hapless whale.

These are but a few of the many maritime proposals offered in an easy fashion by the industrious philosopher, who even thinks of the comfort of chickens taken to sea. The little board with holes in a row, at the lower right, is for their drinking water. He had observed that they were given very little, and that most of this was slopped out and lost because of the motion of the ship. Too many died of thirst—and the rest, a practical footnote to the humanitarian concern, were "tough and hard as whitleather." Indeed, he advised travelers to lay in personal provisions—"oiled eggs," for example, and particularly water bottled at a clear spring—not only for their own comfort but also because when distributed to the poorer passengers they might "restore health, save life, make the miserable happy, and thereby afford you infinite pleasure."

CONQUEST
BY TRADE

DURING THE AMERICAN REVOLUTION, BRITISH SHIPOWNERS HAD HAD A BAD TIME, INJURED about as much by Lord Sandwich as by the privateers. The noble lord, through the folly of his instructions, lost forty-seven West India vessels to a French-Spanish fleet in one batch, and five big East Indiamen in the same convoy; but it was easier to blame the Yankees for the long accumulation of calamities to which they had contributed heartily.

One consequence was an embargo against American ships in the British Caribbean Islands. Another order, working at cross-purposes with the embargo, forbade British merchants to buy shipping built in America. While American vessels lay idle, the British West Indiamen were too few to supply the islands. The worst grades of New England dried fish, a staple diet of plantation slaves, were also cut off. The new orders forbade the shipment of fish even by way of England, which proposed to expand her own deep-sea fisheries. During the clash of policies, the already appalling death rate of slaves in the sugar islands worsened because of malnutrition. Some 15,000 slaves are reported to have starved to death, for want of North American fish and corn, when hurricanes destroyed what local crops there were.

The British government of the day has been defended against a charge that it deliberately loosed the Barbary corsairs to diminish American shipping. Journals and dispatches of American captives and diplomatic agents in the Barbary regencies (Joel Barlow, James Leander Cathcart, William Eaton, Richard O'Brien, and others) reveal that persons on the spot were convinced that such a policy was deliberate. A little later, during the Napoleonic wars, Britain depended largely upon Barbary to provision the Mediterranean fleet. From the end of the American Revolution until shortly before Lord Exmouth's bombardment of Algiers in 1816, treaties with other countries were made and broken by that piratical regency for convenience or at a whim. But the Algerian treaty of accord with England, worded somewhat less shamefully than the others, held firm. At any rate, for eleven years beginning in 1785, it was foolhardy for an American skipper to venture into the Mediterranean. On two occasions American vessels were captured by corsairs outside the Pillars of Hercules.

These severe limitations upon the renewal of trade provoked a response that might have been predicted. Inheritors of the outlook of Phips and Pepperrell, building upon the free-roving experience of a privateers' war, simply extended their trading horizons beyond monopoly and into the disputed seas. Royal patents, moreover, giving chartered companies the exclusive right to trade with areas in the Far East, were not as a rule binding upon the countries in those areas. The Honourable John Company would fight to defend its patent against its Danish, Dutch, and French counterparts. How it might behave toward a roving Yankee was still to be discovered.

In the year the war ended the modest sloop *Harriet* of Hingham, Hallet master, set out for China by way of the Cape of Good Hope. There Captain Hallet encountered some East Indiamen who were solicitous to save him the further journey by buying his cargo and loading him up with fine teas. In February of 1784 the *Empress of China,* a ship of respectable dimensions for the times—360 tons—sailed from New York for Canton and established the China trade which came to a peak of fame about seventy years later in the tea clippers.

While the *Empress of China* was at sea the ship *States* of Boston, with 13,000 sealskins secured in the Falklands, arrived at New York, contributing another element to the inter-weaving, vast pattern of a new trade. Fine furs were acceptable in China as gifts or tribute, by the theory of its proud government which discouraged vulgar commerce. The same proud government, not wishing to seem ungracious, could be counted upon to make presents in return of tea and other merchandise sufficient to fill a ship. The system, greased by bribes, soon was brought under normal laws of supply and demand. A search for sealskins and sea-otter pelts, to be carried as exchangeable tribute to China, sent American vessels farther and farther into seas cluttered with what then were called ice islands.

Representative early voyages were made by the *Columbia Rediviva,* a new 212-ton ship probably built and certainly outfitted for the purpose, at Plymouth, Massachusetts, in 1787. On her first voyage she was accompanied by the sloop *Lady Washington,* of 90 tons. They sailed at the end of September for the Northwest Pacific coast of America, a region fairly well known to the British, who had preferred not to advertise their knowledge by means of maps. The vessels were in company as far as Cape Horn, where they lost track of each other in a gale on April 1, 1788. The *Lady Washington* spent six and a half months crawling up the Pacific to a rendezvous in Nootka Sound, but she was quicker than the *Columbia Rediviva,* which required an extra week.

It was rather to have been expected that the smaller vessel, intended to serve as a tender like the earlier flyboats, would have held back the ship. The difference was in the skippers. Robert Gray of the sloop was immensely enterprising. John Kendrick of the ship was "whimsical and vacillating," by one appraisal, and in Gray's view not "a nimble leader." Perhaps without planning it, he slid little by little into the character of a crook.

While Kendrick dawdled in the sound, Gray took the *Lady Washington* down and up the coast, from Nootka to Juan de Fuca to Alaska. He proved for the world at large what the

The *Grand Turk* punchbowl, brought home from Canton in 1787 in the first of a series of Salem vessels so named. Despite their contemporaneous nature, such representations of particular ships on China ware seldom were accurate. This one, prepared at the order of Pinqua, the eminent Hong merchant who handled the ship's business, may have been more faithful to the original than most.

The Columbia River was named by Captain John Gray of the *Columbia Rediviva,* the second or third Yankee vessel to reach the Northwest coast, and probably the first to complete a circumnavigation in the fur trade with China. The captain's own name survives at Gray's Harbor, Washington. This picture shows the *Columbia Rediviva* in winter quarters, with the sloop *Adventure* under construction on shore.

local residents knew, that the Queen Charlotte Islands did not constitute a peninsula. He traded with great success, at one point securing two hundred sea-otter skins for as many pieces of iron hoop fashioned into rough chisels. Returning, he persuaded Kendrick to go trading with him. Shortly thereafter one of the curiosities of exploratory trade occurred. Gray amicably took command of the expedition. He put all the furs into the *Columbia Rediviva,* left Kendrick in the sloop to continue trading in behalf of the owners, and headed for Hawaii. He disposed of his furs in China and returned to Boston with a debit balance on his books.

The fact that the *Lady Washington* was still to be heard from, and might show a profit for the whole adventure, appears to have encouraged the owners to send the larger vessel out again. With Gray in command instead of Kendrick, the *Columbia Rediviva* cut almost four months from her former sailing time to the Northwest. The ensuing winter was marked by the construction of the first United States vessel built on that coast—the sloop *Adventure,* from a frame brought out in pieces from Boston—and by Gray's giving the name of his ship to the Columbia River. The later claim of the United States to the region, in the days of "Fifty-four forty or fight," rested upon the fact that he was the first man on record to take a ship into the great river.

The *Lady Washington* never came home at all. Captain Kendrick made a sham sale of her, for owners' account, purchasing her himself. Perhaps he intended to remit sooner or later. He took her to China, sold her cargo of sea-otter skins for $18,000, returned at least twice to the Northwest in her, and was killed by an accidentally loaded saluting cannon in the harbor of Honolulu, December 12, 1794. The *Columbia Rediviva* had returned to Boston in the preceding year, arriving on July 29th. She was broken up after fourteen years of hard service. The accounts which give her a career twice as long are in error. The *Lady Washington* was probably the first United States vessel to visit the Northwest coast, although there is a suggestion that the *Eleanora* brig of New York, Simon Metcalfe master, had been there previously.

What evidence we have on this point comes from the log kept by John Boit, perhaps the most phenomenal voyager out of New England in the Federalist period. He shipped as fifth mate in the *Columbia Rediviva,* for her second Nootka voyage, was a first mate in the transatlantic packet service at the age of eighteen, and a year later took command of the 98-ton sloop *Union* for a voyage to the Northwest Coast and China. It has been claimed for Boit that he was the first to circle the globe, westward, by way of Cape Horn, in a sloop. His successful

The Columbia Rediviva attacked by Indians.

fur trading was marred by a sharp battle with Indians in which the inequality of weapons showed cruelly in the casualties. None of the northeastern Americans was injured, 41 of the northwestern ones were killed. The attack upon the visitors, like many others, had its origin in the unprincipled behavior of earlier traders. White men, on the wild shores, too often continued the conquistadores' practice of storing up deadly animosities for the future.

Boit took what became the accustomed westward route, by way of Hawaii, Canton, the Sunda Strait, the Isle of France, Madagascar, and the Cape of Good Hope. He arrived in Boston on July 8, 1796, having been away a little less than two years. On the homeward journey in the Atlantic he was stopped, but treated "with the utmost politeness" by a French warship, and again by a British frigate which, he wrote, "suffer'd me to pass, after treating me in a rough and *ungentlemanlike* manner." Both events were serious portents of the coming involvement of the United States with France and Britain, caught as she again was on the fringes of a mortal struggle between the two great maritime powers.

While Boit was homeward bound, west of Africa, another American citizen who had been longer away sailed for the United States from the North African port of Algiers. James Leander Cathcart, Christian Clerk to the Dey of that regency, had been carried in the capacity of boy on the first United States vessel to be seized by the Algerine corsairs. The early part of his imprisonment had been grim, but he had used his wits to take advantage of the complex status of a slave in Barbary. It was improper for Mahometans to sell wine. He became a wineseller. It was forbidden a good Mahometan to drink wine, but if he were tricked by a Christian who told him it was not wine, then the sin was upon the Christian's head. Cathcart was multitudinously sinful, and his regular customers, the Turks of the garrison, were happy

The large American sloop, a type of vessel which John Paul Jones viewed with misgivings when he was given one for his first command in the Revolution, was in some degree a Yankee answer to British colonial regulations. The lumber trade of Maine, before July 4, 1776, was carried on in British-owned vessels of any convenient size, but residents of the colonies were not permitted to use anything larger than a sloop. The development of very large sloops was the obvious response. This cartouche from Osgood Carleton's Maine map of 1800 shows the loading of lumber in a modest sloop twenty-five years after the practice became optional.

ABOVE. Mauritius was Portuguese in the sixteenth century, Dutch in the seventeenth, French in the eighteenth, and has been English since the Napoleonic Wars. When the circumnavigating American fur traders began to visit Port Louis, Mauritius was temporarily known to sailors as the Isle of France. Off and on it was a rendezvous for privateers, including the famous Robert Surcouf, who captured a heavily armed Indiaman within sight of the Sand Heads below Calcutta. In the 1790s Port Louis, in the Isle of France, was a cosmopolitan market for the redistribution of cargoes and the sale of ships at auction. John Boit paused there in the sloop *Union*, at about the time he came of age, to discharge freight and passengers and to buy coffee and pepper. He was back again a year or two later in a captured English snow, the *George*. "God send me," he wrote, after selling her there, "that I may never sail in the like of her again." RIGHT. Of the world's great ports, Calcutta is the farthest from the sea. Sailing vessels, after finding a way through the perilous Sand Heads, had to await flood tides at least twice to carry them about a hundred miles up the Hooghly to anchorages off the Esplanade, which is shown here as it appeared to early voyagers from post-Revolutionary America. Resident British nabobs endured the climate to make quick fortunes, living luxuriously. Under the Honourable John Company's regulations, American traders were unwelcome. But when offered a bargain the Company's servants found a way. Captain Simon Metcalfe, in the *Eleanora* brig of New York, was one such visitor, at about the time when John Boit of the sloop *Union* wrote of Metcalfe's arrival at Macao "in the Elenora from the N.W. Coast and did then fit her . . . for the Coast again." Other known entries of Metcalfe's voyages make the sequence hard to understand, but if Boit was correct, Metcalfe must have been on the Northwest coast a few months earlier than the *Lady Washington,* the first Northeast American to trade there. This view of Calcutta's Esplanade and part of its anchorage was made about 1790 by Thomas Daniell, who with his nephew William spent ten years in India preparing a series of views published in 1797.

94

BELOW. Crowninshield's Wharf, at Salem, as it appeared to the marine artist George Ropes in 1808. The ship at the far right is the *America*, built in 1804 and later a successful privateer, which once logged 13 knots for two hours. LEFT. The *Harriet* of George Town—so identified on her transom by the Dutch artist G. Groenewegen. A typical sizable American trading ship of the 1790s, probably hailing, at this period, from the South Carolina port on the Pedee River. The print, actually dated 1793, could have been approximately dated by the flag, which in 1795 acquired two extra stars by act of Congress, and two extra stripes as well. In 1818, realizing where this sort of addition might fetch up, the Congress restored the original thirteen stripes. In some of the pictures that follow, fifteen can be counted. Note the resemblance of the little leeboarder in the right forewater to the one in the print of Philadelphia on page 56. The type is still in use.

to pay a modest fee to be similarly tricked every evening. By the distribution of suitable bribes he kept most of his winnings. At the end of eleven years—though still a slave—he rose to be a confidential counselor to the Dey.

When Joel Barlow, the American poet, at last made a practical bargain with the Algerians to release the American slaves, Cathcart was his adviser. The consequent peace treaty involved the payment of perpetual tribute by the United States, "an island in the ocean," and contained clauses which the country has been happy to forget, drowned by the later roar of Decatur's cannon. One provision obliged every American shipmaster to return to the Dey any escaped slave, wherever he might be discovered. But the main point of the treaty was tribute in naval stores, and the tribute was slow in arriving. In the spring of 1796 the Dey became so exasperated that he permitted James Leander Cathcart to buy a ship and sail it to America at his own expense with letters to the President, pointing to the overdue obligation.

It was a long time before the first United States shipment of tribute actually was delivered in Algiers; but the practical poet Barlow in the meanwhile kept the treaty from being torn up and the corsairs from sailing out again by wangling a large loan from the international banking house of Bacri, and by promising that President Adams would build the Dey a magnificent frigate. The money, alas, went mostly for bribes, and the tribute still was owing. But Barlow accomplished his immediate purpose. Five days after the arrival of the sloop *Union* in Boston, more than 120 Americans who had been slaves, some for as long as eleven years, sailed from Algiers for America, and the Mediterranean—at the cost of tribute and bribery—once more was technically open to American sail.

The ship *Monk* was launched at Nobleborough, Maine, in 1805, for Salem owners. She measured 253 tons. One incident of her career was the bringing home of Sylvanus Snow of Orrington, Maine, who escaped to her at Minorca from a British vessel after having served as an impressed seaman at Trafalgar. Here the *Monk* is shown off Marseilles. The painting, by Nicolai Carmillieri, shows an unusually animated scene on deck.

The Navy &
Thomas Jefferson

IT HAS BECOME ALMOST A HABIT AMONG NAUTICAL HISTORIANS TO SINGLE OUT THOMAS Jefferson as a scapegoat upon whom to load all the Navy's early frustrations and send him stumbling inland. They hold him responsible for the ineffective, costly squadrons of gunboats —small craft with one or two guns apiece—and for the lack of ships of the line. The embargo of 1807 was Jefferson's Embargo. As with many other interpretations of history, a case can be made by leaving out the contrary evidence. It is particularly easy if one ignores the origins of the issue and begins twelve years later, when the first great frigates were actually launched. But where did they come from?

The naval issue was precisely drawn in an exchange of correspondence between Adams and Jefferson in the summer of 1786, when their new country's first urgent need for a mobile instrument of force had emerged in the Barbary crisis.

In the autumn of 1785, as a forewarning of ambiguities ahead, twenty-one Americans out of two captured vessels were enslaved by the Algerines, and our attempts to re-establish trade in the Mediterranean came to an abrupt stop. The remnants of the Revolutionary Navy all had been sold. Consequently three of the four most eminent statesmen of the early Republic, on assignments in England and France, were instructed to deal with the problem by diplomacy: Adams, Franklin, and Jefferson. The aged Franklin's departure for home, with his ocean-probing thermometer, left the decisions to the others. Adams advocated intercession, by friendly powers, to persuade the Barbary regencies to accept payments of tribute as the price of allowing our ships freely to pass. It was the common European practice.

Jefferson, in the nub of his long letter of July 11, 1786, replied, "if it is decided that we shall buy a peace, I know no reason for delaying the operation, but should rather think it ought to be hastened. But I should prefer the obtaining it by war. 1. Justice is in favor of this opinion. 2. Honor favors it. 3. It will procure us respect in Europe, and respect is a safe-guard to interest. 4. It will arm the federal head with the safest of all the instruments of coercion over their delinquent members and prevent them from using what would be less safe. I think that so far you go with me. But in the next steps we shall differ. 5. I think it least expensive. 6. Equally effectual. I ask a fleet of 150. guns, the one half of which shall be in constant cruise. This fleet built, manned and victualled for 6. months will cost 450,000 £ sterling." He noted the need for an established "small marine force" if only for its influence in persuading "Pyratical states" to keep a peace once it had been signed. "If it be admitted however that war, on the fairest prospects, is still exposed to incertainties, I weigh against this the greater incertainty of the duration of a peace bought with money, from such a people."

Note the order of emphasis in Jefferson's argument: justice first, then honor, then moral effect, then safety, then cost, and finally practicality. His fourth point deals with the dual problem that was soon to produce our Federal Constitution: the reluctance of states in a loose confederation to support expenditures by a central legislature, and the general abhorrence of a standing army as a means of coercing them. Note also that a fleet of 150 guns, by the standards of 1786, meant six frigates—the number settled for eight years later, but with a significant innovation in size and in number of guns.

Before coming to their opposite positions of policy, Jefferson and Adams had conferred together in London with Abdrahaman, the ambassador of Tripoli, who had candidly explained the Barbary policy: "it was written in their Koran, that all nations who should not have acknowledged their authority were sinners, that it was their right and duty to make war upon them wherever they could be found, and to make slaves of all they could take as Prisoners, and that every Musselman who should be slain in battle was sure to go to paradise."

I quote this from a joint report of Adams and Jefferson, who drew opposite inferences from it. It was the Adams policy that found favor at New York. The first agent sent to Algiers was told to offer $200 apiece for the twenty-one American slaves. The Dey demanded fifteen times as much. Efforts were then made through the Mathurins, an order of monks whose sole function was the redemption of slaves. The general of the order warned that if too much were paid, then the Algerines would never make peace, but would hunt Americans in preference to all others. He suggested trying $555 a man. John Paul Jones bluntly proposed docking all American seamen's wages a shilling a month for the purpose if the United States treasury was empty. This was not tried.

Jefferson was preparing to leave Europe in September of 1789 to report on the French Revolution, one effect of which was the dissolution of all religious orders, even the Mathurins. Just before his departure from Paris, he was asked by Francis Hopkinson whether he was an "antifederalist"—a political question that must be borne in mind because the circumstances of the permanent Navy's founding seem too bizarre for credence unless they are viewed politically. Jefferson replied, "If I could not go to heaven but with a party, I would not go there at all," adding that though he was not a Federalist he was even less an Antifederalist. In this spirit he took the office for which, upon arrival, he found that President Washington had nominated him: Secretary of State. Although the composer of the Declaration of Independence had been out of the country when the Constitution was drafted, he obviously believed, with the men who did shape it, that the new nation could somehow be run without political parties. He soon discovered that those who shared his still favorable opinion of France were behaving like a political party, and that they expected him to lead it, heavenward or wherever.

When Jefferson took up his new duties as President Washington's formulator of foreign policy, a world-shaking quarter century of revolution and readjustment already was under way. It had begun with the storming of the Bastille by the Parisian poor, in 1789, and was to end in 1815 at Waterloo. During this period the United States was to fight two small naval wars—with France, 1798–1800; and with Tripoli, 1801–1805—followed by the sea-and-land war with Britain that began in 1812. All three conflicts, and a belated skirmish with Algiers in 1816, had their origins in naval policy or in the want of it. The founding and early development of the Navy, the dominant weapon in each of them, makes little sense unless we view our alternating naval reluctance and commitment as a continuous response to the vast struggle between France and England which on the waters of the world was relieved only by brief tactical lulls. We, in the same quarter-century, had nearly a decade of non-belligerency before our naval war with France began, and seven more years of dubious restraint between the signing of peace with Tripoli and the declaration of war upon the United Kingdom. It is the second of these periods that has drawn so much irate fire from partisan naval chroniclers. There has been too little effort to comprehend the first one, which seems indispensable to an assessment of what followed.

Jefferson's letter to Adams, quoted above, formulated for an explicit emergency a remedy based on beliefs he had frequently expressed before. An eloquent advocate of naval construction during the Revolution, he had renewed his arguments for a naval force even before the first American seamen were enslaved by Algiers. In February of 1785 he had written to Madison that the United States must either abandon its commerce or protect it. "Otherwise the smallest power in Europe . . . may dictate to us, and enforce their demands by captures on our commerce. Some naval force then is necessary if we mean to be commercial . . . Be assured that the present disrespect of the nations of Europe for us

Algiers at the time of the Barbary Wars. Frontispiece from the journal of Pananti's captivity.

will inevitably bring on insults which must involve us in war. A coward is much more exposed to quarrels than a man of spirit." Six months later he prophetically wrote to John Jay, "I think it to our interest to punis[h] the first insult: because an insult unpunished is the parent of many oth[ers]"—adding that "our first attention" when free of debt would "be to the beginning of a naval force of some sort." Within weeks, the Algerines proved his point.

As Secretary of State Jefferson drew up a full report of the Barbary negotiations, upon which the President asked Congress to act in behalf of the remaining enslaved Americans; six already had died of the plague. Jefferson noted the soaring cost of ransoms, and warned that peace with Algiers might soon be made by Portugal, whose frigates had kept the corsairs corked up inside the Strait of Gibraltar for several years. If so, "the Atlantic will immediately become the principal scene of their piracies. . . . it rests with Congress to decide between war, tribute, and ransom, as the means of re-establishing our Mediterranean commerce."

Congress at first responded to Jefferson's arguments with a committee report that it would be "proper" to have a naval force "as soon as the state of the public finances will admit." It appropriated $20,000 as a "present" to the new emperor of Morocco, and then firmly confronted the naval issue with a resolution favoring tribute of $100,000 a year to Barbary and $40,000 to ransom the captives: not quite $3,000 apiece, the amount demanded by the Dey when he had been offered $200 apiece six years earlier. Since there apparently was to be no navy to enforce his diplomacy as Secretary of State, Jefferson next put his reliance in the man who had won the most famous of recent sea fights with the best part of his own fleet fighting against him.

While in Paris, Jefferson had encouraged John Paul Jones to take the great Catherine's offer to make him a Russian admiral, assuring a maximum of experience to the man most likely to take command of a United States naval force; but both Jefferson and Jones were disturbed by the thought that so ardent a lover of human liberty should serve under a despotism. Jones himself noted that his Black Sea actions were against another tyrant, the Grand Seignior, who was supported by a small fleet from Algiers.

It is not easy to imagine the truculent yet loyal Jones as tribute bearer to Barbary. (Another of our great early captains was to find himself before long in the same circumstances.) Washington and Jefferson made conditions that were meant to take some of the shame out of the sorry errand. It was kept so close a secret that Jefferson wrote Jones's instructions in his own hand. The central condition was, "We will not furnish them naval stores, because we think it not right to furnish them means which we know they will employ to do wrong." The difficulty was that no Algerine Dey—elected head of a murderous Turkish garrison in an economy based upon bribery and plunder—could have survived more than a few hours if he had accepted such a limitation. The slaves, James Leander Cathcart, and Richard O'Brien, had warned that tribute must take the form of naval stores. Whether Jones could again have done the impossible is a futile question. The great American captain and Russian admiral died suddenly in his Paris bedroom, but with "his feet on the floor," before his instructions could be delivered.

The next envoy died on the way to Algiers about six months later. The youngest of the Americans in Algerine slavery had been driven mad, waiting seven years for ransom. Cathcart, the most adaptable, had become the Dey's clerk.

Newly returned from Paris, Jefferson had been astonished at the attachment for England, the late enemy, shown by those who sought to honor him at ceremonial dinners. His approval of even what he later called "the benign stage" of the French Revolution had not

Gibraltar, the key to Barbary. This woodcut is from *A Sequel to Riley's Narrative*. James Riley had the unusually bad luck to be shipwrecked outside the Pillars of Hercules and enslaved in spite of the amicable relations between Morocco and the United States. Portuguese cruisers, standing on and off Gibraltar, at most times kept the corsairs of the other Barbary States inside the Mediterranean.

gone down well with the wine of gentlemen who so recently had made a benign revolution of their own. The new Secretary of State found himself increasingly isolated among Anglophiles. Official communications of the British minister were even routed around him by the influence of Hamilton. As one feature of the fierce symbolic struggle developing between them, it should be remarked that Hamilton, the ardent Federalist and partisan of Britain, wanted a standing army as the main prop of political power, while the reluctant Antifederalist and partisan of France, Jefferson, was the only high official in Philadelphia who urgently advocated a navy.

The position of the Federalists was clear enough. An alliance with England, controller of the oceans, would give American merchant shipping the same sort of protection it had enjoyed in colonial times; a United States navy at best might be a cat's-paw in conjunction with His Majesty's fleets, and at worst would create dangerous incidents. What is hard to comprehend was the solid Federalism of shipowners and merchants, who seemingly would have had a special interest in a navy of their own. Their mounting fear of the libertarian France seems to have forced them into the anti-French party no matter what else it might stand for.

CRISES OF 1793

Early in 1793, year of multiple crises, France declared war upon England. The benign French Revolution turned ruthless. Seizures of American vessels multiplied, as both belligerents enforced their rules against contraband. In an intense effort to maintain sea power, the enslaving of other countries' seamen became more frequent.

Peter Walsh, an American trader at Cadiz, wrote to Secretary Jefferson on October 17, 1793: "whatever English ships of force come into this Bay strip all American Vessels of their Men, the Natives of that Kingdom they take out of them by main force, tho' these always enter as American Citizens, & Swear themselves to be Such, & the Americans they use every endeavor to entice away."

Walsh, himself a naturalized citizen, was being candid about the irreconcilable complication: in the international community of the fo'c's'le, real and former Englishmen mingled with born Americans, but His Majesty's laws did not admit that any Englishman could become former. Moreover, a British captain desperate for men was not always impressed by the documents of the native Yankees.

These were the incidents that Jefferson had foreseen in his letter to Madison. He was also disturbed by a disposition, in the government of which he was a member, to disregard the treaty of alliance with France and to seek one with the United Kingdom. President Washington solved the problem to the satisfaction of no-one by a proclamation of neutrality that encouraged both belligerents to prey upon ships which neither any longer had a reason for protecting.

It was in 1793 that three mingling threads of American interest began to tangle in their movement each toward its seemingly separate war. It was reported to Edward Church, United States consul at Lisbon, that American vessels were returning in ballast from England, "the English not chusing to risk their property in American bottoms, but no reason has been assigned for this mysterious conduct." The reason, as Church soon saw it, "evident Enough here," was that Charles Logie, British consul at Algiers, had been secretly negotiating for the suddenly announced peace between Algiers and Portugal of which Jefferson had warned in his reports to Congress. Church revealed that nine Algerine corsairs had run out through the Strait of Gibraltar on the 6th of October, past the British and Portuguese men of war. Their bag, a few days later, included four ships, five brigs, and a schooner, all owned in the United States. To the fourteen surviving slaves who had waited eight years for their country to release them, 105 new ones were added. Their ransoms, at the rate recently established by congressional appropriation, would add $300,000 to the "price of the peace" —a contemporary euphemism.

Had Logie's instructions really been calculated so as to assure Algerine capture of American vessels whose masters would have no chance to learn of the danger before it struck? It was in the classic pattern of political employment of the Barbary nuisance. Historians of a more civilized interlude, a century later, gave England the benefit of the doubt. Peering back out of the power politics of the mid-twentieth century, it is not so easy to say that all the observers on the spot were wrong. The news muddied the waters at Philadelphia, where the Federalists were less firmly in command of the Second Congress than they had been of the First.

On the other hand, the tactless antics of Citizen Genêt, French envoy, had done far more to ruin the French cause with the American public than Jefferson had been able to do to sustain it. "Never in my opinion," he wrote to Madison, "was so calamitous an appointment made . . . Hot headed, all imagination, no judgment, passionate, disrespectful . . ." Jefferson had resigned over the political mess, in midsummer, but after Washington had intimated he himself had better resign ahead of the chief of his official family, Jefferson reluctantly had stayed on until the end of the year. Just as he left public office, a great objective for which he had striven suddenly came to seem possible. The country was riven over the French question, which was the English question pulled inside out, but no-one was a partisan of Barbary. Peter Walsh reported the continuing enslavement of Americans by Britons in the waters of a third power, but the Federalists found it prudent to concentrate their attention at last upon the appalling news from Algiers.

Although only one high official in the penurious years had consistently urged the creation of a navy, some private citizens had interested themselves. Among these, Joshua Humphreys, the Quaker shipbuilder of Philadelphia, has by almost universal consent been given chief credit for the concept of the renewed Navy. One modern naval historian and marine architect, Howard I. Chapelle, has in his writings repeatedly questioned an excessive concentration upon Humphreys as the father of the Navy's design and thus of its remarkable success. M. V. Brewington, after a careful examination of plans and documents, credited Humphreys with the design of ten of the thirteen original Continental frigates (*American Neptune,* January 1948, page 22). Chapelle responded (same, July 1949, page 161) with strong opinions to the contrary, which were in turn attacked by others.

Chapelle, in the dispute, made a generalization from which all historians can profit: ". . . we look for and always try to establish a dramatic story, with many 'firsts,' of ship development whereas in truth the development was slow, step-by-step improvements: we have made certain individual designers, Humphreys, Fox, Steers, Griffiths, McKay, for examples, important beyond all reason by accrediting them with 'firsts' or qualities of invention they did not possess."

It is beyond dispute that Humphreys participated extensively in the Revolutionary frigate-building program; that he was a prominent builder of merchantmen thereafter; that more than a year before Congress passed the original Navy Act of 1794 he wrote to Robert Morris a famous letter enunciating the theory of a small successful navy; that he was officially appointed under the act to prepare the drafts; that Josiah Fox, whom Chapelle holds in high regard, was assigned as Humphreys's assistant.

The young and able Fox had emigrated from England within the year of his appointment. It seems unlikely that he would immediately have been given the opportunity for a vigorous independent role as a designer.

Humphreys, who would allow no one to paint his picture, must be perceived in his handiwork and letters, such as the famous one to Morris of January 1793. Its essence is summed up in these phrases: ". . . as our navy for a considerable time will be inferior in numbers, we are to consider what size ships will be most formidable and be an overmatch for those of an enemy; such frigates as in blowing weather would be an overmatch for double-deck ships, and in light winds to evade coming to action; or double-deck ships that would be an overmatch for common double-deck ships, and in blowing weather superior to ships of three decks, or in calm weather or light winds to outsail them. Ships built on these principles will render those of an enemy in a degree useless, or require a greater number before they dare attack our ships." Humphreys explicitly discussed an eventual conflict with Great Britain, in his letter, and the way in which such ships as he proposed would have an advantage over a navy of equal weight of metal made up of standard fifth and sixth rates.

Humphreys's references to blowing weather took into account the fact that the lowest tier of guns in ships larger than frigates was too near the water to be used when the waves were high. In these circumstances a two-decker was reduced to a frigate's fire power, but was less handy in maneuver.

First and Last
of the Sailing Navy

The *Constitution*—lonely survivor of the first group of six frigates completed under the authorization of March 1794. Congress had decided that it would be cheaper to pay tribute to the Barbary regencies than to maintain a modest Navy. All six frigates were under construction by the end of 1795, but work was stopped when a treaty between "the American King, our friend," and "His Excellency the noble Vizier and powerful Marshal who sits on the throne of lordship, the destructor of tyranny and injustice and the protector of the country, Hassan Pasha," was negotiated in Algiers at the cost of large bribes and a perpetual yearly tribute in naval stores. Four years to a day after the original authorization, Congress voted to complete three of the frigates to oppose aggressive acts of French ships.

The *Constellation* corvette, one of the two still existing ships of the sailing Navy. The public has at times been encouraged to believe that this vessel is a rebuilt survival of the early frigate, in the sense that the extensively reconstructed *Constitution* has continuously been the same vessel, even though only a small fraction of the original timber remains in her. Patient efforts were made to bring the rotted and hogged "Old Ironsides" back to her planned shape and dimensions; but the *Constellation*, 36, of 1797, after one extensive rebuilding before the War of 1812, and several minor ones, was completely broken up in 1852 and a new vessel of substantially different model was built to carry on the name. The first *Constellation*, in her famous actions, actually mounted 38 guns. The second *Constellation* mounts 24. Some of the first ship's timber probably was used in the second one, but the continuity is no different from that produced when Christian church builders used a few pagan temple stones. The truth makes a more interesting claim: The *Constitution* and *Constellation,* as they now exist, represent the first and the last years of sailing-ship construction under the permanent Department of the Navy: 1797–1853. The *Constellation* corvette was a well-designed ship for her class and period, but she was obsolete when launched—our last fighting ship expected to use sail alone for propulsion.

A NAVY FOR THE
SKIRMISH WARS

ON JANUARY 20, 1794, TWENTY DAYS AFTER JEFFERSON HAD LEFT THE STATE DEPART-
ment and a year after Humphreys had made his lucid proposals, a committee of the House of
Representatives recommended the provision of four ships of 44 guns and two of 20 guns.
It specified particular taxes for raising the money. The credit of the government had been
strengthened by Hamilton's funding policy, but a navy built upon future taxes could have
been had much earlier if a few statesmen besides Jefferson had really seen the need of one.

The resolution passed by two votes. The longest paragraph of the actual bill which
emerged from it prescribed a seaman's exact rations, for each day of the week: "Wednesday,
one pound of bread, two ounces of butter, or in lieu thereof, six ounces of molasses, four
ounces of cheese, and half a pint of rice." Drink? "One half pint of distilled spirits per day,
or, in lieu thereof, one quart of beer per day."

As for those minor matters, ships, powder, and shot, statesmen who knew all about
eating fortunately left the choices to experts of another sort. But the bill could not pick
up a majority until an extra clause was appended: *Provided always, and be it further
enacted,* That if a peace shall take place between the United States and the Regency of
Algiers, that no farther proceeding be had under this act."

The prospect of having bought a peace through ransom and tribute, and of then having
still to pay for a navy for the same purpose, was more than the legislators could bear to contemplate. They probably were moved as well, on both sides of the House, by awful suspicions of what the other faction would do with such a fleet. Thus it was the clear intent of
Congress, on March 27, 1794, that if the tribute bearers could outspeed the shipwrights,
there would be no United States Navy after all. John Adams, the new Vice President, was
able to contemplate at leisure the maturing of the policy he had chosen in 1786, against the
urging of his old friend Jefferson. The two had been forced far apart politically, and neither
one was entirely happy in the company he had to keep.

Aided by Fox and others, Joshua Humphreys prepared drafts and models for the
frigates. He had personal charge of the building of the *United States*. Live oak rather than
white was purchased at his urging. Procurement was difficult and slow.

In Barbary the seasonal plague picked off more and more enslaved Americans. Another Humphreys, David, was hardly nimble in his handling of the ransom negotiations from
his post as Minister to Portugal. Jefferson had instructed him to go personally to Algiers,
and reluctantly had relaxed the stipulation against making a settlement in naval stores.
Humphreys seems to have been greatly relieved when informed that the Dey would not receive any negotiator, but the seizures of 105 additional American slaves brought new
instructions, and he finally sent a gouty character named Joseph Donaldson in his stead.
According to the slave Cathcart, Donaldson managed to infuriate the Dey almost to the
point of murder, while a treaty of sorts was being drawn up. It was signed on September 5,

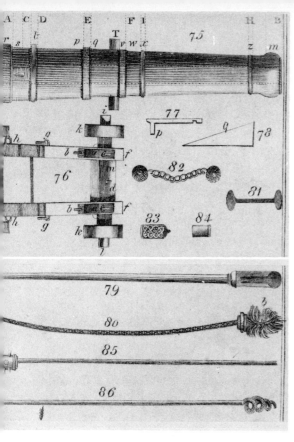

BELOW. Joshua Humphreys, appointed under the Naval Construction Act of 1794 to oversee the design and construction of the first six frigates, built the *United States* in his own yard. It was appropriate that the frigate which, beyond all dispute, was Humphreys's own responsibility, should have been the first to demonstrate the correctness of his principles of design. She had also been the first of the great frigates to be launched, on May 10, 1797, but was damaged in the launching. The fact that she was able to get to sea promptly in 1812, when most of the other ships needed extensive repairs, was at least in part a tribute to his workmanship. All the frigates had suffered under the frugal congressional policy of keeping them laid up "in ordinary" to rot at leisure. Her figurehead, not visible in this quartering view, was the Goddess of Liberty. She is shown here in a detail from the engraving made by Benjamin Tanner of Philadelphia from the painting (facing page 10) by Thomas Birch of her 1812 action with the *Macedonian*.

ABOVE. This naval gun, with its truck, gear, and ammunition, is of the sort used with little change from the early eighteenth until well into the nineteenth century. In the plate, 79 is a "ladle," used to dig the powder out of a gun that has not been discharged; 80 is a double-ended implement, half rammer, half spunge of sheepskin, on a length of rope stiffened with tar and whipping line; 85 is an orthodox "spunge" of bristles; 86 is a worm. It was "indispensably requisite that a gun should be wormed, at least, every third discharge," to take out the bottom of the cartridge which might still be burning when the gun was being reloaded. Numbers 81 to 84 are bar, chain, grape, and canister shot. The pictures are from *The Mariner's Dictionary, or American Seaman's Vocabulary . . . Improved from an English Work*. Most of the material is frankly swiped from J. J. Moore's condensation of Falconer's famous *Universal Dictionary of the Marine* of 1769. The pirated American edition was issued in Washington and Philadelphia in 1805 by William Duane, one of Jefferson's most devoted editorial supporters, an Irish immigrant by way of Calcutta, whence he had been ousted for his criticisms of the regime. It was not surprising that he became a stalwart of the anti-British and pro-Navy faction in his adopted country.

1795. Cathcart claimed that he and the Swedish consul were in fact the real negotiators.

Congress had newly appropriated $800,000 for ransom, "presents," and a start toward the annual tribute for Algiers. David Humphreys assumed that the appropriated money had been made available in negotiable form. His agents, sent to England and elsewhere, could not even get advances against it. The Algerine treaty involved heavy payments in specie for "the peace" and for ransom, with a yearly tribute forever in naval stores. But specie, in a world at war, had gone into hiding.

On March 2, 1796, the Senate ratified the servile treaty signed six months earlier. The tribute bearers appeared to have won the slow race. Work on the half-completed six frigates, because of the short clause added to the bill of 1794 to assure it passage, came to a stop. There was to be no United States Navy after all.

The relaxing of a need for American fighting ships was less obvious abroad. Hassan Bashaw Dey could not understand why the money should be so long in arriving. In Paris, David Humphreys had persuaded Joel Barlow to be his official agent in Algiers. Soon after his arrival Barlow was confronted by Hassan's ultimatum: he must leave within eight days, and if the money had not arrived within thirty days after that, corsairs would be loosed against the American vessels which once more, at news of a peace treaty, were appearing in numbers in the Mediterranean. The paroled American captives would be re-enslaved. Many more would certainly join them in slavery.

BARLOW'S BARGAIN

IN 1796 IT APPEARED THAT THE COUNTRY WOULD HAVE TO PAY HEAVILY AFTER ALL FOR both Adams's tribute and Jefferson's Navy—without profiting from either. A ten-year loss of trade, and of the federal revenue derived from duties, was the chief cost. Against the original, absurdly innocent, notion of "practical" men—that other nations struggling for tactical advantage would be glad to help the United States to compete with their own shipping—the mistrusted idealist Jefferson had assessed the problem with precise practicality. What is even more odd, it took another idealist of the opposition party, the poet and Connecticut wit Joel Barlow, author of *Hasty Pudding* and *The Columbiad,* to push Adams's policy to success with a skillful cynicism that exposed the long moral and strategical bankruptcy of the whole performance.

The principle of giving the pirates nothing "which we know they will employ to do wrong" had been recognized as illogical: whoever bought peace by any means was helping them to plunder and enslave others. Barlow accepted the miserable mess that he inherited, and on the advice of Cathcart, offered the Dey something which he could really employ to do wrong: a 36-gun American frigate. The poet had no authority to commit the $100,000 it would cost, but he perceived the ultimate immoral symbol in an expedient policy, and used it.

Having thus gained time he dashed out and by a complicated financial maneuver borrowed from the Algiers head of the Mediterranean banking house of Bacri more than half a million dollars—money recently deposited by the Dey himself from other ransoms. This Barlow then paid to the Dey, to be redeposited where it came from. When the liberated American slaves sailed at last on July 12, 1796, Joseph Coen Bacri had nothing for collateral but Barlow's head, which would not have saved his own, should this astonishing transaction have backfired. In a nest of vicious intriguers Bacri appears to have been a remarkably upright and generous spirit. A number of Americans recommended him as financially honest and a true friend of America. One or two others turned toward him the standard blinders of anti-Semitism.

Barlow's weird transaction almost did misfire. The ship which at last was sent by David Humphreys, with $225,000 in coin toward the Algerine debts, was captured by the Tripolitan admiral Morad Rais, a Scottish renegade. But from honor, or fear, among thieves it was released after three weeks.

Timothy Pickering, Adams's Secretary of State, was thoroughly unhappy when confronted by Barlow's fabulous bribe, but he saw no other course than to recommend a supplemental appropriation for the frigate, which brought the cost of the Algerine negotiations alone to almost a million dollars. Treaties were still to be concluded with Tripoli and Tunis, and then the tribute payments would begin. Most of the money so far had been spent for bribery and ransom. The 36-gun *Crescent,* to be described at her launch as the finest frigate in the world, was about to be laid down as a personal gift to a piratical former enemy. The country which had declared her independence of mighty Britain, in the memorable phrases of Jefferson, had rejected his warnings to become perpetual tributary to a small Turkish outpost. America was receiving insults continually from both France and England. The year 1796 was deep nadir in the foreign relations of the United States.

THE SKIRMISH WAR WITH FRANCE

HE TURN TOWARD COMMON SENSE HAD BEEN MADE BEFORE THE NEWS OF Barlow's cynical bargain arrived. President Washington, aware that the appended clause of the Naval Act of 1794 would halt work on the unfinished frigates as soon as the Algerine treaty was ratified, had hinted to Congress that "such measures be adopted as may best comport with the public interest." The lawmakers, as anxious not to do one thing as the other, went halfway: they voted to complete two 44s and a 36. Those who find Jefferson indispensable as a scapegoat can here point to his sudden lack of enthusiasm for a navy when one at last began to emerge, early in the period of his Vice Presidency; and here too the background which I have been sketching becomes most significant. Armed services have dedicated adherents who think of nothing else—but to a statesman arms are a means of effecting policy, never a good in themselves. Jefferson's continuous advocacy of a small naval force, in and after the Revolution, had been made more cogent than ever during the long Barbary crisis when there was no dispute over the identity of the enemy. But with the ratification of Jay's treaty with England in 1795, Jefferson knew that the United States had chosen as its friend the country that had wrought the greater and more numerous injuries against our ships and seamen. From his years as envoy in France and as Secretary of State, he knew the French character and saw it as inevitable that France would react against Jay's treaty with sharper retaliatory measures. The pressure from American shipowners to use the new frigates against her might then prove uncontrollable. Under the original rules of the Constitution, Jefferson as second runner had become Vice President, but he could do nothing to represent his party in what was an extremely close division of public opinion. He could hardly have been expected to favor the first use of the Navy he had fathered against France, in his view the diametrically wrong antagonist.

The historical game of What Might Have Been is notably futile. Yet if Jefferson's prediction of 1785 had been heeded, and a fleet in being had been used decisively against Barbary in the late 1780s, the depredations from other quarters might not have occurred. Neutrality, which Washington, Adams, and Jefferson all basically desired, might have been possible. As it turned out, the first of the skirmish wars, in the Adams administration, hardly touched the basic issue. The United States declared a state of belligerency only against armed French ships. The French, while increasing their privateering attacks, avoided outright naval actions. Their ships of superior force were committed off their own coasts, or blockaded by the British. They fought the Quasi War chiefly with privateers commissioned in the Caribbean. Subtle negotiations of Governor Desfourneaux, of Guadeloupe, with his captive Lieutenant William Bainbridge, exemplify French policy throughout the Quasi War, which was simply to force recognition that the French-American treaty of alliance was still in effect.

While the English continued to capture American vessels in large numbers, they exulted over the capture by the new *Constellation,* on February 9, 1799, of one of their primary enemy's frigates. *L'Insurgente,* later added to the American Navy, was the only sizable fighting ship taken by either side during the inconclusive Quasi War; and the action was the first fought by a vessel of the permanently organized United States Navy against another naval vessel.

President Adams resisted the more truculent of his official advisers, who wanted a full war with France. But he began with vigor to strengthen a navy which he had inherited despite himself. The laws for its government were based in those he earlier had devised for the Continental Navy. He proposed solutions of tactical problems arising from the French dependence upon small, shore-based craft. On August 5, 1799, he wrote to Secretary of the Navy Stoddert, ". . . One idea more. I think we must have Bermuda sloops, Virginia pilot boats, or Marblehead schooners, or whaleboats, in one word, some very light small, fast-sailing vessels, furnished with oars as well as sails, to attend our frigates, and pursue the French pirates among their own rocks and shoals to their utter destruction. . . ." Note that his contemporary acknowledgment of the probable Bermuda origin of lines and rig for speed is followed by a stress upon fast and handy special craft which American builders had developed.

Our first three frigates, completion of which was authorized in 1796, got to sea in June and July of 1798, but it was the little *Delaware,* 20, that made the first capture, of the privateer *Croyable,* 12. She was renamed the *Retaliation* and added to our suddenly growing Navy as a 14 with twenty-two-year-old Lieutenant Bainbridge in command. Ten other vessels were added to the fleet in the course of the year. Work was resumed on the remaining three frigates laid down under the act of 1794, but none was in service until 1800. Of the six, only the *Constellation* encountered major opponents, capturing *l'Insurgente,* 40, and fighting an indecisive action with *la Vengeance,* 52, in which both ships were severely

LEFT. The American ship *Planter*, attacked by an unidentified French privateer which was beaten off after an action of "five glasses and a half," or two hours and three-quarters. (The sand ran through the watch glass every half-hour, when the glass was inverted and one more bell struck.) This action came particularly to the notice of the British public because the underwriters at Lloyd's were so pleased at the successful defense that they distributed something over 300 guineas among the ship's people, as well as "elegant gold watches" to two ladies, and "elegant swords" to two gentlemen, passengers who assisted in the fight. The ladies, Mrs. M'Dowell and Miss Mary Harley, passed the powder and attended the wounded. The gentlemen, "with small arms, stood to their quarters with a degree of noble spirit." One was among the eight wounded. Four seamen were killed. The print was made with some care as it gives the reported armament for each vessel, 22 guns in the privateer, 18 in the *Planter*. It is one of two similar prints, published together in England on October 1, 1800, by John Fairburn. The other appears on the preceding page.

BELOW. The famous schooner *Enterprize* supports my assertion that the early Navy was the creation not of a bureaucracy but of knowledgeable individuals. On April 30, 1799, Secretary Stoddert demonstrated that a year in office had not gone to his head. He wrote to Jeremiah Yellot of Baltimore, "Be so good as to have two Schooners built such as you judge best qualified to be usefull in our Navy, and as quickly as possible—with respect to both I rely intirely on your judgment and experience." The *Experiment* got to sea in October, the *Enterprize* two months later. Chapelle says it is "highly probable" that she was "not of the extreme type," but in this exacting water color, which looks like the work of the elder Antoine Roux, the shadow on her topsides under the foremast indicates an extremely sharp entrance. There is an inference that she was "lengthened" in the Mediterranean in 1805, which may account for this aspect in an 1806 picture.

mauled and dismasted. The latter's commander candidly reported that he had done his best to avoid an action, which thus must have been in accordance with his instructions. There were thirty American seamen aboard whom he had impressed for service against the British. When the nationality of the *Constellation* was recognized, he permitted all the Americans to remain below.

About forty vessels, of 24 guns or smaller, were added to the Navy by purchase, capture, or "provision by the citizens." The captured *Insurgente,* 36, refitted, joined the frigates; and eight new vessels were hastily built. These included the *Philadelphia* and *New York,* 36-gun frigates; the *Essex,* 32; the *General Green, Adams, John Adams,* and *Boston,* 28s; and the famous little *Enterprize,* 12. Only the last two fought engagements with opponents close to their own rates. The *Boston* captured a 24 and a 20, unaware that peace already had been arranged. The *Enterprize* took twenty vessels and chastised a larger Spanish armed packet that attacked her for reasons unexplained.

As in the Revolution, both the built and the acquired vessels of the regular Navy were employed at privateering tasks throughout the Quasi War. The *Enterprize* should interest us particularly, having been built on purpose for the Navy at a time, 1799, and at a place, the Eastern Shore of Maryland, to derive the best advantage from both the schooner experimentation of the past decade and the urgencies of conflict that diminish red tape. Her exact lines are not known. She was a square-sterned schooner measuring 135 tons, with a length-to-breadth ratio of almost 4 to 1 on deck. Two later reconstructions, of the sort that could cost more than a vessel built from a new start, indicate the degree in which she was valued.

The Quasi War stretched all around the world. The ship *Concord,* Thompson, of Philadelphia, was taken by the privateer *la Prudente* off the Cape of Good Hope, and the ship *Pacific,* of Norwich, Connecticut, was taken in the Bay of Bengal by the famous privateer Robert Surcouff of Saint-Malo. They were among the many sent to the Isle of France, from which, in December of 1799, six armed vessels were cruising in the capacity of "Marine Force of the Colony." Uncertainty as to just what sort of war, if any, might be under way caused the masters of the captured *Concord* and *Pacific,* with two other Americans at the Isle of France, to petition in August 1799 to buy a ship to go home in because "it is evident beyond a doubt that neither war nor hostilities exists between the two nations." The governor congratulated them if their news were true but said he must wait to hear it officially.

The problem of telling friend from enemy had come to an early issue in the unhappy case of Captain Isaac Phillips. His sailing orders were explicit: to capture "armed Vessels of the French Republic . . . The vessels of every other Nation are on no account to be molested, and I wish particularly to impress on your mind, that should you even see an American Vessel captured by the armed Ship of any Nation at War with whom we are at Peace, you can not Lawfully interfere to prevent the Capture."

Obviously, British ships were *"on no account* to be molested," whatever the provocation. Phillips, in the *Baltimore,* 20, a converted merchantman formerly called the *Adriana,* was convoying merchantmen off the Havana when they were intercepted by a British fleet. The *Carnatic,* 74, Captain Loring, captured some of the merchantmen and sent officers on board the *Baltimore* to seize any British seamen they could find. Phillips protested that in a national cruiser the flag protected every seaman. Loring nevertheless seized fifty-five enlisted men of the United States Navy. Phillips hauled down his flag in surrender to superior force, but this gesture was ignored. When he reached home he was cashiered for obeying his orders exactly.

The friends of England in the United States Government, resigned to the Royal Navy's

The *Columbus* of this print was a promoter's bizarre dream. Congress, in the heat of the Quasi War with France, provided money for the purchase of six frames for 74-gun ships and other "timber for naval purposes." Joshua Humphreys drew the designs for the 74s, and his son Samuel helped to put them into final form. William Doughty and one of the celebrated Huttons of the Philadelphia shipbuilding family assisted in the drafting. No ship of 110 guns was ever authorized, and the 74s were not completed. Howard I. Chapelle has pointed out that if they had been afloat, the exasperating humiliations which provoked a declaration of war upon England in 1812 might never have occurred in the first place. "Anticipated to be built at Portsmouth New-Hampshire about the Year 1800." The print evidently was issued before that date, and after 1795, because the flags are intended for 15-stripers. But the vessel herself, with her spritsail topmast, lateen yard, and big poop lanterns might be a reversed copy of Isaac Sailmaker's well-known print of the *Royal James,* built in 1675. Someone in Portsmouth probably hoped to attract federal money by the distribution of this curious production. If so, he underestimated the technically knowledgeable nautical community of the day, which could only have been warned by it of the promoter's incompetence. The engraving resembles the work of Amos Doolittle.

habit of seizing merchant seamen and merchant ships, had not foreseen that any British officer would act with the tactless arrogance displayed by Loring against a ship of war. Pickering sent a tart protest to the British minister, enclosing a copy of new orders positively forbidding the commanders of public vessels to permit them to be "detained or searched. . . . when overpowered by superior force you are to strike your flag and thus yield your vessel as well as your men, but never your men without your vessel." Phillips had struck after yielding his men. In an unprecedented situation, he had not shown the firmness that tradition would have dictated in an older service. Yet he was dismissed summarily without a hearing or a court-martial, that device which over the years teaches the judges, as well as the arraigned, what the undefinable limits of discretion are in the surrendering of material and men. The instructions were obviously misleading, or they would not have had to be so emphatically recast. A conscientious man's life went down in disgrace, primarily because the true issue was being evaded on the political level, at which the proper use of force, naval or other, has to be determined. The true issue was the right of the human individual not to be seized by anyone for involuntary servitude, anywhere. The French had been seizing many ships and a few men. The British had taken many ships and many men. The Algerines had taken some of both. The two skirmish wars were largely evasions of the true issue, fought in the wrong order. At least they provided a navy, and gave it some training, some tradition, for the central contest that in 1812 could be evaded no longer.

Even before the Federalist administration was defeated, in the strange election of 1800, the Quasi War had dwindled away. But it should be said in justice to brave John Adams that he prosecuted his skirmish war with vigor while mounting at the same time a spirited contest against a conspiring ring of his closest advisers, for the right to make peace. He had to dismiss the most dedicated Federalists in his Cabinet before peacemaking became possible, largely through the agency of a member of the opposition party, Elbridge Gerry. When Adams wrote his own epitaph, many years later, it read, "Here lies John Adams, who took upon himself the responsibility of peace with France in the year 1800." Blessed, and very lonely, are some of the peacemakers.

During the Quasi War British and French engravers had their attention centered upon naval occurrences closer to their own shores. It was difficult to perceive a salable print in the typical action of such a conflict: a ship of moderate force capturing a weak one. But the establishment of what might prove to be a career navy attracted some notice from native-born as well as visiting or immigrant artists. The Englishmen William Birch & Son, in their twenty-eight views of Philadelphia, published as the war was ending, gave a little attention to the waterfront. The younger Birch, Thomas, then aged twenty-one, developed into a marine specialist in time for the War of 1812.

Edward Savage, Massachusetts-born in 1761, was a self-taught artist who had done portraits of the Washingtons. He sent to Washington on June 17, 1799, his two engravings of the recent "Chace" and "Action" between the *Constellation* and *l'Insurgente,* claiming in the accompanying letter to have invented an aqua fortis process of which these were the first examples. Washington, with grave and noncommittal courtesy, replied "the invention is curious" and that something might well come of it. The Savage prints are not particularly good of their kind. I have chosen instead a much more spirited if crude British print of this action and a companion print published on the same day in London, of a privateer action.

The second of the skirmish wars, soon to come, brought forth a number of effective, accurate prints of contemporary American origin, and some foreign ones. Before turning to these, we should note one of the cyclic threats to the existence of a navy which followed the dwindling of hostilities with France. It is standard practice to belabor Jefferson for a drastic reduction of the Navy at the beginning of his first presidential term. The reduction actually originated with the able and loyal Federalist Benjamin Stoddert. On January 12, 1801, he recommended, not a reduction, but a readjustment that would greatly have increased the total force. He advised Congress to sell "all the public vessels, except the following frigates: The *United States, President, Constitution, Chesapeake, Philadelphia, New York, Constellation, Congress, Essex, Boston, John Adams, Adams,* and *General Green.*" Most of the smaller vessels were not built of durable wood, and would be expensive to maintain. He proposed that eleven new frigates and twelve 74-gun ships of the line be added, and that

On June 30, 1798, Congress authorized the President to accept from "any state, body politic or corporate, citizen or citizens of the United States" gifts of vessels to increase the national armament, and to pay in government certificates bearing interest at not more than 6 per cent for not more than twelve others. Vessels built under both plans were acquired to meet the emergency of an undeclared war with France. Philadelphians subscribed $179,349 for a frigate to bear the name of their city. Four others were similarly financed. The *Philadelphia* was designed by Josiah Fox as a somewhat lighter adaptation of the principles that produced the heavy frigates of the *Constitution* class. The keel was laid about four and a half months after passage of the authorizing Act and the ship required a few days more than a year to build. William Birch and his son Thomas were making their fine series of views of Philadelphia at the time, which they published on the last day of the year 1800. What they saw going on in the suburb of Southwark gives us probably the earliest intimate picture of American shipwrights at work. They launched her on November 28, 1799. She had a short career of routine service and a spectacular death when burned in the harbor of Tripoli by Stephen Decatur and his men.

Engraved & Published by W. Birch & Son.

Sold by R. Campbell & C°. N°250 Chesnut Street Philad°. 18(

Preparation for WAR to defend Commerce.

Wall and Water Streets, New York, in 1798. The selective eye of the artist, whether he holds a brush or a camera in his hand, takes him generally to a point of view which brings the object of chief interest into the center and frames out the irrelevant. But the candid-camera technique of recent years has its forerunners. Francis Gay's paintings, in the phrase of John A. Kouwenhoven, "marked an important change in ways of looking at the city." Certainly this is a "composed" picture, but it emphasizes the crossroads of contrast: the sprawling, turbulent commercial life near the waterfront. In the right distance are the masts of vessels tied up in Coffee House Slip. At the left is the financial heart—the Tontine Coffee House— pumping and controlling the flow of investment. Wall Street, then as now, was the center of commercial life; and the clamorous clutter that still marks the streets of lower Manhattan is spread candidly before us in its late eighteenth century manifestation. The name Tontine suggests a life insurance scheme popular in the earlier part of that century, but the chief business of the Tontine Coffee House was marine insurance. Here the proposals for insurance were pinned up for all to see. Those with money to risk subscribed the amounts they would make available, and the premiums at which they would risk their capital on voyages in particular circumstances. The rates rose on the news of captures. There was no concealment possible. It was from these known evidences that Jefferson could prove, at the height of the Quasi War against France, that the English were still the chief enemies of our shipping.

midshipmen be placed on reserve pay—an innovation for any navy—since those in service "possess all the materials to make officers equal to any in the world."

A lame-duck Congress received Stoddert's report. No-one knew at the time which of the two Democratic-Republican candidates who had tied for the Presidency, Jefferson or Burr, would win the deciding contest in the House of Representatives. Some Federalists looked upon Burr almost as one of themselves, but the prospect of handing over to Jefferson the Navy so recently used to chastise his friends the French was an unhappy one for his opponents to contemplate. A year earlier, when the Quasi War was at its height, Jefferson had quoted statistics of Federalist-operated insurance offices to prove what every shipowner who cared to face it knew: that "Insurance is now higher in all the commercial towns against British than French capture."

Congress convened on the 11th of February and balloted day and night, thirty-six times, before Jefferson was elected. It would have been appropriate to leave the determination of naval policy for the next four years to the newly elected Congress, but that would be dominated by Democratic-Republicans. On the last day of the Federalist Congress's existence a Peace Establishment bill was passed, recommending the reductions proposed by Secretary Stoddert, but ignoring his more important increases altogether. It authorized the President to lay up seven of the frigates, to reduce by one-third the crews of the remaining six, and to discharge about three-fifths of the officers.

Historians with nostalgic Federalist sympathies thus are in an odd posture when they rebuke President Jefferson for following the legal directive of the last Federalist Congress. He did decide to keep two of the smaller vessels in commission. He also retained twelve captains instead of the congressionally authorized nine, and a few more midshipmen than the number in the Peace Establishment Act. There was no authorization, no appropriation, to build the extra frigates and the 74s. With a sort of war just concluded, it was hardly the time to ask the new Congress for money for such a purpose. Jefferson had been presiding officer of the Senate throughout the Quasi War, a continuous witness to the attitudes of both parties.

For the unfinished business with Barbary the new Commander in Chief had a fleet ample for his old purpose of keeping up a constant cruise in the Mediterranean.

A MOMENT'S PEACE. The port of Philadelphia, as it appeared to George Beck during the short interlude between the end of the Quasi War with France and the commencement of hostilities in the Mediterranean. The artist chose for a frame the great tree at Kensington under which William Penn signed a reasonable treaty with the Indians. As here reproduced, the print has been trimmed somewhat.

The American
Practical Navigator

SALEM'S BOWDITCH

THE CAREER OF NATHANIEL BOWDITCH, A GENIUS WHO SEEMS AS ABSOLUTE AS HIS OWN mathematics, was the best possible proof of the new American thesis that the world could get on excellently without either privilege or aristocracy to assure and promote learning. The American navigator came to young manhood almost wholly untaught. He was a cooper's son and apprenticed ship's chandler who rose by his own inner qualities to first rank among his contemporaries, and then projected himself into a life beyond life that is as powerful as ever today. A book simply called Bowditch still goes to sea in every American naval vessel, and in most merchantmen: a perpetual best seller, owned literally by all the people of the United States. Our government, often castigated for capricious neglect of the maritime community, had the great good sense almost a hundred years ago to buy the rights to the *American Practical Navigator*. The Hydrographic Office keeps it up to date, as the author would have wished. It has given up the numbering of editions, but has gone on listing it as H. O. No. 9 in a series that now has got beyond fifty thousand titles.

It has been said with justice that Nathaniel Bowditch was the end of a process rather than its beginning. In this his genius was typically American. We have been miscalled a nation of inventors, when we have really been at our characteristic best as improvers of existing ideas or devices. This quality marks pre-eminently the achievement of the self-taught mathematician Bowditch. He was born in 1773 and died in 1838. His youth was spent in extreme poverty. He had less than four years of sporadic schooling, topped off by the glad accident of access to a fine scientific library captured during shipment by a Revolutionary privateer. He taught himself Latin in order to read the *Principia,* and became fluent in many other languages. A Newburyport publisher, Edmund M. Blunt, persuaded him to edit a pirated edition of John Hamilton Moore's *Practical Navigator.* Blunt's Moore was published in May of 1799, "corrected by a Skilful Mathematician and Navigator," otherwise unidentified. Bowditch had brought to light such serious errors that Blunt asked him to do a complete revision, which resulted in his discovery, while acting as supercargo on a Manila voyage, of eight thousand mathematical errors in Moore. The new edition, although it still followed Moore's scheme and used much of his language, was with some justice issued in June 1802, as the *New American Practical Navigator,* by Nathaniel Bowditch. The long process begun at the end of the sixteenth century by Edward Wright, when he "detected and corrected" some errors in the practice of navigation, came to a belated climax in the work of Nathaniel Bowditch, who left almost nothing for anyone else to do in the conceptual or applied mathematics of navigation. New and handier gadgets were to appear. Invisible waves or rays were to replace, for some observations, the ancient light of the stars, the sun, and the moon. Tables were to be elaborated. But in 1802 the laws and applications of mathematics in navigation had been made exact and reliable, for the world and the future, by one phenomenal intellect in the small port of Salem. The new American man, self-reliant, enterprising, practical, had assumed an absolute dimension.

LEFT. NATHANIEL BOWDITCH. A posthumous portrait based on the unfinished original by Gilbert Stuart.

WARFARE WITHOUT COMMUNICATION

THOUGH THE BARBARY CRISIS BEGAN, AND WAS TO END, WITH Algiers, even more distant waters off Tripoli furnished the combat nursery of our infant Navy. "Infant" was the term used by those most concerned for its growth, but the Tripolitan nursery was a long way from parental control.

Readers of later times have to adjust themselves to the complicating effect of remoteness, in this period, upon diplomacy. The merchant shipmaster was given large powers to act in the interest of his owner, who could not know the state of the market in a distant port. Naval commanders had the enormous burden of acting, or of refraining from action, in behalf of the President, the Department of State, the Congress. Young Captain Bainbridge, carrying tribute to Algiers in the United States ship of war *George Washington* in 1800, was confronted by the Dey's ultimatum that he must put the ship at the regency's service to carry to the Grand Seignior, in Constantinople, presents which included jewels, wild animals, male and female slaves. Every part of the stipulation was a court-martial offense. Bainbridge moreover had explicit orders to suppress the slave trade. Yet the alternative was not only to have his ship blown out of the water by heavy batteries a few yards away; the Dey also promised immediately to loose his corsairs to prey upon unwarned American vessels which had been swarming into the Mediterranean following the "peace" with Barbary. Where there had been a hundred slaves to ransom, there well might suddenly be a thousand.

Bainbridge, who had been made the youngest captain in the Navy largely because of his hotheaded exploits, had had one maturing experience at Guadeloupe, confronting the subtle French General Desfourneaux. His decision there had been to save his crew and stand the consequences. It was not his fault that the Federalist administration, which had dispatched him at the age of twenty-six on an ignominious errand, had chosen the policy of servile submission to the piratical regencies. He was the lonely inheritor of full-grown consequences hatched fourteen years earlier by politicians who had taken the expedient advice of John Adams because they wrongly supposed it would cost less. Once more Bainbridge chose safety for his ship's people, and for all the Americans in the Mediterranean, at the risk of his own career. He took aboard the "lyons, tygars . . . male and female slaves."

President Adams had summarily cashiered Captain Phillips for a far less humiliating submission to force, off the Havana. But when Bainbridge returned from Constantinople there was a different president in office, who had suffered himself while Secretary of State and Vice President the discipline of putting into effect a policy in which he had had no faith. Jefferson selected Bainbridge to be one of the captains retained under the Peace Establishment Act, and gave him the fine new frigate *Essex*. There is at least a hint in Stoddert's correspondence that Bainbridge had been sent as tribute bearer, in the Navy's slowest cruiser, as a tempering experience because of the urgency with which he had pressed for promotion to the Navy's highest rank at the age of twenty-five. Jefferson's own correspondence demonstrates no special interest in Bainbridge, but in the early months of his Presidency he had had to act almost as his own Secretary of the Navy. Stoddert had graciously stayed on for a few weeks. The selection of a successor had been difficult because eminent men in the world of shipping were nearly all Federalists. In this state of affairs a show of marked favor to the young captain who had made such a humiliating choice at Algiers could have resulted only from a definite decision by the President.

The State Department had received expressions from the other point of view. The consul at Tunis, William Eaton, when he got the news, wrote to the Secretary:

"Genius of My Country! How art thou prostrate! Hast thou not yet one son whose soul revolts, whose nerves convulse, blood vessels burst, and heart indignant swells at the thoughts of such debasement! . . . I never thought to find a corner of this slanderous world where baseness and American were wedded— . . . Shall Tunis also lift his thievish arm, smite our scarred cheek, then bid us kiss the rod! *This is the price of peace!* But if we will have peace at such a price, recall me, and send a *slave,* accustomed to abasement, to represent the nation. . . . History shall tell that The United States first volunteer'd a *ship of war,* equipt, a *carrier* for a pirate—It is written—Nothing but blood can blot the impression out—Frankly I own, I would have lost the peace, and been empaled myself rather than yield this concession—Will nothing rouse my country!"

Slowness of communication put discretion over the fate of the country in men as different as Bainbridge and Eaton. A crisis would usually have altered by the time means had been sent for dealing with it. A variety of possibilities had to be foreseen. One of the stock complaints against President Jefferson's management of the Navy concerns the orders which prevented Lieutenant Sterett of the *Enterprize* from seizing the first corsair to be whipped by a cruiser of the United States Navy.

The *Enterprize,* fast and handy but small, sailed on June 1, 1801, with the frigates *Essex, Philadelphia,* and *President,* in a squadron under the command of Richard Dale, who had been John Paul Jones's second-in-command off Flamborough Head. On the 6th, Bainbridge wrote in his journal of the *Essex* (a "citizen's frigate" built at Salem): "The *Enterprize* long way astern not able to keep up, the *Philada.* carrying Top gallant sails & stay sails to keep way. I find under low sail we can beat the *President* tolerable easy, on any way I think we are the fastest sailer yet." The *Essex* at this time was probably carrying only four more than the 32 guns for which she had been rated. Her slowness, in the War of 1812, resulted when she was overburdened with 46 guns, all of larger caliber than the 12s and 10s for which Hackett had designed her.

Dale's orders included this statement: "One great object expected from this Squadron is, the instruction of our young men: so that when their more active services shall hereafter be required, they may be capable of defending the honor of their Country. It is particularly requisite, that they should be made acquainted with the coasts & Harbours of the Mediterranean, where their services in all probability will frequently be required."

Shortly after the squadron made its offing, the new President restated his old conviction that peace purchased from the Barbary States was "money thrown away and that there is no end to the demand of these powers, nor any security in their promises. The real alternative before us is whether to abandon the Mediterranean or to keep up a cruise in it." As leader of a party which objected to a large concentration of power in the executive, Jefferson felt bound by his congressional mandate, although he had stretched it a little by maintaining the *Enterprize* and the *George Washington* in service.

"On your arrival at Gibraltar," Dale's orders read, "you will be able to ascertain whether all or any of the Barbary Powers, shall have declared war against the United States." Elaborate instructions followed, governing the use of the squadron in the possible combinations of circumstances thus to be discovered.

James Leander Cathcart, former Christian Clerk to the Dey of Algiers, had become United States consul at Tripoli. The Bashaw distrusted him because he knew too much about Barbary. Cathcart had warned that the treaty with Tripoli was unsatisfactory for a new sort of reason. Unlike the hard-bargaining Dey of Algiers, the Bashaw had been too easily persuaded, and was prepared to fight for a revision: this despite his acceptance of money specifically as the price of continuous peace. As Jefferson had warned from the beginning, there could be no durable arrangement with such military dictatorships. A generous policy provoked their rapacious contempt; a firm one enraged them to the disregard of their engagements. The Tripolitan treaty had been made with a man who had murdered his own brother to assure himself of the throne. The admiral of his fleet was known as Morad Reis, but his real name was Peter Lisle: a Scottish renegade who had with romantic perception married the Bashaw's daughter. Lisle knew a great deal about the European shipping community. He was better able than a native of Tripoli to foresee the movements of the ships upon which Tripoli preyed; but fortunately for the Americans, he lacked the personal courage and religious zeal which marked many Barbary captains.

Commodore Dale, after four days of holding his frigates in leash to allow the little *Enterprize* to keep pace with the squadron, ordered Sterett to make the best of his way to Gibraltar independently and plunged on into the rainy easterlies. When the three frigates arrived, on the 1st of July, they found the *Enterprize* at anchor. Freed of the necessity of keeping the same course that was most advantageous for the larger square-riggers, Sterett had clawed up into the wind and had beaten them by five days.

Admiral Morad-Lisle, in his American-built flagship of 28 guns and 246 men, with a brig of 16 guns and 146 men in company, had entered the bay of Gibraltar a day ahead of the American frigates to secure water: unfortunate timing for him. The weird protocol of our early Barbary relations made an exchange of courtesies between Dale and the renegade a matter of routine. Lisle politely denied that a state of war existed but Dale was convinced that the Tripolitans were on their way into the Atlantic to cruise against American shipping. He consequently left the *Philadelphia* on guard and proceeded up the Mediterranean. The *Grand Turk,* which was also found at anchor near the Rock, loaded with American tribute for Tunis, was taken under convoy by the *Essex*.

This could not have been the so-called "second" *Grand Turk,* built by the famous Enos Briggs, which vanished from the registers because of a change of name when she was sold at New York in 1795. She was more probably the same vessel spoken by the U.S.S. *Warren* on January 24, 1800, and identified as belonging to New London. A Navy agent who was getting her cargo of guns, powder, and other tribute for Tunis aboard on March 12, 1801, described her as "American built, 4 years old, 370 tons burthen," substantially smaller than the Salem second *Grand Turk,* which at this point would have been ten years old.

The *President* and the *Enterprize* followed the Barbary coast eastward, to display the

American pendant flying over American guns. Consul O'Brien, at Algiers, reported that the spectacle did more to keep that regency at peace than could have been expected from the arrival of the again overdue shipload of tribute.

Such were the uncertainties of communication that Captain Bainbridge had spent nine days in the Mediterranean, sailing eastward, before he learned in the second week of July that Tripoli had in fact declared war on the United States sixty days earlier.

Dale's own suspicions were confirmed at Algiers. When the *President* and the *Enterprize* arrived off Tripoli, the Danish consul, as intermediary, intimated that the Bashaw regretted his declaration of war. Dale wrote, ". . . I am sorry to Inform your Excellency—that your Conduct toward the President of the United States, In declaring war against him, has put me under the necessity of Commencing hostilitys against your Excellencys Vessels and subjects . . . I have a Letter for your Excellency on board from the President of the United States and a Present of Ten thousand dollars from himself to you as a mark of his respect and friendship for you—but your Excellency's present conduct towards him put it out of my power to send you either the one or the other . . ."

The Bashaw vacillated, and Dale kept up his blockade. A fleet operating four or five thousand miles from home needed a base. North African weather made most ports unsafe during much of the year. Scurvy, the curse of vessels far from land, appeared in Dale's squadron that had been long in sight of it. Water was the chief problem. Malta, from which the French had recently been expelled by the Maltese and British, had seemed the handiest base for operations off Tripoli. It lay only two hundred miles away, NE by N.

On July 30, 1801, very short of water, the *Enterprize* was sent to Malta under orders reflecting those that Dale had received from the Navy Department: to "sink burn, or otherwise destroy" enemy vessels, if Algiers alone, or if all three states should have declared war. But if only one of the two weaker states, or both together, had done so they should be chastised by blockade, by the recapture of their prizes, and by the putting ashore of captives in evidence that the United States, powerful and humane, considered that it had nothing further to fear from them.

This effort to foresee all contingencies was justified by the domestic relations between the Barbary regencies. Algiers had much the largest fleet, under brave and able commanders. The others' corsairs generally were pariahs following on the flanks of the wolf pack. The Bashaw was soon to make a strong bid for independent power, but United States policy had been drafted in accordance with the best advice available from Consuls Cathcart, Eaton, and O'Brien. Commodore Dale's orders to Lieutenant Sterett consequently contained the following words: "should you fall in with any of the Tripolitan Corsairs that you are confident, that you can Manage, on your Passage to Malta you will heave all his Guns Over board Cut away his Masts, & leave him In a situation, that he can Just make out to get into some Port . . ."

The *Enterprize* was so short of water that she could not safely have brought a prize back to the commodore without first calling at Malta, which had not yet been established as a base. It could not be assumed that the British would receive a prize for adjudication prior to negotiations. Dale's orders to Sterett seem therefore to have correctly reflected the prudently drafted general orders.

Sterett did encounter a Tripolitan, while outward bound, and the ensuing action was the first fought by an armed vessel of our Navy, since the close of the Revolution,

Cap.ˡ **STERRETT** *in the Sch.ʳ* **ENTERPRISE** *paying tribute to* **TRIPOLI**, *August 1801.*

against an enemy that had formally declared war. Here is Sterett's terse report to the commodore:

"Sir, I have the honor to inform you, that on the 1 of August, I fell in with a Tripolitan ship of war, called the *Tripoli,* mounting 14 Guns, commanded by Rais Mahomet Rous. an action immediately commenced within pistol shot, which continued three hours incessantly. She then struck her colors. the carnage on board was dreadful; she having 30 men killed and 30 wounded, among the latter was the Captain and first Lieut.ᵗ Her sails, masts and rigging were cut to pieces with 18 shot between wind and water. Shortly after taking possession, her mizenmast went over the side. agreeably to your orders, I dismantled her of everything but an old sail and spar.—with heartfelt pleasure I add, that the officers and men throughout the vessel, behaved in the most spirited and determined manner, obeying every command with promptitude and alertness. we have not had a man wounded, and we have sustained no material damage in our hull or rigging."

In submitting the above letter to the Secretary of the Navy, Commodore Dale added, "M.ʳ Sterett is a Good Officer, and Deserves well of his Country—"

Sterett was not, however, to be one of the officers developed on the Barbary coast for the more critical contest a decade later. He asked permission in 1803 to make a trading voyage to the Far East, resigned in a huff over seniority in 1805, and died in 1807. His career was shadowed by an episode during the earlier encounter between *l'Insurgente* and the *Constellation,* in which he had served as executive officer under Truxton. He reported it thus to his brother: "One fellow I was obliged to run through the body with my sword, and so put an end to a *coward*. You must not think this strange, for we would put a man to death for even looking pale on board *this* ship."

Such is the spirit that makes an élite corps, and for that reason is insupportable in the armed services of a democracy. Sterett's brother imprudently published the account, which received the comment to be expected in the opposition press of 1799. When the Democratic-Republicans took office in 1801, this other side of Sterett's repute hampered the impulse to give him lavish recognition for the skillfully fought action with the *Tripoli*. The killing of Neal Harvey by his own executive officer also probably influenced the congressional debate over prize money for the crew of the *Enterprize*. Having been sent into her own home port, by explicit orders of Commodore Dale, the *Tripoli* was not a prize within the legal definition.

It was the intent of the law to encourage the commanders of United States fighting ships to sink an enemy or batter one into submission, confident that Congress would provide the sum that might have been got for the same vessel if captured. A too tender regard for keeping a prize salable might otherwise have resulted in escapes, or even in defeats for the United States ships themselves. Despite repeated applications, Congress refused to authorize prize money to the crew of the *Enterprize,* although it did make token payments in recognition of bravery. These were rejected by the indignant officers. Sterett eventually received an "elegant" sword.

In the grim traditions of warfare there is nothing novel in the spectacle of an officer enforcing discipline in conflict by killing a man under his command. John Paul Jones had been widely if slanderously accused of it. But Sterett took a swaggering pride in what he had done. Such episodes, as they accumulated, defined the tradition of the infant Navy. Sterett, if he had been promoted as rapidly as Decatur and Bainbridge, would have become a model not only in his accomplishment but likewise in his deficiency.

The young gentlemen of the Navy were learning by doing. Bainbridge, in his regulations for the government of the frigate *Essex* on her first Mediterranean cruise, stipulated that "Should any person quit his station before he is regularly relieved, or orders to do so, he is to ride the spanker boom three hours the succeeding watch," a punishment involving acute discomfort in moderate weather, and danger to life with a sea running. Yet in general he showed an uncommon solicitude for the welfare of the ship's people. Later in the war, when the crew of the *Philadelphia* was imprisoned in Tripoli, Bainbridge managed the situation with a combination of firmness and humanity hardly to be counted on in an officer still in his twenties.

The humanity of most of our early captains is notable. Extremists such as Sterett were exceptions. The policy underlying his orders from Dale had the most useful kind of effect in Tripoli. It set the Tripolitans against one another, whereas the complete loss of their vessel and her crew would probably have turned all their anger outward. The account in the *National Intelligencer* of November 18, 1801, concludes, "On the arrival of the Tripolitan ship at Tripoli, so strong was the sensations of shame and indignation excited there, that the Bey ordered the wounded captain to be mounted on a Jack Ass, and paraded thro' the streets as an object of public scorn. After which he received 500 bastinadoes.

"So thunderstruck were the Tripolitans at this event, and at the apprehended destruction of their whole marine force, that the sailors, then employed at Tripoli on board of cruisers that were fitting out by the government, all deserted them, and not a man could be procured to navigate them."

Because of an immoral choice made in the first instance, cargoes of tribute were being dispatched to Algiers and Tunis even while the show of force was being made off Tripoli. The immediate duties of the first United States squadron entering the Mediterranean called

William Heath, the Englishman who drew the picture on the left, fought in the Mediterranean theater during the Napoleonic Wars. The details of his picture of a conflict with Barbary pirates are true to the times.

The Non-Contemporaneous View

Alonzo Chappel, a diligent painter of naval portraits and actions, probably was not trying to tamper with the truth when he painted his picture entitled "Reuben James." The upshot, however, is a cluster of historical errors that has bred additional ones. In this action, which occurred on August 3, 1804, in the harbor of Tripoli, Decatur supposedly was saved by "Reuben James, disabled, armless," who "still might show a bloody pirate what a dying man could do," and took the sword blow on his own " 'fenceless forehead." Yet the surgeon's report of the action shows no one killed and no severe head wound except to Daniel Frazer. Reuben James survived to be listed as acting gunner, two years later, in U.S. Gunboat No. 6. An account of the foray published in the *Naval Temple* in 1816 states that the unnamed "hero, however, survived." In Goldsborough's authoritative *Naval Chronicle* of 1824, Frazer is identified as Decatur's savior. The first biography of Decatur, issued a year after the calamitous James Barron killed him in a duel, described the episode in detail. All early accounts agree that Decatur's antagonist was the Turkish captain, not the moorish seaman of this picture, and that Decatur shot him through his own pocket. Decatur's uniform is incorrect, both for his rank and for the period. The sailor blouse being worn by "Reuben" was not issued until about four decades later. And where and how, in this pellmell boarding action, would "Reuben" have got himself fixed up with that flowered sling for his arm? The surviving Reuben James appears to have been a yarn spinner. Someone should have checked before giving his name to a U.S. destroyer.

for the detaching of two frigates, one to keep an eye on the admiral of a supposedly friendly state, the other to convoy tribute through the corsair-ravaged seas to make sure that it reached the specific evildoer whose corsairs it was intended to strengthen.

Why did Jefferson not promptly urge the first Democratic-Republican Congress to reverse the policy that the Federalists had bequeathed to it? There is no clear record of the reasoning behind his forebearance. Probably, in a period of readjustment under Buonaparte's new dictatorship, he was awaiting the best moment for concerted action to break the Barbary system forever. In the meanwhile, as his orders to Dale indicated, he favored a policy of full belligerency if all three regencies made the occasion for it. Unfortunately, at the close of the Adams administration, the United States was the technical malefactor under two treaties—far in arrears in delivery of the promised tribute. It was the third Barbary state, to which our commitments had been fulfilled, that was causing the trouble.

The cruise in the Mediterranean was kept up with reinforcements and exchanges of personnel. A number of vessels were captured without the sort of resistance put up by the *Tripoli*. Bainbridge took the *Mirboka,* a Moroccan irregular. The capture probably quelled a faction in Morocco that had sought to provoke the one consistently friendly North African state into a conflict with the United States. At this time the squadron, in the late summer of 1803, was under the command of Edward Preble. He too had to be his own State Department. After negotiating a reaffirmation of the Moroccan-American treaty of 1786, he gave back the *Mirboka*.

If Tripolitan waters were the nursery of the infant Navy, Commodore Preble was its not too kindly nurse. In his early forties, he complained of being sent on far and arduous duties with a group of boys—his own word even for the captains of his squadron: all under thirty. They disliked him too, but he whipped them into shape with a rigor that they came to value. Bainbridge, Biddle, Chauncey, Decatur, Hull, Jones, Lawrence, Macdonough, Morris, Porter, were his ten most notable young officers.

The outstanding episode of the war began when the ill-starred Bainbridge hung the *Philadelphia* high up on an uncharted rock in the harbor of Tripoli. It ended when the frigate, salvaged by the Tripolitans for their own service, was destroyed at anchor by Decatur. Preble's offshore school for heroes was supplemented, during the following winter, by David Porter's device of keeping his fellow captives busy in Tripoli with a school of tactics and navigation that unquestionably contributed to their later accomplishments. But when news of the loss of the *Philadelphia* reached Washington, one of the many unfortunate results of slow communication itself got slowly under way. Congress concerted with the administration to reinforce the squadron decisively with four frigates. One replacement might have been better. The reason lay in a bureaucratic rigidity which already was chilling the expanded service at home.

The older officers had been hauling at one another on the ladder of rank ever since the original appointment of six captains to oversee the building of the 1794 frigates. Several truculent commanders had set a precedent for Sterett by resigning over questions of preferment. This contest, inherited like other difficulties from the former administration, brought the war with Tripoli to an unsatisfactory close. The law stipulated that frigates must be commanded by officers of the highest rank: captains. Only two captains were junior in rank to Preble, and one of them was already serving under him in the Mediterranean. Consequently, if even two frigates were dispatched, one of their commanders would automatically have to

The seamanlike expertness of this view of the loss of the *Philadelphia* hints at what is in fact true—that it was done by an eyewitness. Charles Denoon observed the action from inside the frigate and so had to imagine a point of view for his engraving, but he was evidently familiar with the form and rig of the Tripolitan gunboats. Note that the lateen sails were brailed up to the yards when the vessels attained the desired position for firing the cannon in their bows. The original caption reads, *A perspective view of the loss of the U.S. Frigate Philadelphia in which is represented her relative position to the Tripolitan Gunboats when during their furious attack upon her she was unable to get a single gun to bear upon them.* The date was October 31, 1803.

replace Preble as commodore. When the appointments were made, there had as yet been no news of the brilliant operations off Tripoli that commenced with the burning of the *Philadelphia*. The concentrated series of achievements, in the late summer of 1804, occurred while the relief squadron was on the way, officered according to the seniority rule adopted from the British service. The commodore had to be Samuel Barron, the elder of a pair of brothers whose commodoreships the Navy managed to outlive, but not without difficulty.

Preble may have been pushed to a special urgency by the tuberculosis that was to kill him three years later. Barron was a routine officer, somewhat incapacitated by a less serious ailment. When he relieved Preble, in September of 1804, Tripoli was staggering from a succession of hard blows. Winter was bad for naval operations in such waters, but Barron declared a winter season much sooner than he had to.

The imprisoned Bainbridge, using invisible ink, had communicated with the squadron through the Swedish consul. The plan for burning the *Philadelphia* had first come from him in this fashion, with a report that the prisoners were not being harshly treated. The Tripolitan prime minister, responsible for this policy, had opposed the war in the belief that conditions had changed sufficiently in the Mediterranean to make peaceful trade more profitable than

February 16, 1804. The *Philadelphia* had been refitted by the Tripolitans, and was at anchor under the heavy batteries when Lieutenant Stephen Decatur drifted up to her in the moonlight in the ketch *Intrepid,* which itself was a refitted Tripolitan prize. Decatur was challenged as he approached. His pilot, the courageous Sicilian Salvadore Catalano, replied that they had lost their anchors and asked permission to tie up to the frigate for the night. When the wind shifted with the ketch still at a little distance, the Turks obligingly sent off a boat with a hawser to meet the *Intrepid*'s boat which took it aboard. In his terse report to the Commodore next day, Decatur wrote: "—at ½ past 9 laid her a long side the *Philadelphia,* boarded, and after a short contest carried her. I immediately fired her in the Store Rooms, Gun Room Cockpit & Birth Deck and remained on board until the flames had issued from the Spar Deck hatch ways & Ports." Midshipman Izard wrote to his mother, "They Tripolitans on board of her were dreadfully alarmed when they found who we were. Poor fellows! About 20 of them were cut to pieces & the rest jumped overboard. . . . It is a miracle that our little vessel escaped the flames, lying within two feet of them & to leeward." In the following cannonade only one shot reached the *Intrepid,* which was in more danger from the double-shotted guns of the *Philadelphia,* banging away as she burned. This crude print, obviously not by an eyewitness, makes the extensive harbor into a little cove. The confusion over Reuben James should not reflect upon his valor. He volunteered for this hazardous adventure.

The 1846 lithograph at the left has interest mainly as an early example of Nathaniel Currier's efforts to celebrate American History for a people creating a romantic legend of their own past. Almost everything is wrong in detail, notably the print's most striking feature: the high-arching bombs. Preble complained of his lack of vessels that could elevate their guns adequately. Frigates were ill adapted to an assault upon shore positions. There were only two mortars in the squadron.

BELOW. A knowledgeable view of the attack on Tripoli of August 3, 1804, by Preble's squadron. The Decatur brothers each captured a gunboat, but James was killed as he boarded the one he had taken. The tussle in which Stephen Decatur was saved by Daniel Frazer is said by some of the participants in this attack to have occurred when he pursued his brother's killer. The frigate is the *Constitution*. The other substantial vessels are, in probable order, left to right, the *Enterprize, Nautilus,* and *Vixen,* schooners, and the *Syren* and *Argus,* brigs. This view was engraved by John B. Guerrazzi and published at Leghorn within a year of the event. The harbor works are about right for the period, according to Midshipman de Krafft's chart and view.

Midshipman Robert T. Spence wrote to his mother, "I made application, as well as Capt Stew't for me, to go in to the Harbour of Tripoli, in an Infernal, containing 150 Barrels of Powder & 300 shells, for the purpose of blowing the Bashaws Castle up; this expedition was Commanded by Capt Sumers—I received no direct answer, from the Commodore. & of course, expected to go; but a favorite of the Commodores, persuaded him, to allow *him* to go. Capt Decatur then made Application for me; But the Commodore reply'd he had already selected the officer, that was to go with Capt Sumers; the Night came—She went in, all were anxious with expectation when Cannon announced her near approach to the Castle. Cannon were fired from all parts of the town. In a few moments she went up—How awfully Grand! Every thing wrapp'd in Dead silence, made the explosion loud, and terrible, the fuses of the shells, burning in the air, shone like so many planets, a vast stream of fire, which appear'd ascending to heaven portrayed the Walls to our view— . . . Poor Sumers a Lieut & a midshipman were gone, no more to return! We conjectured the explosion to have been premature; it has since been confirm'd by information from Tripoli . . . he was boarded by two Gun Boats, 50 men each,—He might have escaped; but he started with a determination never to let so seasonable a supply fall into their Hands; & never to return alive unless he had, satis- factorily, executed his mission. He touched fire himself to match & she went up, sending 100 Turks and 15 Christian souls to eternity. What a Noble Death, & truly characteristic of that Noble Sumers. He cer- tainly was an extraordinary man."

plunder. Barron thus had received an intimation that peace might be concluded on favorable terms. He was empowered to ransom the crew of the *Philadelphia*. Captain Rodgers offered to raise $140,000 to add to the ransom on the condition that the Bashaw would release the prisoners and then go on to fight the war to a finish. But a civilian negotiator, Tobias Lear, favored Barron's policy of negotiation. Peace was finally concluded on June 3, 1805. It involved a ransom payment of $60,000, but in other respects more nearly resembled a compact between civilized states than any so far made with Barbary: no "price of the peace," no tribute. Shore-based forces of the pretender Hamet Karamanli, under the command of William Eaton, were badly let down. But there was always the risk that a final assault from sea and by shore would have resulted in slaughter of the prisoners. Such questions could hardly be submitted to Washington, more than five thousand sailing miles away.

Hindsight says that Preble probably would have pushed the war to a quick victory and installed Hamet on the throne, saving the ransom payment. The seniority of captains determined the issue otherwise; and the skirmish war with Tripoli, like that with France, settled nothing finally because the fundamental issue was not confronted frankly in either case. Involuntary servitude was the issue, more than neutral rights. The first skirmish war was fought against the less likely antagonist, over the more superficial issue rather than the basic one. The second skirmish war, because a ransom payment entered into the settlement, allowed the marauders to go on believing that the seizure of human beings still might be a profitable occupation.

Even so, between the violence of Sterett at one extreme and the caution of Barron at the other, a disciplined but daringly individualistic and self-confident naval character was shaping up.

It has been suggested that this figurehead, in the Marine Museum of the City of New York, may have been that of the *Constitution*. Her log entry for September 12, 1804, states that her original Hercules figure—with a club raised to strike—was "broken to pieces" when she fell afoul of the *President* off Tripoli. She was given a billet head at Malta, a month later, and still carried a simple billet scroll during the War of 1812. Later she was given two different figureheads representing President Jackson, but I find no evidence that a second Hercules which might have been this one ever was shipped. The *Philadelphia* also had a Hercules, with club swung back overhead, shown clearly on the surviving Hutton plan from which she was built. This too was destroyed at Tripoli when Decatur's spectacular raid burned the stranded frigate. *Hercules* was a popular name for ships, in both America and England. The stance and structure of this figure suggest a later date, a stem curving forward in the clipper fashion. In the vessels of 1800 or thereabouts there usually was a beakhead between the figure and the bulwarks of the fo'c's'le—the figure itself being more nearly vertical than this one, sometimes actually vertical. The leeward rails of the head, three more or less horizontal timbers braced by vertical members, served as the traditional, hazardous water closet for seamen: the middle rail for seat, the upper one for backrest, and water in abundance just below. Hence the surviving seaman's name—head—for a latrine that is no longer placed in so sporting a location.

Despite a peace convention, the skirmish war with France had an aftermath of sporadic actions for more than a decade. As the dictatorship of Buonaparte evolved into the empire of Napoleon, new states were created for his relatives and favorites to rule. The authority of marine commissions, particularly of letters of marque and privateers, was often uncertain. The print (right) celebrates the repulse of a French privateer cutter by the brig *Cambrian* of Boston, William Marshall, master. The action occurred on October 23, 1804, a few days after the *Constitution* had completed repairs at Malta. It is one of the more unusual scenes of a sea fight—no effort having been made to depict an overpowering antagonist going down to defeat. The only gun visible in the cutter appears to be a bow chase, but she may have had a rotatable gun amidships, a form of armament that was beginning to be popular. It is not entirely clear whether her boat is towing her off to gain distance from the *Cambrian*'s guns, or turning her to bring a larboard gun to bear. This unconventional and early aquatint was engraved by William Barnard after a painting by Joseph Cartwright. The publisher was C. Cave of Boston, who put it on sale less than four months after the occurrence.

Ship Francis of Salem

The ship *Francis* was one of several built by Enos Briggs of Salem for Joseph Peabody. Briggs earlier had built the *Essex*, Bainbridge's first frigate command. The *Francis* was laid down on June 1, 1807, and launched five months later. She was intended for an Indiaman, and measured 297 tons—about as large a ship as was practicable for the Salem trade. While lying in the harbor of Naples in 1810 she was seized by the French, along with a number of other American vessels. The American consul was obliged to buy her back again from the French authorities as a packet in which to send home the crews of the other vessels requisitioned at the same time.

"JEFFERSON'S" GUNBOATS

IN REHEARSING THE POLITICALLY BIZARRE AND PERSONALLY INSPIRITING ORIGINS OF THE United States Navy I have not been trying to prop up an image of Thomas Jefferson pulled inside out. His correspondence as President reveals his continuing belief that the fleet should be strengthened with ships of the line, but he was never an advocate of a powerful, offensive Navy. He did not try to twist from Congress the sustained naval program which timely leadership might have secured. Under the Act of March 3, 1801, he was expected to reduce crews by one-third in the few vessels to be retained in service. He did nothing to oppose the crippling restriction, but proposed prudently that even fewer vessels should cruise with their complements complete.

"Jefferson's gunboats" has been an easy phrase with which to summarize a large, unhappy subject to the disrepute of the third President. In his special message on gunboats, sent to Congress on February 10, 1807, he supported a concept of coastal defense in which large numbers of gunboats would form one of four interdependent components. What commonly has been ignored is the extraordinary experimentation preceding this attempt to formulate a fresh policy. Jefferson's? They were almost everybody's gunboats. I have quoted President Adams's letter to Secretary Stoddert, urging the provision of some such craft. On May 4, 1798, Congress responded with an appropriation for ten "small vessels . . . equipped as gallies." In political policy and in fact, "Jefferson's" gunboats began early in the Adams administration. It was a gunboat era. Buonaparte was assembling an enormous fleet of such vessels for an invasion of England. A flotilla of little Russian gunboats had trounced a Turkish fleet, sinking several ships of the line. The lack of such craft had severely hampered American operations at Tripoli, where the *Philadelphia* frigate had been run aground while trying to perform what was properly a gunboat's mission. Preble finally acquired six gunboats and two similar bombards from Naples. All eight may be discerned by their flags in the larger of the prints on page 134.

What were these disputatious gunboats? In design and rig they were extremely varied. Most of them were between 55 and 70 feet in length, with lateen rig on two masts. The smaller ones mounted one fairly heavy gun, usually an 18-pounder, as a bow chase. They had sweeps, or large oars, and were at least partially decked over, but shallow. The larger and later ones had two guns, one forward, one aft, or in some cases both mounted parallel amidships on what was called a Hawkins Wheel—a circular, grooved platform from which they pointed in opposite directions. Thus either could be turned to fire from either side while the other was being reloaded.

Jefferson, in his gunboat message, referred to the wide consultation preceding it, among higher officers of the Navy, in which "no difference of judgment appeared on the subjects." Commodore Barron and Captain Tingey submitted concurrent reports approving it. More distinguished younger officers, including Hull, Macdonough, Preble, Rodgers, and Stewart, contributed ideas and designs, or oversaw construction. Gunboats were an international obsession. The President recognized the interest in them of the best professional naval men, and furthered it on the level of policy. The strongest single influence was Preble's. A president would have seemed foolish indeed, in his own time, to ignore the views of the officer in command of the most brilliant operations so far in his country's naval history. The surviving plan of one early gunboat designed by Jacob Coffin carries a notation "Commre Preble's Ideas Adopted."

No law dictates a successful outcome to all experimentation, even when it has the widespread support of able men. It may be noted, for purely military analogies, that gunboats seemed to promise the same sort of breaking of a stalemate between standard weapons that was more recently expected by the proponents of aircraft, poison gas, and submarines. Aircraft and submarines fulfilled expectations. Gunboats and poison gas did not.

The original script caption of this aquatint reads, *John Pierce who was murderd by a Shot from the Leander a British 50 Gun Ship fourth rate Commanded by Henry Whitby, the Cambrian of 44 Guns, & Driver of 20 Guns, within a quarter of a mile of Sandy Hook on Friday at 5.o.Clock P. M. 28th of April 1806.* The three British men-of-war had been searching the vessels that entered and left New York harbor, taking out of them seamen alleged to be British citizens. According to one contemporary account, the sloop *Richard* was already hove to, in response to a shot across her bows, when another shot decapitated her helmsman: the captain's brother. The body of John Pierce was publicly exhibited next day in New York, and his funeral was the focus of intense indignation. The episode probably was the turning point which produced "Jefferson's Embargo." He wrote to Jacob Crowninshield, who had reported the uproar in New York, referring specifically to the hampering effect of the Peace Establishment legislation, so far as the frigates were concerned, and to his new proclamation barring British ships from all American ports. He hoped that New Orleans and New York would be made secure by gunboats and land defenses. "But the building of some ships of the line instead of our most indifferent frigates is not to be lost sight of. That we should have a squadron properly composed to prevent the blockading of our ports is indispensable." The print below is the work of John James Barralet, as designer, engraver, and publisher.

An English view of the action between the *President* and the *Little Belt,* May 15, 1811. The print was published on the 25th of October following. This was the second of two armed conflicts preceding the declaration of war by Congress on June 18, 1812. The first—the *Chesapeake-Leopard* affair—was not of such a character as to move anyone to portray it at the time. It was a repetition, on more nearly equal terms, of the episode of Captain Phillips off the Havana. The English had good information that some of their deserters had enlisted in the *Chesapeake* early in 1807. The *Leopard* left port to require their surrender at sea. The *Chesapeake* was in no condition to fight. The powder horns were empty, and when some priming powder was found there were no matches. Permission to muster the crew being refused him, Captain Humphreys of the *Leopard* opened fire. Only one gun was fired by the *Chesapeake,* just as she was striking. The alleged deserters were seized, but the British captain would not accept the surrender of the *Chesapeake.* Commodore James Barron was suspended for five years without pay for being unready for action. He returned to the Navy in time to kill Decatur in a duel, and regrettably survived to be its senior officer. The *Leopard* had carried about ten more guns than the *Chesapeake.* The *Little Belt,* with 22, had less than half as many guns as her antagonist, all of them lighter. The action was a mistake, occurring after dark, in which the smaller ship was fought with great spirit.

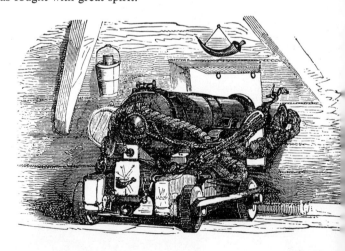

Remembering Chapelle's warning that nautical history reflects slow evolution to which many contribute, and not the sudden inventions of particular men, we might do better to try to understand the appeal of the gunboats rather than bring against their proponents the easy condemnations of hindsight. Jefferson's fruitless advocacy of even a small naval force to chastise Algiers—an outcome for which he had to wait three full decades—had not led him to suppose that Congress would be eager to meet the cost of a navy adequate for the general protection of American commerce. The turning of the first small available fleet against France, while England continued to be the more frequent aggressor, had warned him that the existence of a navy was no assurance of its intelligent use. His letters reveal a deepening personal anguish over the ruined hopes of his own great company of revolutionaries.

France, where his heart lay, had betrayed his world by betraying herself into the brutal projects of Buonaparte. Jefferson, in the year of the gunboat message, was of an aging generation which from birth had seen only scant interludes in the aggressive naval warfare that smashed the most beautiful creations of man and mangled man himself. It went on and on, indecisively. In one letter he calls up a vision of the British Navy as an insensate beast, living on the ships, seamen, and merchandise of all the world, eating everywhere what it must have to survive. That he should have turned with some satisfaction to the gunboat policy—as did many others before him and with him—is a fact that should be viewed against this background.

A different consideration, inevitable in the use of public moneys, was the employment given to a large number of small shipyards, located where the production of major fighting ships would have been difficult or impossible. The political temptations are obvious. For example, Matthew Lyon, the Democratic-Republican Representative who had been jailed by the Federalists under the Alien and Sedition Acts (and re-elected while in jail by his stubborn Vermont constituents) got contracts to build five gunboats on an inland river— numbers 15, 16, 25, 26, and 27. Might it be a bit naïve to think that his weeks of discomfort in a freezing jail in midwinter, shortly before the Jeffersonian electoral victory, had nothing to do with this?

The records are incomplete, but it is likely that 176 gunboats were launched altogether.

Samuel Holbrook, in his *Three Score Years* . . . , tells of having witnessed the punishment of the three seamen who were seized as deserters in the *Chesapeake* by Captain Humphreys of the *Leopard*. Holbrook was at Halifax when Jenkin Ratford, supposed to be the worst offender, was sentenced to be hanged at the fore yardarm of the *Jason* frigate, "yet his punishment was comparatively nothing as viewed with that of the others; for the explosion of the gun instantly kills the victim and his death is easy." The other two were sentenced to be flogged through the fleet. He mentions cases "where the victim has died under the punishment; nevertheless, the number of lashes must be given upon the back of the corpse! . . . At the first three or four blows the cries and entreaties of the poor wretch are heart-rending, crying out, *O God Almighty, save me! O Jesus Christ, have mercy upon me!* . . . while the flesh upon the back was cut into strips."

Perhaps two-fifths of them had been built before passage of the Act of December 18, 1807, authorizing 188 additional ones. Only about a hundred of these were actually constructed. Of the first 92 gunboats, most were built in small communities. Beginning with 93, nearly all the remainder were built in the regular centers of the industry: New York, Philadelphia, Baltimore, Norfolk, and Charleston.

Writing to Tom Paine, one of the sudden horde of gunboat inventors, President Jefferson remarked upon "the ruinous folly of a navy." He had come to believe at last that the only way of starving the great beast, the British Navy, was to withdraw its food from the waters with an embargo upon shipping, and to hold it offshore with impregnable harbor defenses. It was the sort of drastic right answer that becomes right only if enough others are willing and able to concur. That was not the case. The policy was a failure. Yet the wisest of men, in 1807, would probably have been called mad if he had suggested that an American navy even then in existence would be able, a few years later, to challenge the great beast with an outcome distinctly short of disaster.

"Jefferson's gunboats," that were everybody's gunboats, illumine the point which I hope has emerged from this sporadic survey of the curious beginnings of our Navy. The point is that from well before its tentative establishment, and for a long while afterward, the United States Navy resembled the merchant marine in that it took shape and grew despite the government. It was the creation of imaginative, farsighted, individual men. Many of them were impelled by personal advantage. Some were altruistic. A number of the heroic early captains squabbled like vain children for precedence in a service hierarchy. But bureaucracy, with its stultifications, had not yet diminished the American spirit significantly.

One can agree with Chapelle's warning about the function of invention in maritime matters and still contend that it was the Navy of Joshua Humphreys, a Quaker—and of the devoted, upright Federalist Benjamin Stoddert—the Navy of the Philadelphia and Salem merchants who, from a combination of interest and patriotism, privately supplied public vessels. It was the Navy of its earliest stanch advocate, Thomas Jefferson, and of its first Commander in Chief, obstinate John Adams.

It is one of the sweet pleasures of history to watch these two great spirits move together again, after their wintry severance. Adams made the overture, as if in a New Year's Day

Old scores to be settled were numerous in American memory at the outbreak of the War of 1812. Ebenezer Fox and other survivors of the *Jersey* prison ship had not allowed her grim record to be forgotten. Fox's *Adventures . . .*, according to the title page, is "Illustrated by elegant engravings from original designs." The two reproduced left and right show an unsuccessful and a successful attempt to escape from the *Jersey,* which was moored in New York harbor near Brooklyn. Some accounts say that as many as 11,000 men died of disease in her during the Revolution.

resolution on the 1st of January, 1812. He said he was sending Jefferson, knowing him to be "a Friend to American Manufactures . . . two Pieces of Homespun lately produced in this quarter."

He was jesting. The "pieces" turned out to be two volumes of lectures spun from the brain of his son, John Quincy Adams. So began one of the richest interplays of mind and spirit that the world has stored up for the refreshment of the wise: Jefferson using to the last his copperplate grace of phrase, Adams possessing the page just as surely with gnarled and playful integrity. They kept it up almost to the day of their death: the fiftieth anniversary, exactly, of a document that both had signed on July 4, 1776.

The correspondence had been under way for ten years when Adams at last raised "a subject of some delicacy" upon which he had "long entertained scruples." The widow of General Henry Knox had written that she had frequently heard General Washington call the Navy Adams's "child." But, said Adams, "I have always believed it to be Jefferson's child, though Knox may have assisted in ushering it into the world. Hamilton's hobby was the army. That Washington was averse to a navy, I had full proof from his own lips. . . ." In many matters, throughout the correspondence, Adams was patiently putting the record straight for history. Here was a case in point. He did not wish, by the testimony of Mrs. Knox, to gain credit for what another had done.

LEFT. Samuel Leech, an English seaman in the *Macedonian,* after her capture transferred his allegiance to the United States and shipped in the *Syren.* In his reminiscences, *Thirty Years From Home . . .* , he tells of his activities in a press gang. Americans' protections "were often taken from them and destroyed. . . . To prevent the recovery of these men by their consul, the press-gang usually went ashore on the night previous to our going to sea; so that before they were missed they were beyond his protection." RIGHT. Samuel Holbrook issued his memoirs in 1857. His most vivid memory appears to have been of the press gangs, since he chose this scene for frontispiece. Early in the book he comments upon the unreadiness of the United States Navy when Congress at long last was exasperated into declaring war over the impressment of American seamen: ". . . nothing larger than a frigate. No navy yards of any magnitude, except at Washington, no money in the treasury, no materials for ship-building at hand, no preparation on the frontiers, no facilities for transportation or carrying guns, and the necessary articles required in war, including provisions and the numerous requirements for ship building, from the Atlantic States to the Lakes. No army, no horses, scarcely any copper, but a small amount of iron in the country, very little hemp or rigging, and a very small supply of duck fit for warships sails." It was fortunate for the United States that the British ministry, knowing these facts, did not take the declaration as a serious threat, until news of American naval victories aroused the public in England.

Jefferson replied that his "ransacked" papers had furnished nothing definite, but from memory he gave in brief the gist of the account which I have independently taken from the public documents and from correspondence contemporary with the events. Both alluded, in these two letters, to their discussions of 1786. Adams magnanimously remembered Jefferson's position expressed at that time; Jefferson, with an equal magnanimity, merely recorded his memory that they had communicated together at the onset of the Barbary crisis on the subject of a naval force.

The heroic old antagonists had learned how much to value each other, in a world of lesser men. The last words of John Adams, dying, were, "Thomas Jefferson still survives!" He was unaware, as he spoke, that Jefferson had been dead for a few hours.

Prelude to war: The capture in mid-Atlantic, on April 30, 1812, of the American armed schooner *Gipsey* by His Majesty's frigates *Hermes* and *Belle Poule*. The caption of C. Rosenberg's print of the same scene states that, "The schooner was a most superb Vessel of 300 Tons burthen carried Ten 18^{lb} Carronades and one long 18 pound swivel between her main & foremast with a complement of 80 men & 2 Ferocious Dogs. She had twice surrender'd to the *Hermes* previous to falling in with the *Belle Poule* & endeavoured to effect her escape each time by hauling off on a different tack, while the ship was in the act of taking in sail & rounding to. The Crew of the American made a desperate effort to regain possession of their Vessel after being boarded by the boats of the *Hermes* by 20 Armed Men and the Two Dogs suddenly assailing them, which after a severe struggle were overpowered." The schooner's cargo was valued at almost a quarter of a million dollars. The *Hermes* had chased her for three days and nights before the appearance of a second vessel from an unfortunate quarter forced her surrender. The extent of her armament and the tenacity of her defense suggest a state of "peace" so near the exploding point that an American declaration of war a few weeks later was merely a recognition, as indeed it said, that "a state of war exists." This is the original oil painting by W. J. Huggins. A print was promptly engraved from it by Rosenberg which in turn served as the model for several other representations of American schooners. Burton's oil, on page 173, seems obviously to have been derived from this view.

1812:
The Printmaker's War

he American Neptune, A QUARTERLY DEVOTED TO MARITIME HIStory, gave foremost place in its issue of January 1943 to a report upon an exhibit of naval prints at the Grolier Club.

"Proper appraisal," the critic noted, "depends on a true understanding of what the prints are. Essentially they are news pictures recording an incident, episode or action which the public wanted to know about as factually as possible. The literal-minded American wanted his news 'hot' if he could get it . . . a surprising effect of liveliness and truth of feeling permeates the whole group."

The exhibit, supplemented by two books that emerged from it, gathered for comparison the formerly scattered visual records of an extraordinary and misunderstood episode in our national life. Most of the prints were concerned with the War of 1812—dismissed by some as a diversion on the vast perimeter of the Napoleonic Wars, overpraised by others as a contest in which Young America gave Old England a severe trouncing. To say that the truth lies between these misconceptions is inadequate. Each contains a minor element of truth, pulled out of shape, while it misses the central fact of this peculiar occasion altogether. The central fact is that a young nation, which had been bullied up and down the seas for a quarter of a century, bumbled unprepared into war against the most powerful of empires, and emerged three years later, admired and respected, never to be bullied again.

This phenomenal change was worked almost entirely by a dozen sea fights; the American character, which the first Secretary of the Navy had unsuccessfully striven to define, declared itself in action. There was a short while, with Napoleon supposedly well bottled up in Elba, when decision teetered in England toward committing the Royal Navy in force to the Western conflict that had engaged only a tiny fraction of its vessels. The decisive advice was probably Wellington's: his landsman's warning of an endless involvement in the interior wilderness. Many Americans had been willing, at the beginning of the war, to return to a sort of dominion status under the British crown. A great many more would have resisted. But this division itself, within the country, was healed by the inspiriting news of naval victories.

These were the last days of a kind of knight-errantry, surviving in duels on the ocean long after the old spectacle of champions fighting between the armies had been laughed into the past. The victor in a well-fought single-ship action received notice and prestige entirely out of scale with the actual injury done the enemy. British frigate captains, trained up under the example of Nelson, had almost established a world monopoly of this art. The French,

The first notable event of the War of 1812 confirmed the judgment of Joshua Humphreys. The 1794 frigates were designed to whip any standard frigate that could catch them, and to escape from any ship by which they would be seriously outgunned. But what would happen if such a frigate should be pursued by a fleet? Would her extra size doom her? The answer was, "Not if commanded by Captain Isaac Hull." A full-rigged ship is only an extension of the intricate brain that controls her. The *Constitution*, on July 17, 1812, had by great good fortune been under Hull's command for six years. Hull had got to sea as promptly as possible after the declaration of war. Seeking Rodgers's squadron of three frigates, a sloop, and a brig, he came up with four ships near the New Jersey shore and a fifth to seaward of him. It was twilight. His lantern signals brought no response. In the morning he found himself opposing the frigates *Shannon, Belvidera, Aeolus,* and *Guerrière,* with the *Africa,* 74, well astern. Soon the *Constitution* lay in a freakish patch of calm. The others all had wind in their sails. Hull got his boats out to tow the ship. As the calm extended, the pursuers did likewise. At one time they pooled their boats to haul the nearest frigate. Knowing that he was over shallow ground, Hull sent boats ahead with kedge anchors, to which the frigate was hauled by her own capstan. The sails were constantly wet down. The efforts were kept up for about sixty hours of calms and fickle breezes. One of the six vessels would always be getting the best of the light airs; the odds were constantly five to one that it would be a pursuer. Yet Hull kept his ship barely out of long gunshot range during the entire chase, and when a fair breeze came at last, nipped up to windward, distancing them all easily. A few minutes of less than supreme effort, during those sleepless sixty hours, would have ended the great career of "Old Ironsides" before she acquired the name. The escape was a phenomenal victory of seamanship, made possible by the foresight of a marine architect nineteen years earlier. Hull wrote soon afterward that his friends were "good enough to give him more credit . . . than he ought to claim" and requested them "to transfer their good wishes to lieutenant Morris and the other brave officers, and the crew . . . deprived of sleep, and allowed but little refreshment during the time, not a murmur was heard to escape them."

for fifteen or twenty years, seem to have taken it for granted that they would win on shore and lose—gallantly—at sea. When the tiny and ill-prepared United States Navy within seven months won five such actions in a row, before the first defeat, the world was astonished.

The importance of a happening in history lies in its effect. Many battles have been more immediately decisive than the little contest in the pass at Thermopylae. In the long stretch of man's accomplishment, water spilling from an old man's tub may have been more important than the sea fight at Salamis. But Thermopylae and Salamis made room for the mind of Archimedes to have its far effects upon the shapes of ships, and for other minds to shape, in singular freedom amid much slavery, the ultimate liberty of the West.

Although the war that looms pridefully in our own textbooks was little more than a sideshow—in a vast clash of coalitions that shook the world from Copenhagen to the Marquesas—it had the enormous importance of being fought for a pair of clear issues:

Free trade and sailors' rights!

One might carp at the precedence of the economic, but seamen knew that their rights were unenforceable if they had no jobs. The War of 1812 won practically nothing, on paper, for either side. The peace was rather one of mutual understanding between reasonable men weary of the long Napoleonic bloodletting. Although impressment was not mentioned in the treaty, it was not allowed to rise again as a real issue afterward.

The sea duels of 1812 were the first that found American artists and printmakers well prepared, but the importance of these naval encounters on a world scale is reflected in the large number of contemporaneous pictures for which a market was anticipated by print-makers of England, France, and Germany. No later occasion has so explicitly reflected the special American individualism of try-it-and-see. Borrowed traditions had been abraded on our rough frontiers. The national government was reluctant to lead. A brief period when John Adams was supposed by his enemies to have monarchical tastes had given way before a reticent sort of democracy under the example of Jefferson. Madison, not quite so plain, was still a Jeffersonian disciple—acquiescing in the movement toward a declaration of war almost as if in recognition of a law of nature. The ancient evasions fell away, even with the country fantastically unready. Its very unreadiness may have been an important cause of the early victories. British Intelligence had reported a state of affairs over which the ministers hardly could have been concerned. They moved at the standard pace to quell a minor nuisance, which exploded into a series of incredible aggravations.

The printmakers spread the news.

Of the two books which emerged from the Grolier Club exhibition, one was its handsome catalogue, the other an extended volume by the same compiler, Irving S. Olds, called *Bits and Pieces of American History*. Since these are the only comprehensive collections of

lbert Stuart's portrait of Isaac Hull was the basis for an engraving (left) issued by T. W. eeman early in February, 1813. The full sheet includes, below the bust portrait, a tiny advance ndering of Freeman's large print of the *Constitution-Guerrière* action which was issued on arch 8th. The small one was made "from an original drawing under the direction of Captⁿ ll," and the large one "from original Drawings furnished by Capt. I. Hull." This scrupulous graver had found himself involved in a printseller's war of his own. As was customary, he had vertised for subscribers to the battle scene, promising that the picture would be exhibited and at, "It shall be in accuracy of drawing in excellency of engraving and copper-plate printing ual at least, to any Print which ever has been published in the United States." Other proposals ving appeared, he informed his subscribers that "far from abating in zeal or ardor in the osecution of his design, he is determined to spare no expense and pains to produce, not only correct representation but to add to the design in size, making the naval action 24 by 18 inches, thout any additional expense to the subscribers." A number of other printmakers were more ompt; Captain Hull, as was proper, appears to have instructed them impartially. Four paintings the action were done by Michael Corné "under Directions from Commodore Hull & Capt orris." They were engraved, the first print appearing on November 1st. Freeman's and Corné's rried prints of the battle, indifferent in quality, have not been included.

the prints in question, and since both are now unavailable, it has seemed useful to present here an extensive offering of the work called forth in this touch-and-go crisis in the life of our country, when a little less notice, a little less enthusiasm, well might have turned the balance of world history.

Representative prints have been included of all the major actions and of the more significant minor ones, with examples of the Continental as well as of the British response. The entire subject of sea pictures is epitomized in these productions: the questions of structural accuracy of the vessels themselves, and of their tactical relationships at the chosen moment of portrayal; the problem of authority when versions differ, or even when they do not; the date of issue, and the consequent probable public effect.

Varying standards and skills of the printmakers were at interplay with similarly various tastes and resources of the buyers. Some small prints were on the press within two or three weeks of the news. These are usually crude and unreliable. Better examples were made, still quickly, for such magazines as the *Analectic* and *Port Folio*. A majority of those issued outside Great Britain are undated, but printsellers' advertisements indicate that first-rate prints could be made available in less than two months. What seems to have been the earliest large print of the first major action, on August 19, 1812, several hundred miles off the New

LEFT. Thomas Birch's view of the *Constitution-Guerrière* action was produced with care and offered to the public one day less than a year after the event. Cornelius Tiebout, the engraver, used the stipple technique. The print is a large one, 17¾" x 26⅜". It was priced at $5, by subscription. ABOVE. A more spirited French print of the same moment. Note that the artist probably worked directly from one of the several American prints in which the ships have this approximate pose, causing the scene to appear reversed when the plate was printed. The painter was Stradonwort, the engraver Valnest. RIGHT. The later, wry comment on the cost of such a victory, by T. H. Mumford, an industrious illustrator of standard histories.

England coast, between the *Constitution* and the *Guerrière,* went on sale in Philadelphia just six weeks later.

Many prints bear explicit evidence that they were based on sketches received from participants as soon as they reached port. An example is the print here reproduced of the action not far from Bermuda, on October 18, 1812, between the *Wasp* and the *Frolic,* "*Drawn & engraved by F. Kearny, from a Sketch by Lieut. Claxton, of the Wasp.*" The sketch took a strange route to the engraver. During this second considerable action of the war at sea, as reported by Captain Jacob Jones: "Lieut. Claxton, who was confined by sickness, left his bed a little previous to the engagement; and though too indisposed to be at his division, remained upon deck, and showed by his composed manner of noting its incidents that we had lost by his illness the services of a brave officer." The triumphant moments for the *Wasp*'s people were few. Victor and vanquished both were captured about two hours later by the *Poictiers,* 74. The *Wasp* might have escaped to windward if her rigging had not been badly cut up by the *Frolic*'s fire. The *Poictiers* took her prizes into Bermuda, whence Claxton and the other Americans were promptly sent on exchange in a cartel to New York: a portent of less onerous treatment of prisoners, as compared with the experiences of Conyngham in the Revolution.

The original victory of the *Wasp,* over an antagonist slightly superior in metal but less well designed underwater, overshadowed for the public her foredoomed submission to a ship of the line. She had been designed by Fox, and was taken into the British Navy as the *Peacock,* filling the place of the brig of that name sunk by the *Hornet*. Thus the first two close contests of the war reinforced claims for the superiority of American design. The *Constitution*'s victory over the *Guerrière* demonstrated the merit of Humphreys's theory that oversized frigates would have no difficulty in whipping standard ones. The *Wasp*'s efficient taking of the *Frolic* showed the superiority in maneuver of Fox's design, with its sharp floors, over the deep-rolling, brig-rigged 18s which the Admiralty had been turning out on a standardized cheap model. In so far as the War of 1812 can be called a victory for anyone, it was a victory for the individual men in America who had insisted upon making contributions of imagination and of excellence, to overcome the great weight of commonplace superiority in routine maneuver. The British service was not inferior, but it had gone past its heroic Nelsonian peak and was badly overstretched.

Claxton's sketch catches the moment when both ships, somewhat out of control because of damage to their rigging, came together, the *Frolic*'s bowsprit thrust across the *Wasp*'s weather bulwarks. Jones raked with a broadside, and the Americans boarded over the bows of their antagonist, to find all of her officers killed or wounded.

Almost always there are discrepancies between the accounts written by opponents in

One of the several topical caricatures with which William Charles of Philadelphia celebrated episodes of the War of 1812. "I've often heard of your Wasps and Hornet's but little thought such diminitive Insects could give me such a sting! ! !"

LEFT. Lieutenant Claxton's eyewitness sketch of the action between the *Wasp* and the *Frolic*, on October 18, 1812, was the basis of this print, drawn and engraved by Francis Kearny. It gives us an unusually exacting view of the structure of the famous American ship-sloops of the period. The stern differs somewhat from Chapelle's reconstruction of Fox's damaged original plan, still in existence, but the quarter galleries may have been removed when she was refitted. It was an engraver's commonplace to show them, as on the *Frolic* in this case. The omission suggests that Kearny was following Claxton's sketch with care. In this instance a French celebration of the same action (below) by the team of Montardier du Havre and Jean Jérôme Baugean appears to have been made without reference to a reliable sketch or close description. The "*Forlic*'s" bowsprit has come over the starboard side, rather than the larboard; and it is the English who are shown boarding, whereas accounts of the fight agree that it was the Americans who boarded and found no-one on deck who was not wounded. Both prints show the *Wasp*'s maintopmast dangling, but the reversal of her position in the French print puts the wreckage on the wrong side.

Captain Stephen Decatur, a copy in the woodcut technique from the portrait by Thomas Sully. Woodcuts were increasingly to replace other forms of engraving for magazine and book illustration during the nineteenth century. RIGHT. The British frigate *Macedonian* and her captor, the *United States,* passing through "Hurl" Gate on their return to America after the action shown in the painting reproduced opposite page 10. The *United States* had suffered little injury in the contest and might have continued her cruise, but, as Decatur put it, it was important "to see our prize in." He knew the temper of the Essex Junto, the extreme Federalists who had maneuvered themselves into the quaint position of opposing restraints on trade, while still decrying a war that was being fought to remove such restraints. The *Guerrière* having been destroyed after her defeat, Decatur assumed—correctly—that the *Macedonian* would become the first ship of His Britannic Majesty to be added to the United States Navy. Sight of her would further insulate the stubborn defeatists of New England. This rare American print was published by P. H. Hansell, Carver, and Gilder of Philadelphia in 1817.

the same action: differences often appear in those coming from members of the same crew. In the intensity of mortal conflict, men see what they see within a narrow orbit, the sequence of events sometimes being jarred out of order in memory. The historian in most cases has recourse to the transcripts of courts-martial, an invariable formality after the loss of a vessel. Contemporary American newspapers tend to overemphasize the power of the opponent "defeated in a fair fight"—thereby diminishing the most notable single explanation of the series of early victories: that the American ships, on purpose, had been made larger and more powerful than their probable antagonists. It was the only plan by which so small a force might survive.

There was another Lieutenant Claxton in the war, on the British side. In 1816 this officer, Christopher Claxton, published *The Naval Monitor* for the instruction of young officers. On the subject of "our losses in the American war," he wrote, "the neglect shown to gunnery was not the immediate cause of those losses, yet it tended to make the conquests of the Americans more easy, and not only them less fearful, but almost confident of success.

"It is an unfortunate truth, that in all the actions with the Americans wherein they have taken our vessels, the damage done to them has been but trifling in comparison with the great injury we have sustained, although some actions have lasted nearly two hours."

Cautioning disputants against a show of anger (perhaps he was referring to his angry countryman, William James), Claxton points out that he too had been on the American station throughout the war, part of the time a captive. "It is cowardly in an historian to shrink from the dictates of truth. . . . I have possessed myself of facts concerning both sides of the question in most of the engagements . . . ; on the court-martial of the surviving officers and crew of one of the captured vessels, it was proved that her crew had not been exercised at their guns for an entire year and upwards. . . .

"The Americans had wisely paid the most minute attention to the art of gunnery in their vessels; consequently, the cutting up we have received is no more to be wondered at than the very little damage done to them. . . .

"American frigates, in point of size and crews, . . . were wonderfully superior to ours. . . . At the commencement of the war we had not a single ship of one deck in the

navy fit to cope with their three largest frigates—the *President, Constitution,* and *United States.*"

Several causes contributed to the first major American loss, that of the *Chesapeake* to the *Shannon;* one factor surely was that she was the first of the 36-gun frigates of 1794 to go into action. The victories over the *Guerrière, Macedonian,* and *Java* had been won by two of the 44s, against smaller opponents. Humphreys had planned it so. He designed the *Chesapeake* also as a 44; she was described as such by her builder, Fox, when he had her keel laid. But somewhere along the line she was reduced to a 36, and was duly lost to an excellently managed 38 in her first worthy encounter.

The concern of the British public over several defeats at sea finds some measure in the fact that the printmakers of London had three large prints of their *Shannon-Chesapeake* victory on sale in August. A fourth was issued on the 1st of September, three months to a day after the fight. More followed. Deck-scene caricatures, that made no attempt to reflect the facts, were published in London as early as July, a few days after the news arrived. I have included two such for special reasons, as noted in the captions. The persistence of interest in this action appears in a fine series of four prints issued seventeen years later. A London publisher even produced a print of Captain James Lawrence, "respectfully dedicated to the British Nation, whose philanthropy is such as to esteem the Brave and Virtuous even in an Enemy.—"

Lawrence, second in command when Decatur burned the *Philadelphia* in the harbor of Tripoli, had had his own 1812 triumph when his *Hornet* defeated the *Peacock*. It is not true that he wagered his country's ship, the *Chesapeake,* and sacrificed her people upon an antique notion of chivalry. Captain Broke of the *Shannon* did send a challenge in to Boston, but Lawrence had sailed out to meet him before it arrived. It is clear, however, that he erred in taking his ship out to do certain battle with an equal when most of the *Chesapeake*'s officers and hands had been in her for only a few days. A frigate was an intricate fighting machine, dependent upon concurrent skills of maneuver and gunnery. Mahan, who studied the action with minute diligence, thought that Lawrence and his crew did very well after the original calamitous decision was made.

Broke won, coolly and swiftly, an action he deserved to win. He well might have won

1.
Pocock, after Buchanan.   The *Constitution*
3.

nd the *Java*.

See text page 162

2.

4.

This stipple engraving from Gilbert Stuart's portrait of Captain William Bainbridge was done for the *Analectic Magazine* as one of a series that included Hull, Decatur, Jones, Lawrence, and Perry.

BELOW. This American print of Bainbridge's victory over the *Java* has a liveliness of human action that is unusual. Note the men aloft and on the jib boom, trying to bring under control the sails which have had their rigging cut up. The picture was "Drawn under the direction of a witness of the action by W.G." Engraver, publisher, and date do not appear. Can some reader identify "W.G."?

even if the *Chesapeake* had had the three weeks of sea drill in which Captain Isaac Hull had shaped up his green crew in the *Constitution,* before her second encounter with the *Guerrière.* It was Broke who had come nearest to catching the *Constitution* in the famous sixty-hour kedging and towing race. He had been at sea almost constantly for six or seven years in the same frigate, looking for any Frenchman to fight, encountering none. When his chance came he used it valiantly, and led his own boarders. The elaborate American explanations of the defeat of the *Chesapeake* are sound enough. The inference that Broke would have lost if Lawrence had been less hasty is egregious.

It was basically a naval architect's war: the superior ship won on every occasion. It

Just before his action with the *Java*, Captain Bainbridge had tried to persuade the captain of the *Bonne Citoyenne*, a British ship-sloop, to come out of Bahía, Brazil, and fight his escort: the *Hornet*, Captain James Lawrence. The Briton had a large amount of treasure aboard, and properly refused to put an antique notion of gallantry above his duty to deliver it. Bainbridge consequently left Lawrence to blockade the port. This wood engraving is from the *Naval Temple*, 1816, and is probably the work of Michael Corné.

The *Hornet* sinking the *Peacock*: February 24, 1813. Early retrospects upon the War of 1812 had a rugged honesty like that of the picture in the upper corner of this page. Below is an illustration from J. Fenimore Cooper's *Naval History of the United States of America*, a large-paper reissue of 1847. Cooper had an adequate knowledge of the sea and a good sense of factual appraisal. He seems to have seen to it that the illustrations were based upon reliable earlier prints. Some are close copies. But even when the memories were accurate the American public was beginning to put them into an ornate frame, a crude reversion to the nautical baroque.

HORNET SINKING THE PEACOCK

Free Trade & Sailors Rights you old rascal!

Boo-o—o—hoo!!!!

Or, JOHN BULL IN DISTRESS.
Entered according to act of Congress the 27th day of March 1813, by A. Doolittle of the State of Connecticut.

JOHNNY BULL in a Fre[t]
Oh these Wasps & Hornets! the dreadful little Insects, how they Sting & Oh how why did I disturb their Nest!!

was only when ships were approximately equal that maneuver and gunnery became decisive. Our one 44 that was lost, the *President,* was hogged when she ran aground in getting to sea. Even so she knocked the *Endymion,* her nearest pursuer of a squadron of four, out of the fight in a difficult leading action off Long Island before succumbing to the others on January 15, 1815. The reports of the commanders, toward the end of this action, are precisely contradictory. The discrepancy is so marked that falsification, on one side or the other, seems probable. The remaining pursuers were the *Majestic* razee, and the light frigates *Pomone* and *Tenedos.*

Despite an acrimonious haggling over statistics, Americans continued to claim victories for secondary reasons. Not so elsewhere. "Our valiant tars" had indeed been valiant, and this was recognized with a new respect; but it was the doing of so much with so little that turned the serious attention of the world upon American shipbuilding. As in the Revolution, the oceans had been haunted by a horde of swift and weatherly privateers. This time, however, the American Navy had made a far more effective showing. Most of the officers had been of the same high order, in skill and judgment, as England's best. The freely enlisted crews had been at least as disciplined as those largely made up by impressment. Their gunnery, in general, had been superior; but it was the ships themselves that had overcome the enormous odds which threatened them.

ABOVE. Quick, crude caricatures helped the dominant party in the United States to neutralize the Anglophile opposition. The one on the left was registered on March 27, 1813, by "A. Doolittle of the State of Connecticut," and may have been inspired by William Charles's rapier-tailed wasp (page 151) in an undated print that probably appeared earlier. In the right-hand print above, Charles again depicts John Bull, gripping a scroll with ten blank spaces, in the fourth of which is the name *Java.* The fifth entry reads, *Hornet Sunk the Peacock in 15 m.* The remaining five blank spaces were not to be filled as uniformly to the discomfiture of John Bull. RIGHT. An oil of the privateer *Providence,* perhaps by A. Williams. The only *Providence* in Lieutenant Emmons's list of 517 privateers of 1812–1814 was an 8-gun schooner of 94 tons, captured September 11, 1812, by the three-masted schooner *Dominica,* 14. If this picture represents the same *Providence,* some of the guns may have been dummies.

"The American schooner bore down on the Pylades Sloop of War, mistaking her, but on receiving a Shot made sail & escaped hoisting a white flag at her fore 'Catch me who Can'—G. H." These words are written below a water color probably painted by an officer of the *Pylades*. It seems likely that this was the Baltimore privateer *Catch Me if You Can* that soon was caught off Cape Sable by H.M.S. *Colibri* on July 26, 1812. A first rush of American privateers got to sea with inadequate equipment, to try to capture unwarned British ships: one of the advantages of being the declarer of war, as the Barbary pirates had well known. But the improvised privateers, with too many men and too much metal crowded into small vessels, were soon picked up. Bad weather was their chief danger, when a man of war in pursuit could stand up to a press of sail. The losses were worth while, from a national standpoint, as more British ships were sent in than the combined losses of American privateers and merchantmen. During the war a heavier type of privateer, designed for the job, was perfected. Baltimore was blockaded, but her shipbuilders moved to the open ports. The success of large privateers on the fast Baltimore-clipper model was so striking that the Secretary of the Navy asked Congress for twenty such vessels, but the war was over before they could be provided.

The *Shannon* and the *Chesapeake*

1. "H.M.S. Shannon, commencing the Battle with the American Frigate Chesapeake, on the 1st June 1813."
2. "the American Frigate Chesapeake, Crippled and thrown into utter disorder by the first two broadsides fired."
3. "H.M.S. Shannon, carrying by Boarding the American Frigate Chesapeake, after a Cannonade of Five Minutes."
4. "H.M.S. Shannon leading her Prize the American Frigate Chesapeake, into Halifax Harbour, on the 6th June, 1813."

Seventeen years after the *Shannon,* 38, Broke, took the *Chesapeake,* 36, Lawrence, this first British frigate victory of the War of 1812 still seemed sufficiently noteworthy to justify the publication of four large sequential lithographs, each dedicated "To Captain Sir Philip Bowes Vere Broke, Bar^t and K.C.B. . . . by his obliged and most grateful Servant, R. H. King." Their manner of production has a number of aspects interesting to the print viewer. John Christian Schetky, who painted the scenes, was Marine Painter to His Majesty, and had a reputation for "unsurpassed" precision in nautical detail. Louis Haghe, who rendered them on stone, was a young man at the outset of a career as one of the foremost lithographers of the century. An accompanying cover claims that the paintings were executed "under the inspection of Captain R. H. King, R.N." King had begun his naval career under Broke in the *Druid,* 32, in 1805, and had stayed with him in the *Shannon* throughout the frustrating years from 1806 to 1813 when no worthy opponent ever turned up. On March 8, 1813, he was transferred into the *Sylph* as acting lieutenant in an apparent emergency on the Halifax station, but rejoined the *Shannon* on July 12th. It was in this short interval that she fought her famous action, and the faithful Lieutenant King missed it, a fact which may help to explain his desire to commission these handsome prints. The English were tardy in turning to the lithographic process. Few early works on stone were done as skillfully as these.

In the mystical long run of naval morale, the phrase "Don't Give Up the Ship" probably has been worth more to the United States Navy than the frigate *Chesapeake* whose loss it failed to prevent. There is some question as to the precise words spoken by the mortally wounded Lawrence as he was carried below; but these express, with a terser eloquence, and a more effective rhythm, the same sense as "Don't surrender the ship," which one of his officers thought he heard. Less notice has been given to Lawrence's last words on the action: "—then the officers of the deck haven't toed the mark—the *Shannon* was whip'd when I left." This engraving, by William Strickland, heads the membership certificate of the Lawrence Benevolent Institution of Pennsylvania, issued a year after the captain's death.

To say this is not to underrate the free seamen and their officers, who were extraordinary. Long public humiliations endured by their country unquestionably fired them to establish her dignity when the dual issue of freedom, for ships and for sailors, was confronted at long last. The frigate captains had been men of an almost heartbreaking patience, who flared suddenly into their own hurtful kind of greatness, the kind that uses a lifetime of scrupulous preparation to direct with the utmost skill a few minutes of splintering cannonade.

Isaac Hull had begun the great series of single-ship actions under a familial comparison that did not bode well for the land forces. His tergiversating uncle, General William Hull, on August 16, 1812, had surrendered an American army on the Canadian frontier without a fight. Three days later, nephew Isaac snapped the long chain of British naval triumphs by taking the *Guerrière*.

William Bainbridge, who had endured mortifying calamities at Guadeloupe, Algiers, and Tripoli, ran down his own bizarre opportunity at last in the South Atlantic, where in the *Constitution* he so battered the *Java* on December 29, 1812, that she had to be sunk. It is significant that the finest prints of this defeat for Britain were published in England on January 1, 1814, while the war was still in progress. The set of four (pages 154 and 155) was drawn and etched by Nicholas Pocock. In the judgment of A. G. H. Macpherson, who assembled the finest collection of nautical pictures in the world (now in the National Maritime Museum, Greenwich, England), "Pocock stands by himself in the quality and accuracy of his work." Each of the four was derived from "a sketch by Lieut. Buchanan," of the *Java,* who had got home on parole in time to advise the artist. Pocock's unusually precise renderings of the *Constitution* (note the billet head) suggest that Buchanan must have drawn her with care during the five days when she lay at San Salvador, mending her wounds, before sailing for home. The schooling of young sea officers of the period included draftsmanship. Many were artistically competent, and most were technically scrupulous even in crudity of effect.

Land forces of the United States, throughout the war, were able to do little of consequence—and that little required naval support. The battles of the lakes, a year and a day apart, were the only notable fleet actions. Both were fought to control vital waterways needed to supply land forces on the two principal invasion routes from Canada. The Battle of Lake Erie nullified the advantage gained by the British from General Hull's easy capitulation and gave to American history one of its more stirring phrases: Commodore Oliver Hazard Perry's "We have met the enemy and they are ours." The Battle of Lake Champlain, fought on September 11, 1814, removed an invasion threat which could not have been

ABOVE. An undated but obviously hasty print of the second British victory in a row, that of the brig-sloop *Pelican* over the American raider brig *Argus,* off the coast of Wales, August 14, 1813. When the convoy system diminished captures in the open ocean, the *Argus* was sent to raid British coastal waters. In one month she captured nineteen vessels. The *Pelican,* sent out to find her, tracked her by the smoke of her last two burning victims. Captain Allen, whom Decatur had so warmly praised as a subordinate, probably could have avoided a fight, as the *Argus* was fast and weatherly, while the *Pelican* was a standard, workhorse brig. Allen waited for her to close, and was mortally wounded in the first exchange. The American gunnery this time was poor, the British was good. As usual the vessel of slightly superior weight of metal won. BELOW. A duel off the Maine coast, between the *Enterprize* and the *Boxer,* served to even the account after the loss of the *Argus.* Again the brig with slightly heavier metal won, but this time the American had the advantage. Both captains received their death wounds in the first exchange of fire. This wood engraving, from the *Naval Temple* of 1816, shows the *Enterprize* preceding her captive into Portland, where "the bodies of the two commanding officers, lieutenant Burrows and captain Blythe, were brought on shore in ten oared barges, rowed by masters of ships. . . . the interment took place with all the honours that the military and civil authorities at the place, and the great body of the people, could bestow." The game of war was still being played ceremoniously. A like punctilio had been observed when Allen was buried at Plymouth with eight captains of the Royal Navy as pallbearers. The famous *Enterprize,* at some time before 1811, had been rebuilt as a brig. Her original armament of twelve 12-pounders had given place to fourteen 18-pounder carronades and two long 9-pounders. Her sailing qualities suffered under the change.

renewed until after the winter season. News of Sir Edward Pakenham's defeat on Lake Champlain arrived in Europe in time to strengthen the faction of the great Wellington, who had developed a jowly cynicism toward the notion that the abdication of Napoleon I had finally settled the affairs of a distracted continent. No-one could have been wise enough to foresee the course of the "Hundred Days" of the following spring, that were to culminate at Waterloo, but Wellington was convinced that there would be more plausible uses for most of his Peninsula veterans on the plains of Europe than in the forests of America. The result was that happy rarity: a peace negotiation with counsels divided on both sides. Instead of the usual outcome of war—an imposed peace which wearies the victor and infuriates the vanquished toward a new violence—the result in the Christmas season of 1814 was a compromise that began a century and a half of unbroken peace between the combatants.

It is startling to realize how little the Americans had to bargain with. News of the burning of Washington had left them without military pretensions. Victories at sea, in the second year of the war, had all involved minor vessels: sloops and brigs. In the technical state of peace, with Napoleon tucked away on his island, scores of major fighting ships had become available for use against the now blockaded American frigates. Commander Thomas Macdonough's victory, on a lake in the woods, reopened British memories of Perry and of the eight American single-ship victories to set against British captures of two frigates, one by a fleet, and of two sloops, one by a 74. On October 21, 1814, the British Secretary for War wrote to the Secretary of State for Foreign Affairs, "Had it not been for this unfortunate adventure on Lake Champlain, I really believe we should have signed a peace by the end of this month." The proposal was made that Wellington be put in command to wind up the American business in style. To this the Iron Duke, never much hampered by modesty, responded that the Americans would be far too exhilarated by any such compliment to their power. He noted further that he should want naval command of the lakes before attempting a final campaign with his land forces. How were vessels to be built on the shores of waters already patrolled by large fleets? How launched, when ready?

Of course it could be done, by the creation of a major fortified base to protect a shipping basin. Lord Castlereagh looked at his already forbidding budget, and across the Channel at the troubled adjacent continent, and settled for a peace of accommodation. It is difficult ever to foresee the one action, out of several, which will prove decisive. Correspondence that passed between troubled statesmen three thousand miles away remains to show how the timing of Macdonough's victory made a reasonable peace possible. Again, in this climax, it was the indomitable individualism of a young sea officer that prevailed on an inland lake.

Macdonough, another of "Preble's boys" who had gone in with Decatur to burn the *Philadelphia*, had had to cajole the necessaries for his Lake Champlain fleet from a government much more worried about Captain Isaac Chauncey's Great Lakes. Treasonable Vermonters had obligingly tried to deliver masts for the British fleet; Macdonough had intercepted them. Treasonable New Yorkers had fed the British, who offered better prices; this aid and comfort to the enemy Macdonough had had to endure. Most of his land support was diverted to the Niagara frontier shortly before the battle. Perhaps the worried statesmen were so fully persuaded of an impending defeat that they wanted to surrender as little as possible.

Macdonough chose the position in which to be defeated with a masterly strategic acumen. He anchored his vessels with a system of cables and kedges laid out to rotate them even without wind for the best direction of their fire. In his dispatch, he attributed his

What's in a name? Oliver Hazard Perry's name was euphoniously suitable for the risk-taking hero he suddenly became to the American people. LEFT. Detail from a late, sentimentalized woodcut of Perry's victory, published in 1856.

The two major fleet actions of the War of 1812 were fought far from the ocean. Although smaller vessels were engaged than in the famous frigate duels, the effects upon morale were at least as notable, and the actual military gains of the two American victories on the lakes were much more decisive. In each case an army poised for invasion of the United States was made helpless by a naval action. Lieutenant Oliver Hazard Perry's victory on Lake Erie, on September 10, 1813, was the pivot of the war, opening the way for serious peace negotiations as an alternative to a ruinously extravagant rebuilding of British power in the interior of the continent. Macdonough's victory on Lake Champlain, a year later, persuaded the peacemakers that the time had come. The rare print above shows, in a somewhat collapsed perspective, the most famous moment in the battle when Perry transferred his flag as commodore from the *Lawrence* to the *Niagara*, which had loitered at long range while the original flagship was being shot to pieces by the two sizable British vessels, the *Detroit* and the *Queen Charlotte*. The British thought they had won and that Perry was escaping, but he returned promptly in the uninjured *Niagara* and began a raking fire which concluded the action. Perry's victory was his second, in a sense. His first had been the creation of a slightly superior force, on an inland lake, starting with almost nothing. He was twenty-eight when he directed this substantial shipbuilding enterprise, producing and arming the brigs *Lawrence* and *Niagara,* of 20 guns apiece, six schooners, and a sloop. A large proportion of the "seamen" were Kentucky riflemen.

Com.r Oliver H. Perry
of the U.S. Navy

165

Naval warfare sputtered on Lake Ontario, where the New York shipbuilder Henry Eckford quickly produced a number of fine vessels launched in the summer of 1813. The best of these, probably the most powerful naval vessel on any of the inland waters, was the *General Pike*, a flush-decked heavy corvette built in sixty-three days. She measured twice the tonnage of the famous *Hornet* and *Wasp* examples of the ship-sloop, but Commodore Isaac Chauncey employed her with a prudence bordering upon caution. This print is of the beginning of her only sharp contest, with the *Wolfe*, a ship-sloop about two-thirds her length, although one would not know it from the print. Chauncey damaged the *Wolfe* severely, but she was able to flee before the wind, and the American decided not to pursue her toward a lee shore held by the enemy. Peace put an end to a curious shipbuilders' war on Lake Ontario, in which technical advantage shifted with the splash of new launchings. At the end of it the Americans were building two huge ships of the line, to carry 130 guns apiece. They were never completed. This print was published in Connecticut, Chauncey's home state, thirty-three days after the action.

LEFT. An anonymous water color of the taking of the *Meteor* by boats from the *Endymion* frigate, which later was instrumental in the capture of the *President*. This action occurred off Nantucket, February 7, 1814. The *Meteor* was a letter-of-marque: primarily a merchantman but authorized to make prizes. Her commission rated her at three guns with 29 men. The script caption states that she had four guns and 40 men when taken.

Most of the surviving American frigates were bottled up before the war was over. The *Essex,* farthest ranging of all, was finally blockaded in Valparaiso by two British fighting ships that hardly could have had less appropriate names: the *Phoebe* and the *Cherub.* Before this occurrence she had ranged for seventeen months, from the Delaware to the Marquesas, and captured fifteen prizes. Strickland's engraving above, from a drawing by Captain David Porter, shows her in the process of being rerigged in a bay at Nukahiva, using materials from her prizes, all of which were finally recaptured by the enemy. Her own fate was decided principally by her armament, to which Porter had objected before his departure. Her main battery was of carronades, which threw 32-pound shot a short distance. The *Phoebe*'s main battery was of long 18-pounders. Porter was blown from his anchorage in a sudden gust and had to accept battle with the blockaders, which stayed at long range (as the *United States* had done, under similar conditions of armament, when she took the *Macedonian*). The result was a terrible punishing for the crew of the *Essex,* which early lost her main topmast, as shown in the woodcut below, and could not maneuver handily. More than half the American crew was killed or wounded. The British had fifteen casualties.

RIGHT. Perhaps the best of the promptly made woodcuts, this shows the action between the *Peacock* (a new American ship-sloop named after the British vessel sunk by the *Hornet*) and the *Epervier,* a standard British brig. Lieutenant Warrington got his prize safely into Savannah, with frigates in pursuit, and sailed again to take fourteen more prizes.

167

ABOVE. The "third" *Grand Turk,* privateer brig, engaging the Royal West India Mail packet *Hinchinbroke,* on May 1, 1814. Robert E. Peabody, in his *Log of the Grand Turks,* numbered four of the vessels so named, with textual references which indicate his belief that there had been no others. There actually were at least two between his "second" and "third," and at least four more between his "third" and "fourth," a circumstance which makes this sort of numbering more of a confusion than a help. This print, published five years after the action, is dedicated by the artist, W. I. Pocock, to William James who commanded the *Hinchinbroke.* The inference is that James commissioned the print and would have taken some care to see to it that the technical details were accurate. The scene expresses well the somewhat different reports of the action written by the two commanders. The *Grand Turk's* log reported that the enemy "was very much cut up in his hull . . . whereas we had no shot in our hull except a few grape, the enemy directing his fire at our spars and rigging"—a logical tactic of the slower vessel to disable the swifter one. Although the *Grand Turk* was more heavily armed and manned, the action, fought in the Atlantic on the Tropic of Cancer, was indecisive. This Maine-built *Grand Turk* made five privateering voyages during the war and took more than thirty prizes. RIGHT. The name of William Strickland has been recurrent in these captions. It was probably in the summer of 1814 that he drew and engraved this cumulative celebration of nine American naval victories. News of the latest of them, the *Peacock's* taking of the *Epervier* on April 29th, would not have reached him in Philadelphia until about a month later. Since the *Wasp-Reindeer* action of June 28th is not included, and particularly because there is no notice of Macdonough's decisive action of September 11th on Lake Champlain, an approximate time of publication can be assumed. There had been at least two earlier, somewhat smaller pictorial summations. Both were "school sheets," with a central space for a composition. But as the number of victories mounted, Strickland was moved to fill the entire sheet with pictures. Some of these scenes bear a close resemblance to separate prints, but Strickland seems not to have been content merely to copy them. The print cost $3.

SPRIGS OF LAUREL.

PERRY'S VICTORY.

CONSTITUTION & GUERRIERE

WASP AND FROLIC

UNITED STATES & MACEDONIAN

CONSTITUTION AND JAVA

HORNET BLOCKADING BONNE CITOYENNE

SINKING OF THE PEACOCK

ENTERPRISE AND BOXER

PEACOCK & L'EPERVIER

Drawn & Engraved by W. Strickland.

BATTLE OF LAKE CHAMPLAIN.

Cooper, selecting a model for illustrating the Battle of Lake Champlain in his reissued naval history, approved the large and handsome print which had been engraved by Benjamin Tanner from Hugh Reinagle's contemporaneous painting. Tanner had published his print on July 4, 1816. This smaller and somewhat simplified drawing reduces the number of visible British gunboats in the offing, and removes a few foreground figures—one of them a disinterested dog. Otherwise it closely follows its model.

This idealized portrait justifiably reminds us of the youth of most officers who in the War of 1812 were not only adept and courageous leaders in battle but often, as in the case of Thomas Macdonough, were possessed of extraordinary powers as executives. Macdonough was not yet thirty when he set about the creation, from almost nothing, of an inland fleet with which he fought the decisive victory of the war. The "American character" reached its able and confident zenith in such young men.

Heroe of Lake Champlain

Commodore McDonnough

victory to the Almighty. There have not been many occasions when the Almighty has been so ably represented by a thirty-one-year-old sailor on the spot.

Here was the ultimate affirmation of a quality of accomplishment which brought the United States abruptly into the world of major nations, despite Congress and its policies. Yet such individual action was made possible in the first place by the early American concept of a government which left the free individual largely to his own devices.

Rodgers and Hull had both got to sea, in the early days after the declaration of war, in a desperate effort to outrun their expected orders. They knew that the administration had decided to keep its precious few frigates safely in port, to use as floating batteries. Bainbridge and Stewart, by an impassioned plea, had caused a reconsideration of that calamitous policy. The free-ranging frigate captains did not wait to see what would replace it. Hull got his offing just in time to set the pattern for the war with his escape from Broke's squadron and his re-encounter with the *Guerrière*. It would have been a fantastic way to operate a career navy in the long run; but it took such acts of vigorous, confident individualism, performed under personal discipline of the strictest sort, to hoist the young country into a free and independent future out of a first quarter century of humiliation and disgrace.

The men who did it were the young past masters of American sail.

Captain Nicholas Lockyer, R.N., attacking the gunboats on Lake Borgne, December 14, 1814. Peace had been signed, and was soon to be ratified; but no one knew it in Louisiana. The Battle of New Orleans kicked one more prop out from under the notion that it was profitable for Great Britain to conduct military and naval operations at a great distance against enemies of a similar heritage. The same sort of amphibious operation that had succeeded, to no great purpose, in the Chesapeake and Potomac this time was a disaster. A minor naval delaying action on Lake Borgne, a local defeat, was the key to the American triumph. One cannot be sure how rapidly Lockyer would have moved troops up through the backwaters if Lieutenant-Commanding Thomas ap Catesby Jones had not drawn across his path a line of five of the despised "Jeffersonian" gunboats. But in the few days while an assault adequate to eliminate them was being prepared, Jackson was strongly reinforced and the guns of the U.S.S. *Louisiana* were got ashore to form an enfilading battery that put the British field pieces out of action. The print, from a drawing by Lieutenant T. M. Williams, a British participant, shows 24 of the 45 British boats that contained six times as many men, and almost twice the number of guns, as were in the Americans. Nothing was in doubt but the amount of time the operation would require—and it took a little too long. Lieutenant Jones's flagship, No. 156, is identifiable in the center by her broad pendant. She and two of the others were built on Barron's plan by James Marsh and Francis Saltus in South Carolina. One of the gunboats was No. 5, built at Baltimore by William Price on Fox's design. She had been sailed to the Mediterranean and back in the latter days of the war with Tripoli. The fifth gunboat, No. 23, was also on Fox's model but may have been built in West Virginia. Lockyer, following tradition, made for Jones's flagship, and both commanders were severely wounded. The losses were similar, in an hour of fierce fighting: about a hundred casualties on each side. No. 5 and No. 23 surrendered only after the guns of the other captured boats were turned against them.

The ultimate development of the American clipper-privateer. An oil done at the war's end, in 1815, by C. Burton.

Peace had been signed, but was not yet ratified, when a spectacular naval action occurred, similar in nature to the long chase of the *Constitution* with which the serious war began. Blockaded in New York, Decatur tried to get the *President* to sea, but his pilot ran her aground. She was hogged by the mishap: her keel bent upward amidships. Aided by a snowstorm, Decatur eluded the British squadron, but encountered it at dawn of January 15, 1815, south of Long Island. After an all-day chase in which the hogging seriously slowed her, the *President* began to be hit by the *Endymion,* 40, which repeatedly luffed up to rake from astern. The tactic was to force Decatur to wear, to bring his broadside to bear upon his nearest pursuer, thus allowing the others to cut a corner and creep up. As darkness deepened, Decatur could endure the heavy casualties no longer without replying. He stood southward for the broadside-to-broadside action shown in these prints, using dismantling shot to strip the enemy of his sails. In this he was successful, but as the *Endymion* dropped out of the fight the light frigates *Pomone* and *Tenedos* gained. One or both of these fresh ships caught his battered one at midnight, and Decatur surrendered after receiving three more broadsides. Mahan believed the *President* could have knocked the *Pomone* out before the *Tenedos* closed. British writers contended that the battle had already been won by the *Endymion,* which had merely dropped astern to rerig. It seems clear that Decatur could have turned to demolish the smaller *Endymion* early in the action if there had been no other pursuers. Because of flat contradictions in the contemporary testimony, continued recriminations will never settle the controversy. British printmakers regarded it as the *Endymion*'s victory. The crude print at the right was published only forty days after the action: at least half of that time would have been needed to bring the news across the Atlantic. The aquatint above, "Drawn by an Officer of H.M.R.N.," is one of the most graceful representations of single-ship actions. It is in error in suggesting that the close action occurred before dark. The publication date was May 1, 1815. John Hill was the engraver.

BRITISH VALOUR

CAPTURE OF THE UNITED STATES FRIGATE PRESIDENT COMMODORE DECATUR BY THE ENDYMION FRIGATE CAPTAIN HOPE
after an anxious chase of eighteen hours and a desperate fight of Two hours and a half, Jan.r 15, 1815.

American Force
60 Guns 490 Men

British Force
46 Guns 340 Men

HATRED OF SIN.

Holy Lord God! Shew thy truth,
Nor dare thy least commandment slight
Yet pierc'd by sin, the serpent's tooth,
I mourn the anguish & the bite.

But though the poison lurks within,
Hope bids me still with patience wait,
Till death shall set me free from sin,
Free from the only thing I hate.

Had I a throne above the rest,
Where angels and archangels dwell;
One sin unslain, within my breast,
Would make that heaven as dark as hell.

The prisoner, sent to breathe fresh air,
And bless'd with liberty again,
Would mourn were he condemn'd to wear,
One link of all his former chain.

But ah! no foe invades the bliss,
When glory crowns the Christian's head,
One view of Jesus as he is,
Will strike all sin for ever dead.

Josiah John Shaw,
June 26th, 1815.

The Gallant Captain Hope
giving orders to his Crew.

Crippled state of the Enemys
ship at the close of the Action.

Commodore Decatur ordering the
Anchors to be thrown Overboard

Commodore Decatur giving up
his sword to Captain Hope.

Published by J. FAIRBURN, Jun.r Fountain Court, Minories, sold also by Champante & Whitrow Jewry Street.

The above school sheet expresses the standard British interpretation of the capture of the *President,* 44. Three other ships of the pursuing squadron are shown at the right, but there is no hint in the captions of their participation. By all accounts the actual capture, which Captain Hope in the *Endymion* made possible, occurred only after his ship had dropped out of the action, and after further fighting. Hope handled his smaller frigate brilliantly. This school sheet may be compared with the American one on the dedication page. The calligraphic exercise in the middle has no direct connection with the action.

"Old Ironsides" also had a post-peace encounter. On February 20, 1815, she was courageously attacked by two small British ships of war, the *Cyane* and the *Levant*, which together could throw about the same total weight of shot as she could. But again it was carronades in the smaller vessels against long guns. Captain Charles Stewart, in the *Constitution*, fought at his own best range. By swift backing and filling he overcame the tactical advantage which could have allowed one enemy to rake him while he directed his own fire against the other. This contemporaneous woodcut shows him taking his two prizes into a port of the Cape Verde Islands, whence he escaped with one of them just in time to elude two British 50-gun ships and a 40-gun frigate. The historian James's comments reflect one aspect of the temper of the times: "While on the way to these islands, Captain Stewart had caused the *Cyane* to be painted so as to resemble a 36-gun frigate. The object of this was to aggrandize his exploit, in the wondering eyes of the gaping citizens of Boston: not one of a hundred of whom, he knew, would trouble themselves to inquire any further on the subject." Stewart more probably hoped to make an enemy more reluctant to attack him, since he did not have the men to handle the *Cyane*'s guns: that at least is what resulted. The log of one of the pursuing ships, the *Leander*, notes "apparently frigates."

LEFT. Another encounter, after peace treaty was ratified, occu in the Indian Ocean, when Ca James Biddle in the little *Ho* by jettisoning all his armament anchors, escaped from the *C wallis*, 74, in a long chase.

176

POSTSCRIPT: 1815

EELS SCARFED IN 1795—SIX OF THEM—WERE ALMOST ALL WE HAD to carry the newly evident American character, twenty years later, past the hazards of a small war that came close to ending the very identity of the United States. Backward-looking romantics have obscured the inept beginnings of American nationality, the festering internal contentions that had to drain before our external expediencies could be corrected in this conflict. Charles Cotesworth Pinckney, who knew enough about the Barbary treaties never to have said, "Millions for defense, but not one cent for tribute," was made to say it after he was dead, on his own monument. What he really said had been published promptly in an official document, but improvers of the truth have preferred the phrase of a congressional toastmaster. Throughout the first three Presidencies, and part of the fourth, we endured plunder and insult by our supposed friends. We paid tribute.

A patriotic urge to evade sorry truths, such as the giving of four fine naval vessels as bribes to piratical scoundrels, is understandable; but it deprives later men of a lesson in history helpful in the solution of recurrent problems. The Barbary coast of the late eighteenth century is not the only place and time that have confronted America with an utterly alien ideology, contemptuous of Western notions of civilized behavior, and spoiling for a fight. Politicians who have had only filtered glimpses of prior occasions are likely to fumble the problem all over again when it turns up with a look of newness among history's refurbished surprise packages.

Historical candor is needed also if we are to do simple justice to a small group of phenomenal individuals. The war of 1812 was, in its successful phases, an enterprise of disciplined young seafarers who had the wit or the luck to get out of reach of the shoreside statesmen. But if the ineptitudes of our first two or three American decades are blamable upon the representative system, centering in Congress, it must be reaffirmed that no other system could have forced statesmanship upon the sailors. The rougher criticisms of our young captains, made by as thoughtful a historian as Mahan, reinforce this thesis. His simmering rebuke to Decatur, for having surrendered the wounded *President* before she was knocked into splinters, is an instance. With two fresh frigates on his flanks, and a 74 coming up, Decatur could not possibly have won. The British were not so stupid as to sink a useful ship that was within their grasp. Slaughter of still more of the *President*'s people by deck-level, raking broadsides, and by an eventual boarding in superior force, was the only prospect. Decatur, who had lived as a popular hero since his burning of the *Philadelphia,* made the unlikely decision: the choice of a mature man. His country had matured also: it approved.

Fenimore Cooper implies that the process of naval statesmanship, which operated negatively through the luckless Bainbridge at Guadeloupe and Algiers, had become positive by 1805. "The temporary control of events had been taken out of the hands of timid politicians at a distance, and had passed into those of men on the spot. . . . The navy, the ablest of all negotiators in such matters, had completely reversed the ancient order of things, for, instead of an American agent's being compelled to solicit the restoration of prizes, illegally taken, in Africa, an African agent was now soliciting the restoration of prizes legally captured, in America."

Cooper, writing shortly before the death of Commodore John Rodgers, was referring to Rodgers's firm, swift settlement with Tunis that in 1805 squashed yet another threatened Barbary war before it could get under way. I believe Cooper was inaccurate, however, in giving credit to the Navy as an organization. It was not until many years later that the sort of naval negotiations became possible which proceed from the deeply inculcated traditions of an armed service, transcending personal judgment.

The American public character seldom has expressed itself in the conduct of public servants who have been told exactly what to do. Representative government, proclaiming liberty while evading central responsibility, has tended to force individual statesmanship to emerge, approving its accomplishments, and—most unfairly—making scapegoats of the individuals who have failed.

An English officer in Revolutionary Boston set up the burlesque character of Yankee Doodle to identify the adversary and laugh him back to the farm. The straw man misfired. By 1815 Britain and the world knew quite clearly what an American really was. Even the "British Valour" school sheet, reproduced on page 175, glorifies Captain Hope in the act of receiving the sword of a gallant, distressed antagonist. Where else would gallantry lie, for the British victor? Not in the deflating of a clown like Yankee Doodle. A newly dignified American character emerged in the defeats as well as in the victories. In the trial and error that had refined this character, Sterett had offset his fine contribution with impulsive brutality. Bainbridge had firmed up the thews of restraint under extraordinary trial. Although there was as yet no service tradition in 1815 to guide Decatur in his own use of restraint, example had been provided by a few individuals.

The year 1815 was the swivel upon which the American future turned. Behind the great young captains were the able and imaginative shipbuilders—farsighted men who, with remarkably few examples of their skill in naval architecture, forced revision upon vast navies of the old world. If the print-celebrated single-ship victories had had no other effect, they still would have spread an advertisement for Yankee shipyards among all maritime

The taking of the *Mashouda* by Decatur's squadron, June 17, 1815, about twenty miles off the southeastern promontory of Spain. Rais Hammida, perhaps the most eminent of the latter-day Algerine naval commanders, handled his 46-gun frigate bravely. Although wounded early in the action, he kept to his quarter-deck, directing the action, until he was chopped in two by a cannon ball. The picture, apparently the work of an Arab, brings nine of Decatur's ten vessels into close range during the fight. Six of the American vessels actually were at too great distance to participate. The picture has puzzling aspects. It seems to distinguish knowledgeably between the squadron's three frigates—off the bows and to starboard of the *Mashouda*—and the brigs and schooners of the fleet. Progressive action may have been intended, the same vessels shown more than once at different points. The frigate at the left must be the *Guerrière*, 44, as she is flying the commodore's broad pennant. The little sloop-of-war *Epervier*, which nipped in to circle the crippled Algerine and give her nine close broadsides, is shown on her larboard quarter, but has the rig of a topsail schooner rather than that of a brig, which she is said to have carried at the time. Compare the pictures of her on pages 167 and 169.

nations. The enterprising shipwrights who loosed hundreds of sizable schooner-privateers upon the oceans probably had a more immediately revolutionary effect upon the commercial fleets of Europe.

The spring of 1815 witnessed a sort of final grace note, putting an end to a long disgrace. Thirty years after the first enslavement of American seamen on the Barbary coast, twenty years after negotiation of the first tributary treaty, ten years after the inconclusive Tripolitan War and the conclusive Tunisian peace, Thomas Jefferson at last saw his Barbary policy put firmly into action. He was seventy-two when the successor whom he had converted from Federalism decided to act while the country's naval prestige was at its height.

Jefferson had written to Barclay, in 1791, "We prefer war in all cases to tribute under any form, and to any people whatever." He should have said, "*I* prefer," because tributary treaties were still in technical effect when President Madison, six days after the ratification of peace with Britain, asked Congress for a declaration of war on Algiers. Congress obliged on March 2nd, unaware that one day earlier something had happened in Europe to confirm the wisdom of Wellington in keeping himself and his Peninsula veterans out of the back woods of America. Buonaparte had landed from Elba. The famous Hundred Days, terminating at Waterloo, were about to begin. If the peace negotiations at Ghent had been in-

N. Jocelin and G. Munger engraved this print and published it in New Haven seven months after Decatur's call at Algiers on June 30, 1815. The city is portrayed with an unusual accuracy, suggesting the use of a sketch brought home in one of the ships which arrived at New York on November 12, 1815. But the American artists were less accurate than the Arab of the last drawing in particularizing the squadron, here comprising nine ship-rigged vessels and one brig. The actual force was made up of three ships, one ship-rigged sloop, four brigs, two schooners.

conclusive, strong British forces would probably have been diverted during that winter toward a still active American enemy. What then would have happened at Waterloo, or at an equivalent decisive European action? The question merely emphasizes the balancing importance of the "little" American war: the reason why, within that little war, the independent action of a few young men had a tremendous final effect upon history. Their achievements made a peace possible which freed Britain for a full concentration upon the Napoleonic tyranny, and freed America to deal with the strip of tyrannical Turkish regencies along the Barbary coast.

At the conclusion of the War of 1812 the American Navy showed a substantial net gain despite losses. The first of the 74s was afloat; there were more frigates available than at the beginning. Well-found smaller fighting vessels were added to make up two fleets, of ten under Decatur and nine under Bainbridge. Decatur got away first, on May 20th. Soon after entering the Mediterranean he took the *Mashouda* frigate, 46, after an unequal action marked by the spirited infighting of the sloop-of-war *Epervier,* 18, commanded by John Downes, another former midshipman of the Tripolitan War. Downes, in command of the *Essex Junior* off Valparaiso, and forbidden by Porter to engage in the action when the *Essex* was captured, evidently was getting in his licks to compensate.

Decatur proceeded to Algiers where he concluded a new treaty without further fighting. "It has been dictated at the mouths of our cannon," he informed Secretary of the Navy Crowninshield, "And I beg leave to express to you my opinion that the presence of a respectable naval force in this sea will be the only certain guarantee for its observance."

Thence he proceeded to Tunis, to exact from the startled Bey a payment of $46,000 for two vessels, sent into Tunis by an American privateer, which the Bey had allowed the British to recapture in neutral waters. At Tripoli he collected $25,000 on a similar claim and forced the freeing of ten slaves—two Danes and eight Sicilians—in gratitude for help given the United States at that port by nationals of these countries ten or twelve years earlier.

Such hard bargains might have caused explosive consequences soon after the squadron had passed from view. A few weeks later Bainbridge's even stronger squadron, following the same route with a 74 as flagship, confirmed for the regents of Barbary the news that they could no longer employ their traditional methods against one suddenly self-confident maritime power. The example was felt elsewhere. Brenton's *Naval History of Great Britain* remarks, "It was not to be endured that England should tolerate what America had resented and punished." Lord Exmouth was sent to ransom twelve hundred slaves in Algiers, from countries under alliance with England. The British public clamored for something more decisive, and Exmouth returned a few months later to deliver the terrific bombardment that was the last major action against Barbary before its occupation by forces from Europe.

Modest United States fleets in the Mediterranean held the Barbary regencies to a minor level of chicanery until they ceased to have much military significance. It was in these years, the beginning of a third of a century of peace, that a bureaucratic department settled into the routines of a career navy. The world-startling American contribution to the practice of sail had been made in naval craft and privateers for the most part. Thereafter the imagination of naval constructors received little encouragement. Two ships of the line, the larger variously described as a first rate of 120 or 130 guns, were left in frame on the stocks at Sackett's Harbor. A purchaser for the timbers of one of them was found seventy years after her construction began. The little Navy that had led the world at its beginnings became imitative. Two frigates laid down in 1820 and 1822 were not lauched until 1855, when they were obsolete. One of the 74s laid down in 1818 was not completed until 1845; another remained on the stocks for forty-six years before being launched as a store ship; a third, after fifty-six years of intermittent construction, was broken up on the stocks. It should be noted, however, that some of the 74s produced in and soon after the War of 1812 had remarkable careers apart from combat. The *Independence*, the first American-built 74 in our own Navy, was not sold out of the service until 1914. The *Vermont*, although not launched until

LEFT. The sailmaker.
RIGHT. The *Vermont*, 74. Keel laid, 1818. Launched, 1845. Sold, 1902. From a woodcut published in 1855.

1845, continued in service until 1902. The *Ohio,* built by Henry Eckford, had been in commission for sixty-three years when she was sold in 1883 for commercial use.

Eckford had been one of the most notable constructors of naval vessels for the War of 1812. His following career is an instructive example of the repute gained by American builders as a consequence. He resigned as Naval Constructor in 1820, shortly after completing the *Ohio,* and was soon launching ships of war for foreign countries. A frigate built for the Sultan of Turkey in 1831 brought about Eckford's appointment as chief constructor for the Turkish Navy, but he died in Constantinople in 1832.

The individual enterprise which had developed such remarkable fighting ships, public and private, was turned promptly after the War of 1812 with an equal confidence to the world of trade. Jefferson's old request for a regularly scheduled packet service was one of the first objectives. The whaling fleet, ruinously diminished by captures, was increased by 150 per cent in the first five postwar years. The sporadic sealing industry attained a sudden importance, and other specializing endeavors followed. Ingenuity which for so long a time had centered upon the task of making ships swift and handy in combat began to develop varieties that forced a revision of commercial concepts in the post-Napoleonic world. This was only one influence in a cluster of altering economic conditions; but it may have been the most decisive of the external pressures that turned the theories of the Physiocrats and of Adam Smith into realities of British law. While it is true that the War of 1812 settled none of its major issues on paper, the first half of the slogan, "Free Trade and Sailors' Rights," was called to world attention by it and became the dominant world policy before the middle of the nineteenth century.

Not all the retrospective views of the War of 1812 stressed its glamour. This wordless comment was drawn and engraved on wood by T. H. Mumford for a biographical history published in 1844.

In the decade between the close of the War of 1812 and the opening of the Erie Canal in 1825, New York became decisively the foremost port of the United States. The canal, and a generation later the railroads, only emphasized the prior natural advantages of its position: midway on the more populous part of the coast, with a spacious harbor nearer the sea than those on the bays of the Delaware and Chesapeake, yet better protected from weather and from enemies than any of the New England ports. What was most important, it stood at the gateway of the easiest route through the Appalachians to the plains of the West. In the above aquatint (one of a series of twenty painted by W. G. Wall and engraved by John Hill, offered as *The Hudson River Port-Folio*) the martial mood still is dominant in 1820. But the view below, offered independently at about the same time by the same artists, is full of the new mood of peaceful confidence. The upper view is from Governors Island, past Castle William. The lower is from Brooklyn Heights. The area of sky has been reduced in both reproductions.

WAR into PEACE

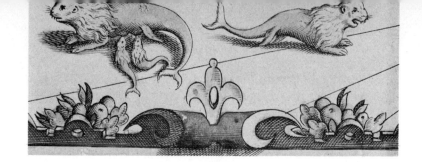

"The Skinning Business"

SEALING, MARKED BY THE DRAMA AND VIOLENCE THAT GO WITH EXCESSIVE COMPETITION beyond reach of established law, exemplifies many ventures to which American seamen turned in their search for new trades after the War of 1812. It was not new in itself, any more than the whaling industry was new when the Nantucketers so largely pre-empted it; but unlike whaling, it was marked by the ancient human dispute over real estate. Sealing in the Americas is at least as old as the first voyage of Thomas Cavendish, an episode from which was used by De Bry for the 1595 engraving reproduced below. Violent conflict, as here between the English and the Indians, marked it from the outset. The sealer's club, five or six feet long, seems not to have altered much in the more than three centuries separating this picture from the one on the next page. De Bry's charming if bizarre seals evidently inspired an engraver who did the index-page decorations (*above*) for the great Mercator-Hondius *Atlas* a quarter of a century later. Note the similarities between the nursing seals in both pictures. The fact that the later one is reversed is an indication of copying, directly upon the plate.

A sealers' encampment—one of the early examples of lithographic illustration in American books. Another from the same work, Edmund Fanning's *Voyages and Discoveries in the South Seas,* 1833, appears on page 10. An error by Fanning, writing from recollection about ten years later, is partly responsible for the dispute over Palmer's "discovery" of Antarctica. Fanning put in the wrong sequence two Stonington voyages of 1820–1821 and 1821–1822.

A newly found seal rookery was worth a substantial fortune to the shipmaster who could exploit it secretly. For this reason the early records of "the skinning business," as nineteenth century Americans often called it, are scanty. Substantial records of New England sealing operations date from about 1820, but there are published inferences that the trade had flourished in secret from the beginning of the century. A persistent controversy over the discovery of Antarctica has evolved from the terseness of the sealers' accounts. Reputable American scholars argued for many years that the famous clipper-ship captain Nathaniel Brown Palmer had sighted the continent in 1821 when he was twenty-two years old. An encounter with the Russian Admiral Bellingshausen, shortly after the event, supposedly proved it. I should take this occasion for cautioning readers of my own book *Clipper Ship Men,* published in 1944, that the account in it needs revision in the light of later researches which have been ably evaluated in *The Voyage of the* Huron *and the* Huntress, by Edouard A. Stackpole, 1955. The claims made for Palmer always were inferential. Evidence turned up in the last few years, although it does not flatly disprove them, does make them seem dubious. The well-documented log entry of Captain John Davis, for February 7, 1821, in which he wrote, "I think this Southern Land to be a Continent," should take precedence. Davis also was a New England sealer, about whom little is known.

An 1846 wood engraving of a variation in approach to the unchanging work with the long sealer's club.

Evolving technical confidence in the medium of wood engraving, in the nineteenth century, is reflected in these pictures of the hunters and the hunted. The two in the upper corners are details from a large natural-history plate in *Ballou's Pictorial and Drawing Room Companion*, February 10, 1855. The scene of a boat attacked by walruses appeared in the same journal, May 30, 1857. The walruses attacked by a boat appeared in *Harper's Weekly*, October 23, 1875. The seal-hunting picture is also from *Harper's* for April 16, 1881.

Most accounts of "the skinning business" substantiate Stackpole's summary: "Despite their brutal trade, which made them realists in the fullest sense, the captains, officers, and men were not all reckless, cynical and dissolute. True, they lived a hard life of necessity, but their fragmentary records reveal them as resourceful mariners, fully aware of their danger but willing to risk their lives in their hazardous calling."

What was it that sent the sealers, in their modest craft, down from New England and New York to probe the fracturing edge of the Antarctic ice? Why were they willing to live in comfortless fo'c's'les or to camp on ironbound, icy beaches while waiting for the occasional frantic clubbing of inoffensive animals to death? Money was a part of it, but an even sadder insight into the complex nature of man is needed to explain the lure of such a ruthless enterprise for the foremasthand. A merely economic explanation appears in the fact that the sea otter, valued in China, had been almost exterminated on the more temperate coasts of the Pacific Northwest. There were few articles of trade which the obstinately self-sufficient Chinese wanted. They were willing to accept sealskins when otter pelts were no longer available. Outward cargo was necessary to make a circumnavigation profitable; seals supplied it.

The British discovery of the South Shetlands in 1819 leaked out despite efforts to monopolize the rookeries. Two years later there were more American vessels than British off the islands. Competition became so fearsome that both sides mobilized for a midget war

—fortunately averted. But the circumstance typifies the obstinate push of the Yankee seafarers to the ends of the earth, developing some trades by themselves, insisting upon a share in others.

Wisdom in matters of conservation came too late. Unregulated private enterprise slaughtered the seals so vigorously that the rich venture dwindled to an intermittent and much less profitable one. It was varied by the pursuit of walruses: animals of a wider commercial application, valued for their oil, ivory, and heavy leather for shoe soles and harnesses. The techniques of sealing continued almost unchanged into the twentieth century, but the walrus hunters promptly adopted the whaler's harpoon gun.

INSTRUCTION and CALAMITY

The crudity of most early American wood engravings reflects the effort of unskilled artists to use a readily available material which actually presents more difficult problems than copper does. Then as now, the public was less interested in useful knowledge than in calamity. Perils of seafaring, the risks of the wild shores, appear to have been the subjects in dominant request throughout the first half of the nineteenth century. The earnest wit of the pedagogue appears in the page (upper right) from a schoolbook of 1831. The essential, if squeezed-up, truth of its hand-tinted woodcut of Table Mountain may be noted by comparison with W. I. Pocock's undated water color above. Pocock also did the *Hinchinbroke* vs. *Grand Turk* plate on page 168. Turn the page left side upward for a glance at the rock-sculptured African queen.

A

NARRATIVE

OF THE

SHIPWRECK

AND

UNPARALLELED SUFFERINGS

OF MRS.

SARAH ALLEN,

(LATE OF BOSTON)

ON HER PASSAGE IN MAY LAST FROM NEW-YORK TO NEW ORLEANS.

Being the substance of a letter from the unfortunate Mrs. ALLEN to her Sister in Boston.

THE SECOND EDITION.

BOSTON—Printed by HENRY TRUMBULL.
1817.

WRECK AND SUFFERINGS OF SARAH ALLEN LATE OF BOSTON.

This primitive folding frontispiece of 1817 shows the manner in which woodblocks sometimes were prepared in sections, in this case four. Mrs. Allen's treatment by American "savages" was by her own testimony gentle and humane, nothing like the automatic enslavement that awaited castaways in Africa.

Episodes in the African shipwrecks of Abel Sampson and James Riley on the coasts of Africa.

A PROMONTORY

Is a point of land stretching into the sea, and, if it be considerably elevated, the end of it is called a Cape; as the Cape of Good Hope, a view of which I shall do myself the pleasure of presenting, in the good hope of giving you a more clear idea of a Promontory and Cape than you have hitherto had.

The primitive in art often makes a comic effect far from its creator's intent. But there are instances, such as the one above, when simple dignity and a good sense of design triumph over technical limitations. This is the frontispiece from an account published in New York, in 1830, of the loss of the English brig *Neptune* north of Newfoundland. It was written by the American mate, John Smith. At the beginning of January of that year the sails and rigging of the *Neptune* became so thickly coated with ice that she drifted, unmanageable, for ten days and struck in a snowstorm. Smith, the captain's wife, and one of her two sons, each selected by lot, got ashore in an icy boat with a line attached. It was hauled back to the brig but capsized on a second attempt. The captain swam to shore, then plunged in again, trying to rescue his second son. Both were cast up drowned. The cook had brought "fire-works" in his pocket and made a fire. After thirteen days the castaways encountered an Eskimo hunter who, like the Indian rescuers of Mrs. Allen in Florida, demonstrated the gentle nobility of the unprovoked American "savage." Smith describes him as "of small statue [*sic*], inclined to corpulency, and of a tawny complexion—his face very broad, with a large mouth, and with black hair and eyes." He fed and cared for them in his skin lodge, gave the woman and child moccasins and deerskin blankets, and when they had sufficiently recovered from starvation and exposure conducted them to Belle Isle. BELOW. A less successful attempt to strike pity and terror. Castaways conquering an improbable sea elephant. Lithograph, 1847.

THE WILD SHORES

Survivors of the *Doll* at Cook's Bay being carried ashore by Marquesan natives. Visible above the boat's stern is a waterfall mentioned in the logs of whalers as one of the most convenient sources in the Pacific at which to refill their casks. Mendana, who "discovered" the place long after the great Polynesian voyages of discovery, named it Mother of God Bay. But the name of Cook, who visited the anchorage nearly two centuries after Mendana, appears on some charts. Resolution Bay celebrates his ship on others.

William Torrey is not the only American who has sat for a portrait so as to exhibit tattooing on the back of the hands, but his picture antedated a better-known one by more than a century. When the brig *Doll* was wrecked near Cook's Bay in the Marquesas in 1835, the survivors were kindly received by the cannibals. Most of them attempted a hazardous voyage to Tahiti in the brig's small boat. Torrey and two others remained. Soon he was made a warrior by the tattooing ceremony. His account of his life as a native, published two years after Melville's *Typee* had set the fashion for South Sea narratives, stands up well under anthropological inspection. Such accounts, stressing the hardships of a sailor's life afloat and on the wild shores, often seem deliberate warnings against the folly of going to sea, but they had the opposite effect. Wild hogs, in the islands, were both peril and sustenance. Hunting them "was found to be a dangerous service, and proved nearly fatal to some of the crew," according to George Little, a blind seaman from Baltimore, whose reminiscences of 1843 provide the picture at the lower left. Torrey's escape from a hog, after he had given up his sailor's garb, is shown at the lower right. Torrey reported the foremasthand's usual experience of captains: occasionally a kind one, but more that were brutal. In a misunderstanding with natives at the Mulgraves, one captain needlessly "fired, wounding one of them in the legs, who fell upon the ground, yelling loudly, and taking up sand rubbed it on the wound. This to the Captain was much sport, but it would not be sport to the next unsuspecting crew that might touch there . . ."

191

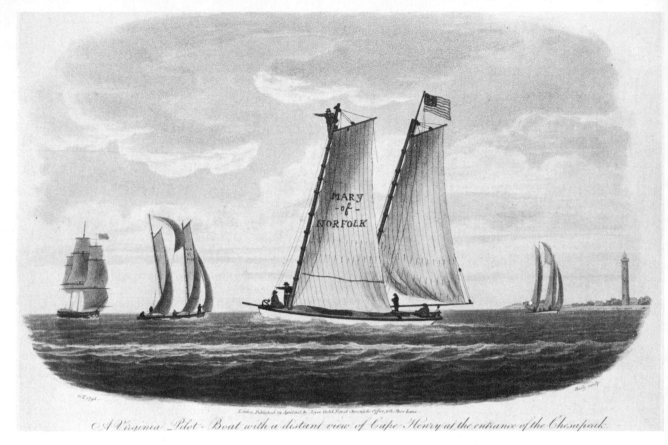

A Virginia Pilot-Boat with a distant view of Cape Henry at the entrance of the Chesapeak.

Interest abroad in the American schooner rig, at the close of the War of 1812, is indicated by publication in the English *Naval Chronicle* for 1815 of the above picture drawn twenty years earlier by George Tobin. Charles Vignoles, an English surveyor employed in Charleston, South Carolina, about 1820, drew the original view of that port from which the engraving below was made. Note that schooners outnumber any other class of vessel by five to two.

THE ORIGIN OF
The SCHOONER

THE EXTREME DURABILITY OF PLEASANT ERROR, AGAINST ABRASIONS OF MERE FACTUAL evidence and common sense, may be marveled at in most printed accounts of the schooner's origin. More than half a century has passed since T. F. Day, editor of *The Rudder,* challenged in 1906 the hazily documented myth that the schooner was "invented" in 1713 by a local hero in a specific New England town. In January of 1911 the first issue of that light-heartedly learned British quarterly, *The Mariner's Mirror,* devoted its research note Number One to this subject. Professor L. G. Carr Laughton submitted a print of a schooner made from a painting by one of the Van de Veldes, the younger of whom died in 1707. This seemed adequate to demolish the 1713 date, but the sturdy old yarn persisted.

In 1927 Professor E. P. Morris of Yale, a professional historian and amateur naval architect, tried again. He devoted about eight pages of his study *The Fore and Aft Rig in America* to a careful review of the evidence, concluding, ". . . the Gloucester tradition leaves us exactly where we should be if the story had never been recorded."

The argument turns partly upon a definition of "schooner," and upon the word's etymologically baffling origin. Carr Laughton opened his 1911 discussion by declaring: "The true schooner rig comprises two gaff sails, the fore being less than the after sail, and a headsail. These are the essentials; all beyond is accidental." Evidently he thought of the square-topsail schooners of the eighteenth century and the multi-masted ones of about 1900 as embellished by "accidents." That his sense of the distinction between the "true" and the "accidental" was sound is indicated by working schooners and schooner yachts of today. If

Detail from "The Capture of Cadiz . . . ," a Dutch print including what E. Keble Chatterton called "one of the earliest two-masted schooners to be shown by any of the engravers." But this usually careful scholar relied upon what turns out to be a re-engraving based only roughly upon the original Hondius print, which had been published prior to 1650. The one used by Chatterton was published in 1730 by Zacharias Chatelain. The "early" schooner, or speeljacht, near the right margin of the detail, was a capricious addition of the later engraver. Nothing resembling it appears on the Hondius version of the scene.

we substitute "headboard" for the headstick or short gaff of the first depicted schooners, Carr Laughton's definition once more is as good as ever.

An occasional upholder of the Gloucester myth who has bothered to glance at contrary evidence has found comfort in Carr Laughton's amiable hint that a finer form of hull rather than of rig might have been developed in Gloucester's cherished year. For this there is no evidence. The schooner rig has been carried on a variety of hulls—sharp, blunt, with or without after drag, given little or much dead rise, some fin-keeled, others almost keel-less. It seems plausible that pre-Revolutionary American schooners should have had finer lines than those of the contemporary brigs and snows. Much of the advantage of the rig would otherwise have been lost; but such drafts as survive do little to encourage that thesis. As Benjamin Franklin noted, soon after the Revolution, the interrelationship of sail plan and lines under water was still being neglected by designers.

Throughout the history of sail it has been the rig that has distinguished different classes of vessels—and this has continued to be true in spite of the perversities of naval usage, such as the ship-rigged "sloop." The part visible above water revealed a vessel for what she was—to those who needed to know from motives friendly or truculent. For example, the famous Freeport privateer *Dash* (her lines are reproduced on page 200) was launched as a schooner but listed later as a brigantine after changes of her foremast canvas. The shape of her hull had not made her a schooner in the first place; it did not prevent her from being a brigantine later on.

An inadequate presentation of pictorial evidence has hampered the discussion of the schooner's origin. Some writers who have warned of the risk in trusting redrawn pictures

Detail from a line engraving by D. van Bremden of the capture by Piet Hein of the Spanish silver fleet in sight of Havana, in 1628. This is perhaps the earliest well-identified print showing what appears to be a schooner (lower right). It was published by Z. Roman about a year after the event.

have used the device themselves. Carr Laughton's reproduction of a Van de Velde schooner was not made from the original painting (of uncertain date but surely earlier than 1707)— it was photographed from Richard Houston's engraved copy. Houston appears to have been a raffish character. One printseller kept him "for many years" in debtors' prison. As he was not born until 1721, any evidence from his burin that concerns the date 1713 should have been checked against the original painting. If it was, Carr Laughton did not say so.

The reason for care in such matters is advanced in a positive instance by Morris, who noted in Alexander Brown's scrupulously edited documentary collection *The Genesis of the United States* an "apparently careful reproduction of the 1616 print of London" containing "several very curious rigs." Morris later compared Brown's reproduction with the original print in the British Museum "and discovered that no such rigs were in the picture." Brown's engraver had depended upon an intermediate copy of 1848, in which liberties had been taken with the original. (This warning in Morris was one of my reasons for securing directly from Simancas a photograph, reproduced on page 32, of the stolen map with a marginal picture of what may be the *Virginia* of Sagadahoc of 1607. Certainly it is one of the earliest authentic views of a sloop with a headsail set.)

The dating even of original pictures or prints is often uncertain. The detail reproduced on page 193 is from "The Capture of Cadiz, 1596," a print in the Macpherson Collection reproduced entire by E. Keble Chatterton in *Old Ship Prints,* 1927. He identified it merely as "early Dutch," noting that it includes "one of the earliest two-masted schooners to be shown by any of the engravers." How early? Professor J. G. van Gelder of Utrecht, who has advised me generously on several such problems, thinks the original print of this scene may

This is the oldest exactly dated picture I have so far found of a fore-runner-schooner under sail. It appears on the great world map issued in sections in 1648 by sons of the pioneering cartographer Willem Janszoon Blaeu, a Dutchman.

be the work of Pieter van der Keere, who is mentioned in 1624 and thereafter disappears. It was published by Hondius, at an uncertain date between 1597 and 1650. Unfortunately, the Macpherson print turns out to be a 1730 rerendering, which badly distorts the topography of the bay and inserts the little "schooner" where there is no such vessel at all in the primary Hondius print. Chatterton's "one of the earliest" really is a relatively late example of the pictured speeljacht, or forerunner schooner.

The De Bry fishing sloop of 1594, given on page 30, includes a sort of headsail. Thus the one on a sloop in the 1730 Cadiz print (upper left, headed toward shore) is not an anachronism as such. I should perhaps mention that the *Mariner's Mirror,* as recently as 1957, published a note that seems to have been written by Carr Laughton twenty-one years earlier: "There is one doubtful representation of a jib in 1588 . . . but apart from this the jib is not known to have been used before 1600." The De Bry engraving indicates that some kind of triangular headsail was available before 1600, for possible use on a two-master, but pictorial evidence of such use poses a different problem. Philip Molenvliet published in 1625 a view of the waterfront of Amsterdam showing two vessels under sail, side by side, which between them carry all the elements of a schooner's rig. One is a sloop with a long gaff and a headsail set, the other a two-master, "the fore being less than the after sail," but wanting a sprit. This I have not reproduced.

In 1628 a Dutch fleet captured the Spanish plate galleons off Cuba. Van Bremden's engraving of the achievement, issued about a year later, presents us with what may be the earliest closely dated picture of a vessel rigged to carry a schooner's sails. In the detail which we reproduced on page 194, the two men aboard her will be seen to have been drawn to an exaggerated scale, but this is true of all the other people in the print.

A similar little vessel appears often enough in seventeenth century pictures to suggest that the type was a standard tender or dispatch boat for fleets. The Blaeus' vast world map of 1648 places such a forerunner-schooner in a fleet action at 10° N., 130° W., in the Pacific. Here again no headsail is set, although bowsprit and forestay are ready for it.

It was just after mid-century that an event occurred which produced satisfactory pictorial

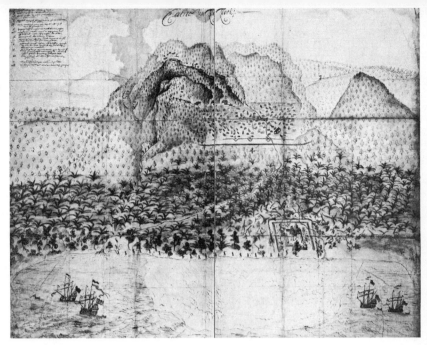

LEFT. This is perhaps the earliest representation of a schooner with all requisite sails set—in this instance with one more headsail than would be necessary to satisfy the basic definition of schooner rig. It is an enlargement from the scene below (a unique drawing from the van der Hem "secret atlas," which was completed prior to 1678), celebrating the capture of Loki, in the Celebes, in 1652. RIGHT. A sketch of the capture of Loki, Celebes, in 1652, made on the spot and perhaps used some years later as a model by the more sophisticated artist who drew the view below.

evidence: the small port of Loki in the Moluccas was captured by Arnold de Vlamingh van Outshoorn. His personal "verbael" of the action, sent to the Dutch East India Company's headquarters at Batavia, mentions by name two "chaloupen" that accompanied him, and refers to the later arrival of the "yacht" *Leeuwerck*. Although the Dutch company guarded all maps and views most jealously, one or more of the contemporaneous sketches, made of this action on the spot, came to the notice of a wealthy cartographical magpie of Amsterdam named Laurens van der Hem. With his copy of the eleven-volume, sumptuous Blaeu *Atlas Major* as a basis, van der Hem had decided to make up his own personal supplement, particularly of maps and scenes of the Dutch East India Company's conquests. He employed artist-cartographers to produce, in a uniform style and in rich colors, many unique charts and views based upon drawings which he somehow wangled from the company's servants who sketched them during their voyages. One depicts the capture of Loki, and includes in the center foreground the schooner enlarged on page 196

When was the atlas picture made? The artist may have set to work as soon as evidences of the 1652 battle reached Amsterdam. Dr. F. C. Wieder, who revived interest in the van der Hem "secret" atlas in 1933 after it had lain almost forgotten in Vienna for two centuries, believes that the major part of the work on it was done about 1670. The anonymous artists appear to have copied, in a uniform script, all dated notations on the original sources. Most of these dates fall in the 1650s and 1660s—the latest in 1666—and it is on record that Cosimo de' Medici examined van der Hem's atlas on a visit to Amsterdam in 1668. A sub-

stantial part of it must have been finished at that time, but since the Loki drawing is itself unsigned and undated it is prudent to use the year 1678, when van der Hem died and the atlas was turned over to his daughter, a nun. Using this sure date we still have proof that a developed form of the schooner, with two headsails, was in use thirty-five years earlier than the date claimed for its "invention" by Captain Robinson of Gloucester.

How accurately did van der Hem's artist follow his models? To judge by the two Moluccan korakoras, at the left and in the right forewater, he was a respecter of precise detail. Except for a leeboard and a spritsail yard, the schooner shown off Loki in 1652 does not differ in any significant structural way from what is perhaps a schooner on the Blaeu map positively dated four years earlier. The view of the latter on page 195 is enlarged to about twice its dimensions on the map: Blaeu's draftsman could not have attempted the degree of detail employed by van der Hem's. It is possible that the heavy line of the forestay—much heavier than that of the flagstaff—is intended for a jib furled to the stay. A faint vertical line, making a tiny triangle at the foot of this heavy "stay," could represent the bunched broad foot of the jib itself. (Compare the furled staysail of the three-master on page 201.) The use of two headsails on the Loki schooner suggests a mature model, preceded in evolution by others with a single headsail. The curious fact is that the earliest indubitable depiction of a schooner that I have noticed, with the minimum of necessary canvas set, has more than enough sails to answer to the definition.

Can we identify her further? The "secret" atlas view shows eight vessels. De Vlamingh's fleet numbered sixteen, including three jachten, two galiooten, and two chaloupen. The schooner standing in on the port tack, across the bows of the anchored ships, is not meant for a shallop because de Vlamingh calls these "open." The distant vessel, left of center, answers to that description. The two korakoras probably are his "galiooten." On his list this leaves the yachts *Delffshaaven, Leeuwerck,* and *'t Sas van Gent.* My guess is that the artist meant to portray the second of these, the late arriver. The scene jibes well with details of the verbael itself. The korakoras, with their well-observed tripod masts and outrigger structures, must have been derived from an eyewitness drawing or a model. But we still have no evidence that the view in the van der Hem atlas is a close representation of an actual picture made on the spot.

In the January 1929 issue of the *Mariner's Mirror,* R. C. Anderson referred to "a view of a tropical island with a number of Dutch vessels and one of these was a distinct schooner." Ascribed merely to "Peeters," it had been recently auctioned at Christie's. Possibly this gives us a clue to the identity of van der Hem's artist, or to the model he used for the unique drawing in the atlas itself. Two artists named Peeters worked in the seventeenth century. Bonaventura Peeters died in the year of the capture of Loki, but where or how I have so far been unable to learn. His brother Jan, who died in 1677, was employed by van der Hem. The tempting inferences are obvious, but let us hold to the facts.

Two drawings of the capture of Loki, made at the time, were sent by de Vlamingh to Batavia with his verbael. One shows no vessels. The other, reproduced here, could have been the topographical model for the atlas picture, with perspective adjusted by a more sophisticated draftsman. The main features of the two are similar, but there are notable discrepancies—and no schooner appears offshore.

There is a chance that the view sold at Christie's is the prototype of the atlas picture, but when or where "Peeters" drew it seems not to be known. I should like to see a photocopy if anyone knows where it now is. For the present it should perhaps be assumed that the schooner in van der Hem's sumptuous atlas, while certainly drawn by 1678, and probably drawn about a decade earlier, was inserted in the scene by an Amsterdam artist who used a variety of materials for his guidance.

Because of this prior example it becomes unnecessary to review Morris's evidence, given with inadequate pictorial support, that schooners were in use between 1690 and 1707. But since the addition of a headsail to the shallop creates the schooner type, I should mention one bit of testimony that seems in error. In his knowledgeable book *The Yankee Whaler* (1926) Clifford W. Ashley supported the case Carr Laughton had made in 1911; but he also referred to prints by the older Peter Brueghel in which he had noticed "triangular headsails (staysails or jibs)." This would date the jib's emergence before Brueghel's death in 1568, but I think Ashley was misled by indifferent reproductions in the collection he cites, edited by Rene van Bastalaer in 1908. I can find no true headsails in the Brueghel etchings. Anyone who looks at his well-known "Fall of Icarus" painting might well suppose that the distant small craft have headsails, but the brushwork is too broad for a confident decision. Details of this foreshore-seascape appear in some of the etchings, with what seem to be the same craft drawn in sharp detail. In these, the canvas that suggests a jib and mainsail in the painting can be seen precisely to be parts of a single spritsail. There are two etchings in which the tack of a spritsail appears to have been carried forward, abaft the mast, and made fast about halfway between shroud and stem. This permits a triangular portion of the sail to take the quartering wind forward of the mast—but the forward edge of the sail is free, the after portion constituting the luff, a circumstance opposite to that of the true headsail. I believe there is no instance, in the Brueghel pictures or prints, of a sail carried on a headstay with the leech free.

It should be clear from even this hasty review that a quest for the "inventor" of the schooner was always chimerical. Small craft described as shallops, carrying fore-and-aft canvas on two masts, were in use around the year 1600. Some had two sails of equal size, but the foresail tended to become the smaller. Single-masted boats, later to be called sloops, were in use at the same time. Before 1628 the two-masted shallop had acquired a sloop's bowsprit, which may at first have been intended only as a support for the forestay, but which later was used to set a sloop's headsail as well. This may have happened early in the century. The first good pictorial evidence I know of shows that it occurred not later than 1678.

Thus the Gloucester myth is disposed of by at least a thirty-five-year margin—but most of us go on believing what we want to believe. In 1944 one of our naval officers published a history based in a series of lectures which he had been authorized to deliver at the United States Maritime Service Officers' School. In it he wrote, "Gloucester distinguished itself over two hundred years ago by the invention of a brand new rig, that of the schooner. There may have been accidentally similar rigs in Holland at an earlier date, but . . . ."

Shipping in Montego Bay, Jamaica, 1770. A sloop with the sort of jib-headed topsail that became standard for schooners more than a century later, and a schooner almost identical in rig with that of the "Loki" schooner of about a century earlier.

THE DEVELOPMENT OF
The Schooner · 2

I HAVE PRESENTED PICTORIAL EVIDENCE THAT THE SCHOONER HAD BEEN DEVELOPED BY the Dutch not later than 1678 and that a small vessel with the schooner's essential structure and standing rigging was used by them at least thirty and perhaps fifty years earlier. There is credit enough for the young colonies that became the United States in their pragmatic further development of a handy rig which the Dutch seem to have employed around the world. All early pictures that I have seen of the forerunner-schooner, and of the eventual Dutch schooner itself, show a little vessel acting in concert with larger ones. It was the American contribution to make the schooner a free agent at sea. Her dimensions were increased and her rig expanded to include square sails aloft. These too were borrowed from the Dutch. Sloop yachts built in Holland for Charles II, as depicted by one of the Van de Veldes as early as 1672, have square topsails.

The American schooners sometimes set square topsails on one mast, sometimes on both. The lower yard crossed on the foremast was soon being used to set a forecourse as well, as may be seen in the logbook drawing of the *Baltick* on page 58. Loftier sails were safer, with the wind aft in a rough sea, when long, low booms thrust outboard added to the risk of broaching to. Square topsails also constituted fighting sails for armed schooners that had to take care of themselves in hostile waters. Fore-and-aft canvas, on low booms, often obscured the opponent from the best point of vantage: upwind. It was more likely to be slashed by enemy fire. Square sails aloft also could be backed to stop a vessel with little or no change of course, an extremely important aspect of maneuver when fighting at sea.

The great advantage of the basic schooner, over any other rig moving the same tonnage with as much canvas, was the smallness of a minimum crew needed to work her. The fore and main sails could be set or taken in one at a time, by fewer hands and with lighter rigging than would be needed for the same amount of canvas in a sloop's single mainsail. (I have mentioned John Paul Jones's dislike of the tall brute of a sloop that was his first command in the American Revolution.) The schooner's main boom, being shorter than that of an equivalent sloop, is less of a hazard thrust outboard in a heavy sea.

To trace the schooner's early development after its migration to America we seem to be dependent upon harbor views such as those of Burgis and Roberts. The Burgis view of Boston, in about the year 1722, has a schooner with the three requisite sails drawing. She looks very much like those in the Dutch pictures made in the last quarter of the preceding

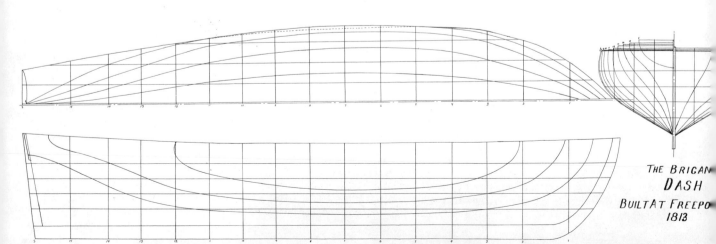

THE BRIGAN
DASH
BUILT AT FREEPO
1813

An early American three-masted schooner, from a lithograph by J. Rogers published in England in 1825. Note the pronounced rake of the short mizzenmast, by comparison with that of the developed form of the "tern" rig on page 204.

century. There are topsail sloops in the same view that are close cousins to King Charles's Dutch-made yacht, the *Mary,* of 1660. The engraving of Charleston done by Roberts before 1739 contains the same two types: basic schooner, topsail sloop. (See page 51.) Here is a situation similar to that of the minimum forms of shallop and sloop, sailing side by side in the Molenvliet print about a century earlier. In both cases, the date at which the available elements were combined to make a handier and more versatile vessel is uncertain, but the topsail schooner does not appear among the many varieties of craft in the Heap view of Philadelphia in 1754 (pages 56 and 57) and does appear in the *Baltick*'s log drawing eleven years later. Paul Revere included one in his Boston harbor of 1768 (page 58). Thereafter the type became commonplace, in deep-water employments, although pilot schooners and others that spent most of their time on soundings had less occasion for using square sail, and seldom carried it.

Privateering experience, in the Revolution and the War of 1812, perfected a number of American topsail schooner types. The most famous became known as the Baltimore clipper, later notorious as a favorite with slavers and opium smugglers. Concurrently, beginning at about the turn of the century, the same logic that had evolved the schooner from the sloop was extended to experiments with three masts in order to enlarge the vessel again without undue size in the single sails. This experimentation occurred on both sides of the Atlantic. An American example of 1825, observed by an Englishman, is reproduced on this page. Despite a renewal of piracy, the need for extreme weatherliness and large capacity for freight in

A reminder that the rig is paramount in a classification of sailing vessels: lines of the topsail schooner *Dash,* taken off from the original hawk's-nest model followed by master carpenter James Brewer when he built her for use as a letter of marque in the War of 1812. At a time when most privateers were hastily converted merchantmen, the *Dash* was designed for the most versatile aspect of her truculent function. She was both cargo carrier and commerce raider: running the blockade of Portland, Maine, with a lading of vital freight each way, on every one of her seven wartime voyages. She sent in fifteen prizes, losing none by recapture. She carried one 32-pounder on a pivot amidships and was pierced for sixteen guns. Of her original armament, ten were dummies. In 1814 the six small-caliber guns were removed in favor of two 18-pounders. Her lines are notably unusual for her period, with a length-to-breadth ratio seldom met with until mid-century: 4.13 to 1. Originally rigged as a schooner with square topsails on the foremast and a gaff topsail on the main, she was rerigged after her first voyage to cross four yards on her foremast, with an enlarged gaff topsail and a ringtail to balance on the main. Thus she became a brigantine, but the mere unbending of her fore course would have made her in effect a schooner again. I am indebted to Myron Hilton, of Freeport, Maine, for this rendering of her lines.

ABOVE. Reefing a square topsail: an illustration accompanying instructions in the 1843 American edition of *The Young Sea Officer's Sheet Anchor* by Darcy Lever. LEFT. The "pilot-boat built" topsail schooner *Sea Serpent* of 139 tons, off Cape Horn in a blizzard on February 3, 1822. The lithographer Gildemeister may have worked directly on stone under the supervision of Captain George Coggeshall, from whose memoirs published in 1851 the picture is taken. Details are faithful to the text—bulwarks deliberately smashed open to allow heavy seas to spill quickly from the deck; the square yards had been sent down in anticipation of dirty weather. Note the simplicity of the schooner's minimum rig under the worst conditions. Her single foresail has been reefed downward to the foot, near deck level. A square sail, by contrast, had to be reefed up to a lofty, plunging yard in a fashion that required many more hands. See above.

A great deal of experimentation went into the perfecting of fore-and-aft topsails manageable entirely from the deck. Here is a nock staysail bent to the topmast jumper stay of the pink-sterned schooner *Sea Flower*, sketched off Portsmouth, New Hampshire, in 1836. She has the general look of an Eastport pinkie of a slightly later date. The name *Sea Flower* was a favorite with Maine shipbuilders.

the same vessel subsided after the end of the Napoleonic Wars. The somewhat safer power of square sail, in brigs and ships, continued in favor for general trade. With the curtailment of navies, more seamen were available for the merchant services. The strategical and economic pressures which had produced the three-masted schooner relaxed for several decades. When a sharp competition between steam and sail developed, in the 1850s, there was less reason than ever to strive for weatherliness at the expense of carrying capacity. Throughout most of the nineteenth century the versatile, two-masted topsail schooner of modest size persisted as a perfected type all over the world with little further alteration, except for the shift to fore-and-aft topsails when the problem of manpower once more became acute, after mid-century.

America's chief eighteenth century development in marine architecture, above water, was a modification of Dutch elements. If others had been as diligent as the Dutch in keeping an intimate pictorial record of their mechanic arts in action, a different historical truth might have emerged. But that elusive ideal, the truth of history, is dependent upon records that happen to survive from among those that chanced to be made in the first place. Our information on the underwater shapes of the smaller sorts of vessels is seriously unsatisfactory. Some writers, as a consequence, when confronted by great ragged holes in the contemporaneous evidence, succumb to the pleasures of supposition: a harmless activity when labeled for what it is. There was a Dutch shipwright in a vessel wrecked on the Bermudas before 1620, who built some boats for the governor: good reason for inferring a direct connection between Dutch shallops of the period and the distinctive Bermuda sloops; but little else is as well documented.

Later traffic between the British and Dutch islands in the West Indies may account for the spread of certain features. A print of Montego Bay, in northwestern Jamaica (page 199), includes a small schooner. Drawn in 1770, it differs hardly at all from the little Dutch schooners of a century earlier. A hundred years later the triangular topsail of the sloop upon which the unknown artist centered his chief attention had replaced square topsails in most American schooners. Such hundred-year leaps are a reminder that the main features of sail plans are persistent through a few major and a multitude of minor variations. Gaff and jack topsails, even jumper staysails, have varied the pattern aloft and once more have vanished, bringing the essential schooner back to her origins: the bald-headed or jib-headed two-master. The only surviving "accident" is a yachtsman's gorgeous extravagance to which America can make no honest claim, the spinnaker.

But before her return to her origins the schooner did undergo a last, extraordinary period of experimentation, charateristically American. In the constant moving of large quantities of durable materials of widespread and steady use—such as fuel and lumber— speed in transit becomes relatively unimportant. Another consideration is the economy of stowing and discharging large quantities of homogeneous cargo at one time. When steam seemed finally to have won the contest, the usefulness of sail was extended for two or three decades by a diligent process of trial and error centering in the state of Maine. It was based

". . . the versatile, two-masted topsail schooner of modest size persisted as a perfected type all over the world . . ." Here is one off the Peruvian guano islands in 1852.

There was no single line of schooner development. Both types on this page were contemporaries of the 1850s. The revenue cutters below were the final overexaggeration of the square-topsail schooner. The last impulsive defiance of steam on its own terms, which produced the oversparred clipper ships, also produced eight schooner-cutters of the *Morris* class that were built for the ultimate in speed. An admiring writer for *Ballou's* noted that they could "eat right into the wind's eye." But Thomas Dunham of New York affirmed in the *Eckford Webb* the rigging principle that was to survive longest: a "tern" schooner with masts of equal height and rake, which could be increased in number like standard parts to propel a bigger hull without enlarging the crew appreciably. The *Eckford Webb*'s masts were 84 feet tall, in a hull measuring 137' x 30' x 11' 6". A speed of 16 miles an hour was claimed for her, and a day's run of 309 miles.

UNITED STATES
REVENUE CUTTER

Special forms emerge from particular uses. While the great many-masted schooners were evolving, the Banks fishermen evolved at least two distinct types of their own which persisted into the twilight of sail. One was the double-ender, like the nearest of these several schooners of the 1890s, reefed down and running from a storm. The pinkie influence is evident in the narrow, long stern, which had advantages both for the working of fishing gear and for keeping the decks dry. In the rolling seas of these ocean shallows the pronounced scoop-shaped sheer of the fisherman made her more comfortable to live in than the almost sheerless examples on the opposite page.

upon these two considerations, and the only group of sailing vessels still making a steady living, early in the twentieth century, was almost entirely composed of multi-masted schooners in the coastwise lumber and fuel trades.

This last phase of the evolutionary process had a built-in difficulty comparable with the antlers of another oversized Maine phenomenon, the moose. An asset was extended into a handicap. Nagged by a competitive need for ever-enlarging capacity, designers increased not only the number of masts but their height as well. At the same time the hulls under water began to resemble huge floating boxes that canceled the original weatherly virtues of the fore-and-aft rig. When the three-master had been pushed to what most builders regarded as its ultimate economical size—about 800 tons—a trial was made of a four-mast schooner-rig in a converted steamer. Soon afterward, in 1880, the first schooner designed as a four-master was launched at Bath: the *W. L. White.* The extra mast made her measurement of just under a thousand tons seem feasible; but it should be noted that while the addition of a fifth, a sixth, and in one instance a seventh mast was being tried, the tonnage measurement for each class of schooner was also increasing. The first five-master, the *Governor Ames* of 1888, measured 1,788 tons; but by this time four-masters were being built that were nearly as large; and nine years later the biggest four-sticker of all, the *Frank A. Palmer,* pushed the tonnage figure for its class above 2,000.

A partial explanation is the development, early in the 1880s, of the steam donkey to haul the running rigging; but this device, humane as well as economical, encouraged owners to ship inexperienced, small crews: a practice responsible for catastrophic losses. Of the last fourteen schooners added to the great Palmer fleet, beginning with the *Marie Palmer* (of 1,904 tons, built in 1899), two foundered with all hands lost, four others foundered some-

A famous marine photograph: Dry Dock No. 2, Newport News Shipbuilding and Dry Dock Company, September 12, 1906, with the three-masted schooner *Sallie I'on,* the four-master *Malcolm Baxter, Jr.,* the five-master *Jennie French Potter,* the six-master *Eleanor A. Percy,* and the unique seven-master—the *Thomas W. Lawson*—all in view. The photographer barely missed a two-master, seen under sail in the river when the significance of the gathering first was noticed.

what less calamitously, two were sunk in collisions, two ran ashore and were wrecked, one was burned, one is accounted for merely as "lost at sea," and two survived for endings more nearly normal: one to be sold for scrap, the other to be sunk by a U-boat. This was the hard-luck fleet, in which all kinds of disasters that others suffered were concentrated.

These disasters seem persistently related to the effort to economize. Even when a donkey engine would do a seaman's backwork, an able seaman's experience was particularly needed to guide its pace in dangerous weather. It could do what no amount of manpower could accomplish—part a halliard or the strap of a block by adding its insensate power to that of the seesaw lunge of the sea. When men had no choice but to relax, the donkey could dig in its iron-shod hoofs and hold on too long. Skilled hands knew how to compensate when they handled the little monster, but enough skilled hands, in a marginal enterprise, meant the difference between a little profit and a loss. Too often the consequence of this sort of accounting, in the big schooners, was total loss to the underwriters and some loss of life.

The yards of square-riggers had ropes to brace them firmly at both ends. When one or both parted, a yard was still balanced at its center. But the booms of a big schooner could swing back and forth across the deck uncontrollably, and the very effort to check them might snap the only rope with which it could be done. In the trough of a heavy sea, it would not take much of that sort of random battering to start the seams or even to invite a capsizal. Testimony of survivors indicates that some of the big multi-masters simply could not be put about on the other tack in heavy weather and were driven on a lee shore for that reason. Thus the tag ends of schooner experimentation threw into mocking reversal the two great original virtues of the type: weatherliness, and ease in coming about.

The extent to which economy in manpower had become a controlling factor can be gathered from a comparison between the ill-fated *Thomas W. Lawson,* the only seven-sticker ever built, and some of the great square-riggers of the 1850s. Donald McKay's largest clipper, the *Great Republic,* originally measuring 4,555 tons, was designed to be worked by a crew of 130. The *Thomas W. Lawson,* 60 feet longer, measuring 5,218 tons gross, carried on her fateful first transatlantic voyage a crew of seventeen, including officers. She went on the rocks in the Scilly Islands and was lost with all but two of her people. McKay's *Sovereign of the Seas* of 2,421 tons carried 80 able seamen on her maiden voyage, in a crew of more than 100. The six-masted schooner *Wyoming,* 71 feet longer and with a tonnage about half again as great, had a crew of 12, not excluding the skipper. In a comparison with square-riggers of the last days of deep-water sail, tonnage for tonnage the schooners' crews usually numbered about a third as many as were needed in even the most parsimonious ship.

Two- and three-masted square-topsail schooners, as perfected by Americans, proved useful as deep-water carriers for more than a century. The large, multi-masted schooners were a transient, coastal type. As fore-and-afters they should have been suited to the tricky navigation of shoal estuaries leading to the coal ports of the Middle Atlantic States, and to the task of clawing sharply offshore in bad situations of current and wind. When structural compromises, particularly of sheer size, lost them these advantages, some efforts were made to put them into competition with the last of the square-rigged Down-Easters in deep water. The result was calamity. Some got around the Horn for use in the Pacific, but it was a costly experiment. Captain Frank W. Patten of the big *Kineo,* a five-master built for deep-sea service, had a grim voyage taking her out to Manila with coal and home again with Hawaiian sugar. Pleasant breezes in the enduring deep-ocean swells were often his most exasperating problem. In his log at these times he made such entries as, "Lowered down everything to save sails from slatting to pieces," and, "Don't like this lowering sails while there is a wind, but the rig is at a disadvantage." Heavy weather proposed different problems: "Often times the schooner has been obliged to sail N.E. when her course was S.E. and my experience in the *Kineo* off the Horn is a repetition of what the *Gov. Ames* went through and what every other big schooner will go through." He lost fourteen sails. All his mast hoops chafed to pieces.

The big schooners were a gambler's response to intermittent restatements of the economic odds: to the business cycle of prosperity and depression, the belated development of a small but highly economical steam collier, the emergence of the towing barge as a dominant

The *Thomas W. Lawson* represented the ultimate overstretching of the schooner principle. A process which began by adding more masts, each of which would still be as easy as ever to man, ended with this colossus in which the rigging alone, for each mast, weighed three tons. This was insignificant by comparison with her carrying capacity of 8,100 tons, but her length-to-breadth ratio of 8 to 1 was out of keeping with her rig. Her designer, B. B. Crowninshield, candidly wrote in retrospect, "Light, she was all right with a leading wind, but tacking in moderate weather was sometimes difficult and occasionally impossible." Thus in his effort to achieve the ultimate economy he lost the very virtues that had made the schooner into the last practical survivor of commercial sail. She was built at Quincy, Massachusetts, by the Fore River Ship and Engine Company, and launched in May 1902. In 1907 she was converted by the Sun Oil Company into a 14-compartment tanker. Despite her great sail power, her first voyage with oil took six weeks to the mouth of the English channel, where she went ashore with great loss of life. The names of her masts have been a subject of stoveside squabble among old salts. One of her captains, who should have known, listed them as "Fore, Main, Mizzen, No. 4, No. 5, No. 6, and Spanker."

TOP. The *J. R. Teel,* photographed at sea by Captain Elliot. She was built at Newburyport in 1889, in the first great surge of interest in the four-sticker, and was at sea, listed as a schooner barge, in 1913. BELOW. Shipwrights in the frame of a schooner in the Dunn & Elliot yards, Thomaston, Maine.

Captain Arthur J. Elliot of Thomaston: shipbuilder, shipmaster, ship owner, photographed by the author in 1959. ABOVE. A schooner's transom eagle on the Dunn & Elliot sail loft at Thomaston, Maine.

Two pictures that testify to the enduring technical economy of wooden shipbuilding. At the left is the launch, at Thomaston, Maine, in 1901, of the *William H. Yerkes*. She was built by Dunn & Elliot, in the heyday of the big schooners that stepped one or two more than her four masts. Seventeen years later the same firm launched the slightly smaller but otherwise similar *Margaret Throop* (right). Despite a desperate need for tonnage in World War I, and a shortage of officers, there was no disposition in the last artificial boom in schooner building to produce any more unmanageable monsters. The four-sticker had proved herself the ultimate practicable enlargement of the basic schooner design.

type, the growth of the case-oil trade in competition with coal, and the perfecting of large steam colliers. Ignoring the one seven-master as a dubious freak, we can get a reasonably clear view of what happened from a glance at the anonymous figures. In Maine's pyramiding of tonnage for efficiency, 311 four-masters were built—45 five-masters—10 six-masters. The great surge of production in four-masters occurred about 1890, when a hundred of them were built in a little over three years. The first five-master had been launched in 1888, but it did not prove convincing: a decade was to pass before the next one was hazarded. Then, for a six-year period beginning in 1899, the production of five-masters averaged six a year. The huge six-masters, representing more of an investment problem, were launched at an almost even rate of one a year from 1900 to 1909.

It may be more significant that, during the turn-of-the-century heyday of the five-masters, there was a renewed demand for four-masters as well. Another hundred of them were launched between 1900 and the middle of 1905. Because nearly all of the big schooners were built for the same purpose, and were financed by widely held shares, it would have been feasible to consolidate more of the investment in the largest sizes. That this was not done is an indication of contemporary doubts of their success in the long run, even while some of them were earning good returns. In the years around 1906, before calamity struck it, the Palmer fleet paid an average yearly dividend of 14 per cent to its investors, but the financial community was not persuaded of the endurance of the trade. The year 1904 had been the peak for the construction of big schooners, comparable only to 1890 when a few more had been launched but with none having more than four masts.

Careful students of this enterprise, particularly in Maine, note that these final years of commercial sail were made possible only by a remarkable organization of resources, an intermingling of the life of the coastal carrier with the whole life of a region. Shipyard wages in Maine towns were far lower than they could be in a large industrial center because the Maine shipwright had continued throughout three centuries to be a versatile farmer, fisher-

Although the four-sticker was the most successful adaptation of the schooner principle for the bulk cargo trade in coastal waters, the basic two-masted schooner continued to be the most versatile craft of all. This is the *Teddy Bear,* an Arctic trader identified by Stefansson as the first to make contact with the Copper Eskimos. Her auxiliary power had to be carefully hoarded in remote seas far from fuel supplies. Sail consequently was vital to her operation long after engines in normal competition had won out. The date is 1910.

man, and woodsman who was not dependent upon the steadiness of any one trade, or upon high wages to compensate for periods of idleness. The general practice of keeping capitalization spread within the local community also contributed the small saving which allows a marginal enterprise to last a little longer. But when more and more of the big schooners were stripped down for conversion to towing barges, it was the very flexibility of this sort of economy that brought the entire production of wooden sailing vessels for commerce to an abrupt end. Abnormal conditions of the First World War stimulated a brief revival, with four-masted schooners again the type most favored.

There is one more affirmation of the practical judiciousness of Benjamin Franklin in the fact that the last examples of working sail in general use—four-masted schooners with three headsails—used the same division of canvas into seven approximate triangles which he had advocated in his "nautical budget" of 1786. Despite a different system of spars, his three reasons still applied: ". . . more or less sail may be made at pleasure . . . swiftness would be very considerable . . . the vessel would lie nearer the wind."

"Total Loss" is the caption written on this photograph taken by Captain Arthur J. Elliot near San Juan, Puerto Rico, in 1917.

Oystermen:

One of the Last Trades To Use Sail by Preference

The working schooner returns to its origins. The last of the sail-powered oystermen in Delaware Bay, photographed by the late Graham Schofield. Their job was dredging for oysters, an operation which kept a fleet of schooners in being up to the beginnings of World War II, partly on the theory that they did less damage than motored craft would do to the oyster beds.

PIRACY

HERE IS NO LOGICAL DATE AT WHICH AN ACCOUNT OF PIRACY CAN BEGIN or end, no place in which to localize it except, by basic definition, the high seas. Odysseus, sacker of cities, appears to be so addressed in admiration by the primary chronicler. The public has never since known quite how to react to this phenomenon, which slides from the ruthless sea king of Ithaca —so sympathetic and woebegone a fellow when he is in trouble himself— to the self-made sovereign like Eric the Red, and thence into such figures as Hawkins, Kidd, and John Paul Jones, who in their own time were regarded by some as pirates, by others as patriots.

Piracy is a cyclic activity, less prevalent in wartime than one might assume, because much which would otherwise be called piracy is made legal, under antique international law, by a declaration of belligerency. The same act, if you announce you are going to try to commit it, becomes nicer. The enlargement of regular armed services also tightens the control of centralized authorities over waters sometimes neglected. The freebooter is under pressure to take sides, if only because his usual prey is more likely to be under convoy, or in a state of military preparedness for assaults from the sea. Lafitte's fleeting days of virtue at New Orleans produce an example.

Piracy has often been a by-product of peacemaking. The brutalities of warfare, with its sanctioned pillage, have not been easily shed by some participants. This was notably true among privateersmen. Seldom sure of the legality of their seizures, and sometimes disappointed by the prize courts, individuals found it easy to drift from privateering into piracy. Men pressed into naval services occasionally worked off their legitimate grievances by this illegitimate route.

On the American coasts, piracy followed the general pattern. Notable raids in the Caribbean tended to occur when the European nations whose peoples were involved enjoyed a technical state of peace. The shipping of the English colonies was beset by pirates until the French and Indian Wars began. Then, for a period extending through the American Revolution and the Napoleonic Wars, piracy was a minor problem. The end of privateering, at the close of the War of 1812, and the political confusions of a rebellious South America, stimulated a renewal of piracy. It became so virulent that in the 1820s the United States maintained regular cruises of its fighting ships in the Caribbean to control the situation.

LEFT. Lafitte the pirate negotiating with Governor Clairborne and General Jackson. RIGHT. Captain Jacob Dunham tells, in his *Journal,* of encountering a pirate named Mitchell who boasted that he had entertained his captive, Governor Gonzales of St. Andreas, for ten days "with wine at his dinner, and plenty of Spanish segars" before hanging him at a moment's whim.

Captain Dunham (left) who was told by its perpetrator of the act depicted at the bottom of page 214, had an unnerving encounter of his own (right) with the Rhode Island pirate Charles Gibbs: ". . . finding all my entreaties unsuccessful, and my strength much exhausted, I took a firm stand in the ring marked out for me, hoping to receive a ball through the heart, fearing if I was wounded I should be tortured to death to make sport for the demons. Two of the pirates with loaded muskets took their stand and fired them toward me, when I cast my eyes down toward my feet looking for blood, thinking I might have been wounded without feeling the pain." But Gibbs by this method was trying to frighten his captives into telling him where their money was hidden, and consequently kept them alive.

LEFT. The account of the piracies of Charles Gibbs, given in *The Pirates Own Book,* is taken with little change from a pamphlet published at Providence in 1831 which purports to be his confession written before he was hanged in New York. In it he seems to deny any complicity in the seizure and subsequent poisoning of a young Dutch girl taken to a pirates' rendezvous where she "received such treatment, the bare recollection of which causes me to shudder!" Although he claims to have tried to protect her, the illustrators both of the pamphlet and the subsequent book gave the episode their major attention. RIGHT. Gibbs was fifteen when he first went to sea in the *Hornet.* He was aboard when she took the *Peacock* off Pernambuco and followed Lawrence into the *Chesapeake,* playing by his own account "a very distinguished part" in the engagement with the *Shannon.* Some years later, in an Argentinian privateer, he participated in a mutiny and turned pirate. He confessed to a share in the murder of almost four hundred persons. After a period of seeming respectability ashore, he and an accomplice named Wansley again mutinied in a small schooner, and were taken and hanged. Here they are burying the schooner's moneybags.

Gibbs and the steward Wansley murdering Captain Thornby of the brig *Vineyard*, November 23, 1830. A woodcut from *The Pirates Own Book*, published when the upsurge of piracy that had so unhappily distinguished the 1820s was being brought under control.

Another source of piracy was the harshness of shipmasters. Some mutineers, who may have wanted only to end an intolerable state of affairs, then found piracy to be one of the outlaw's few options for a brief survival.

The most curious aspect of this activity is the manner in which it has been romanticized by those safely beyond its reach. The accounts of eyewitnesses, in and out of court, show it almost uniformly to be the work of sadistic creatures whom it would be wrong to call brutes. They were human, with a deepening of the inhumanity found only in man. Being human, many had moments of compassion that have been pounced upon by yarnspinners. Most of the accompanying pictures are taken from a book published in 1837, when the post-war renewal of piracy had once more been brought fairly well under control: *The Pirates Own Book, or Authentic Narratives of the Lives, Exploits, and Executions of the Most Celebrated Sea Robbers*. It was widely popular and went into many editions. The polite prose mutes in euphemism, but does not evade, the sickening aspects of its subject. These were diminished by later writers to the point at which the unimaginative could wear a black hat with a skull and crossbones at a fancy-dress party without giving a thought to its ferocious origins.

Captain George Davis's *Recollections* . . . include this 1844 skirmish with pirates while at anchor in the Kumsingmoon Passage near Canton. Piracy was often a hereditary profession in the East.

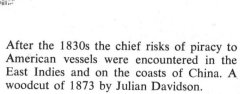

After the 1830s the chief risks of piracy to American vessels were encountered in the East Indies and on the coasts of China. A woodcut of 1873 by Julian Davidson.

The romanticizing of a hideous evil, which culminated in Long John Silver, began while the fact was still prevalent. The above three personages were being viewed retrospectively, over a past century and more, when they were engraved for *The Pirates Own Book*. Kidd the scapegoat, who probably never overstepped the limits of his privateer's commission, had to be cloaked in legends. Here he is burying his Bible. Teach, a privateer who became the indubitable pirate Blackbeard in 1716, did justify some of the later lush accounts by his remarkable behavior. The romantics have had difficulties with Low. Philip Gosse complains that he was "a repulsive, uninteresting, and bloody pirate . . . not a sympathetic figure." The picture celebrates one of his milder moments, when he gave Captain Graves the choice of drinking his health or of being shot. An ultimate for silliness was reached by Auguste François Biard, whose oil of disguised pirates decoying an American ship—exhibited in 1855—became so popular a model for engravers and lithographers that cartoonists assumed the public would recognize the original when they in turn used it as a model for political satires. See, for example, *Harper's* for November 9, 1872, and *Puck* for September 23, 1896.

THE LAW OF STORMS

A PUBLIC UNCOMFORTABLY FAMILIAR WITH THE BEHAVIOR OF AFFECTIONATELY NAMED hurricanes perhaps needs to be reminded that it was an American practical scientist who had the original clarifying insight into their full nature and its significance for the management of sailing ships. Scattered observations, beginning in the latter part of the seventeenth century, hint at an understanding of the circular nature of some storms. William Hickey, a Calcutta barrister, noted in his diary in the 1780s that a terrific storm, after a brief lull, had blown back where it came from just as violently. Franklin had earlier observed that northeast storms on the American coast seemed to progress backward, starting in the southwest, moving as a whole toward the direction from which the wind was blowing.

In meteorology, as in ship design, improvement resulted from the patient contributions of many observers and theorists, but it remained for William C. Redfield, in the 1820s, to evolve a hypothesis harmonizing all the important evidence. Being less of a pure scientist than a practical mechanical genius—which is to say, being a scientific American of his time—Redfield concerned himself with the immediate utility of his theory to shipmasters. In 1831 he contributed to the *American Journal of Science and Arts* a remarkable paper analyzing a mass of factual reports of several storms, gathered from observers ashore and from the logs of ships. A chart accompanying the article develops the observed track of a hurricane of August 1830, with a pair of lines to show the path of its center, within an outer pair tracing the broadening limits of its effects. The chart shows the great counterclockwise wheel of wind centered southeast of New York, moving northeastward, having followed a roughly parabolic course from the Virgin Islands across the Bahamas, encountering the coast at Savannah, skirting it to Cape Hatteras, thence proceeding close to the Gulf Stream to dissipate south of Newfoundland. The location of the storm center is given for the nights of August 12th, when first observed, August 14th, 15th, 16th, 17th, and 18th. Another track is given in less detail for the offshore hurricane which two weeks later passed over Bermuda.

Apart from its orderly and final perception of phenomena thitherto imperfectly understood, Redfield's account is pivotal in the history of practical meteorology because of its conclusion: ". . . it would seem also that a pretty correct estimate may be formed of the bearing, and probable course of the *heart of a storm,* and of the course also which, if steered, will have the best tendency to lessen its violence, or duration; and that those navigators who find in any of the more moderate storms, an adverse wind, may, by pursuing a course transverse to that of the storm, often modify its direction in a manner favorable to their wishes." The italics are Redfield's. He was stating the gist of what later came to be known among alert seamen as the Law of Storms.

Redfield invited seamen and scientists to send their observations of violent gales to Messrs. E. & G. W. Blunt, Hydrographers, in New York. Drawing partly upon the submitted data, he published in the twelfth edition of Blunt's *American Coast Pilot* in 1836 a revised paper providing practical seamen with five clear rules of thumb for keeping out of the center of a hurricane. They were all based on the single fact that a rotating wind would in its very rotation betray to the mariner the side of his own course upon which its center lay, and on the following inference that he could then use the power of the storm itself to shoulder him away from the center instead of letting it scoop him into it.

Redfield's new principle for navigators was taken up promptly by the more intelligent shipmasters, but his collaborator George W. Blunt still thought it necessary, in a work on the subject which he issued thirty years later, to open his preface with the statement, "A belief that much loss of life and property on the ocean might be prevented by a proper knowledge of the character of our severe gales, and how to avoid them, has induced me to prepare this work . . . from the labors of our countryman, Wm. C. Redfield, the discoverer of the Law of Storms . . ." Despite the emergence in the 1840s of a large scientific literature on the subject, "practical" shipmasters continued to do what they thought best up to the moment when wireless telegraphy could tell them what to do without even thinking. At that point the Law of Storms, one of the notable American contributions to practical science, passed out of memory among even able shipmasters of the sort whose journals and reminiscences prove that they had relied upon it in many instances to minimize calamity and perhaps to save their ships.

LEFT. The American ship *Rotunda* breaking up on Nantucket Shoals in a September hurricane. RIGHT. Henry Piddington, curator of the Museum of Economic Geology of India, published in Calcutta in 1844 a "Horn Book" for sailors. It did more than borrow the name of the old primers which had their type and pictures protected by sheets of horn: it incorporated, in pockets fore and aft, two horn cards based upon drawings by Redfield. One indicated a counterclockwise wind rotation, for the northern hurricanes. The clockwise one at the right was for the Southern Hemisphere. Horn cards, when placed on a chart, greatly simplified the practical seaman's effort to locate the storm center and choose the best course.

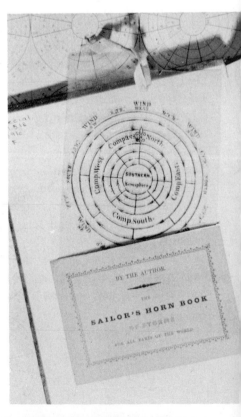

William C. Redfield, 1789–1857, has been too much muted by historians of science in America. No-one prior to the younger Josiah Willard Gibbs came closer to the conceptual processes of pure science, save Franklin, the exception to all cozy generalizations. Yet where Franklin tossed out an idea and a sketch for others to exploit, Redfield was an enterpriser as well as a theoretician. When boiler explosions became a chronic menace in steam navigation, he conceived the idea of putting the passengers in a towed barge, and the device persisted as the original freight carrier of the sort. Redfield turned from the laying out of railroads to the task of organizing the American Association for the Advancement of Science. But his primary contribution, generously recognized by such foreign meteorologists as Piddington who worked concurrently on the same problem, was the Law of Storms. The above picture, from *Popular Science Monthly* for November 1896, is a fine example of the fully developed woodcut technique in American magazine illustration.

The United States brig *Washington* had the ill luck to be engaged in surveying the coast and shoals off Cape Hatteras on September 8, 1846, when a hurricane arrived. Whether the Law of Storms was understood by her officers is not hinted at in the record of the consequent disaster. Since her task kept her close to shore, she may not have been able to claw off when evidence of the approaching storm's nature became apparent. A. Hoffy's unusual lithograph of the scene was advertised as having been done "under the immediate supervision of some surviving officers." It thus makes a special claim to authority as a contemporaneous view. When a hurricane's center followed the coast a bit offshore, the wind was first felt as a northeast storm which blew with increasing violence, against the shore, until the center had passed. The normal reaction would have been to stand offshore on the port tack, but this piece of routine prudence, in a circular storm, would probably have drawn the vessel right into the hurricane's eye.

THE YANKEE PACKET SHIPS

FED UP WITH CONSTANT TAMPERING WITH HIS OFFICIAL MAIL, WHEN IT HAD TO BE CARRIED in British and French vessels, Thomas Jefferson wrote to Richard Henry Lee, from Paris, on July 12, 1785, proposing the establishment of a line of American packets between New York and Havre: "To send a packet from each port once in two months, the business might possibly be done by two packets, as will be seen by the following scheme, wherein we will call the two packets A. and B.

> Jan. A. sails from New York, B. from Havre.
> Feb.
> Mar. B. New York. A. Havre.
> Apr.
> May A. New York. B. Havre.
> June.
> July B. New York. A. Havre.
> Aug.
> Sep. A. New York. B. Havre.
> Oct.
> Nov. B. New York. A. Havre.
> Dec."

He thought the French could be persuaded to send their packets in the intervening months, and that this would provide "a safe conveiance every two months" for his official mail, and greater regularity for all mails. It would look, he wrote, like the beginning of a small navy (a matter thus shown to have been on his mind a year in advance of the Barbary crisis that caused his exchange of views with Adams on naval policy). A navy, he reminded Lee, would be "the only kind of force we ought to possess." He opposed a standing army as firmly as he favored a small navy "in constant cruise." He had a twelve-year wait for the first launchings of the fighting ships he had advocated, and 33 years had passed between his

LEFT. The *Francis Depau*, of the Havre Old Line, flung ashore by the violence of the gale as she entered the French port on March 28, 1836. The ship *Harriet & Jessie* of Charleston slipped in. When built in 1833 by Brown & Bell, the *Francis Depau*, of 595 tons, was one of the ten largest packets in service. RIGHT. Christian Bergh's little shipyard, at the corner of Water Street, as seen by the artist William Chappel in 1809—a year or so after he had produced five gunboats for the Navy. Bergh's design, which used the "perry-auger" rig popular in New York harbor, was followed in the building of nine more gunboats in other New York shipyards. Ten years after this picture was made, Bergh launched the *Bayard*, the first of thirty-one packets which he built for the major lines.

ABOVE. The Smith & Dimon shipyard at the foot of Fourth Street, New York, as painted by James Pringle in 1833. In that year the *United States*, 650 tons, the largest packet so far, was launched here. Smith & Dimon had built three of the early packets, the *Corinthian*, the *Howard* and the *Florida*, all in 1822, and all for different lines. Later the yard launched four of the most famous clippers: the *Rainbow*, the *Sea Witch*, the *Memnon*, and the *Mandarin*. A year after Pringle painted the above picture, Stephen Smith, senior partner in Smith & Dimon, launched on his own account the *Independence* of 734 tons. This painting was made in 1836 by the British artist Samuel Walters. The scene is the English Channel. The *Independence* once ran from New York to Liverpool in fifteen days. Here she is flying the blue swallowtail of the fourth Liverpool line. After 1847 she flew for five years the red swallowtail of the London line. She was wrecked in the China Sea in 1862.

The Collins's Dramatic Line packet *Roscius,* not dramatically speedy, but reliable for fifteen years in the service. She was built by Brown & Bell in 1838. Another lithograph from a Walters painting.

recommendation and the actual founding of the first Atlantic packet line which as a matter of policy was to keep to a fixed schedule.

"Packet-boats" had been in use, and so called, since the middle of the seventeenth century, usually as government-owned carriers of the mails and of important passengers. For such vessels, sailings on a reasonably steady schedule were not new, between nearby ports of England and the European continent. When conditions in the colonies had made it desirable, monthly sailings on His Majesty's business to America had been provided for, but it had long been understood that there was no obligation to put out into angry weather. Lesser excuses often caused delays.

Americans, here again, did not invent anything really new in the Yankee packets. They improved upon an indifferently managed prior arrangement, gave it an almost absolute reliability, developed better ships, and soon were commanding premium rates which more than offset the predicted losses implicit in a policy of sailing on the dot, "full or not full." The repute of the packet liners actually guaranteed, over long periods, that they would not be the losers by such a policy. All passenger and cargo space often was taken, for an upcoming outward voyage, before the vessel arrived from its last one.

The service began with the Black Ball Line of four ships: the *Pacific, Amity, Courier,* and *James Monroe,* owned by five associated merchants. The last was the largest, 424 tons. All but the *Pacific,* which was eleven years old, had been launched within a year or two, and all but the *Amity* became whalers when a demand for more spacious packets developed. As a whaler, the very first packet, the *Pacific,* completed the longest career of any of them—seventy-five years in all. She was a Black Baller for only one of these years. The *Courier* might have proved as durable, but she was sunk deliberately with the "stone fleet" in the Civil War, in an attempt to block up the entrance into Charleston.

It was the original schedule that a Black Ball liner would sail from Liverpool for New

The great storm of January 7 and 8, 1839, off Liverpool. The blue Swallowtail *Pennsylvania*, left fore-water, with her flag inverted, was lost. The Red Star liner *St. Andrew*, extreme left, was wrecked a day or two later. A lithograph by T. Fairland after Samuel Walters.

York on the 1st of every month, and then another would sail from New York on the 5th. The schedule recognized the difference in average time to be expected between the "down-hill" and "uphill" passages, with or against the prevailing westerly winds. After ten years the line published an analysis of passages indicating a highly predictable time for the eastbound Atlantic crossing: almost always between 18 and 26 days. The westbound passages were more varied in length, and averaged 38 days. Consequently the sailing date from New York had been shifted from the 5th to the 10th of the month. The Black Ball Line operated 39 regular packets during the great packet period, ending with 1855. William H. Webb built the last ten packets acquired by the line during this period. Of these, three were still in use in 1878 when the Black Ball Line ended its operations: the *Isaac Webb, Great Western,* and *James Foster, Jr.* A fourth, the *Columbia* (II), was registered out of San Francisco in 1887. The *Yorkshire,* the first of this group of ten to be supplied, was launched in 1843 and "went missing" in 1862. It seems likely that she met a Confederate raider, but no record of the occurrence has turned up. She was consistently the fastest of the packets, and made one astonishing westbound passage in 15 days.

The Black Ballers increased steadily in size, from the *Courier* of 381 tons to the *Charles H. Marshall* of 1,683, built by Webb in 1869. In nearly every case the line's newest ship was a little larger than the last one. Ten of the best Black Ball liners were built by Brown & Bell.

Two competitors for the Liverpool packet business began operations in 1822—the Red Star and Blue Swallowtail Lines. They had respectively about 21 and 25 packets in service in the great period. Both ended their service in 1867; the latter transferred some of its ships to the London Red Swallowtail Line. The *St. Andrew,* built by Christian Bergh in 1835, and the *John R. Skiddy,* built by Donald McKay ten years later, were among the well-known Red Star liners. The Blue Swallowtail ships included the *Henry Clay,* launched by Brown & Bell in 1845, and Donald McKay's *New World* of 1,404 tons, a huge ship for the time, launched the year following.

The Dramatic Line began operations to Liverpool in 1836, by acquiring the *Shakespeare,* a former New Orleans packet, and then ordering others from Brown & Bell, her builders. The first four of these also were given dramatic names: *Garrick, Sheridan, Siddons,* and *Roscius.* The Liverpool New Line operated more briefly than the others, from 1843 to 1849, when the surviving four of its five ships were acquired by the Blue Swallowtail.

Liverpool, as the most accessible major British port, got most of the earlier packet business. But the third line to be established was the London Black X, in 1824, just ahead of the Blue Swallowtail. The Black X packets operated for forty-five years, despite the disadvantage in time of having to bite their way up the English Channel and to cope with the tides of the Thames. Most of the ships were built by Christian Bergh and by J. A. Westervelt and his partners. The *Devonshire* and *Ocean Queen* were Westervelt products.

The Blue Swallowtail packet *Henry Clay,* 1,207 tons, was said at her launch to be the largest merchant ship afloat. Later she went ashore with three hundred immigrants on the same beach where the *John Minturn* came to grief, but Captain Ezra Nye saved all of the *Henry Clay's* people with a breeches buoy, and got her off to continue as a packet until 1865.

The packet ship *Devonshire*, 1,149 tons, built in 1848 by Westervelt & Mackey for the Black X line, in which she served thirteen years. Her best westward passage, 19 days, has seldom been bettered. Her thirteen-year average of 30 days for all westbound passages was bettered only by the *Yorkshire*'s 29 and the *Amazon*'s 28.

The Red Swallowtail Line, also founded in the enterprising year 1824, but slower to expand its service, was the other London line. Among its distinctions was to end operations in 1880 with the old *Liverpool* (II) still in service. She had begun in 1843 in the Liverpool New Line, from 1849 to 1855 had flown the Blue Swallowtail, and then for twenty-five years had worn the red one to complete the longest continuous liner service on record.

Lines to Havre were started in 1822 and 1823, the "Old" and the "Second" Lines. The first was discouraged out of business by the Civil War, when it sold its surviving ships to Norway and England. The second kept two or three ships moving in a desultory way until 1870. The Havre record is complicated by the founding of a third line, also in 1823, by William Whitlock, Jr., who unlike the other packet enterprisers for a while preferred to operate without partners, but later placed his ships in service with those of the "Old" Line, which became known as the "Union" line.

A number of coastal packet lines also were founded in the early 1820s, operating out of New York to the cotton ports, sometimes with a triangular service by way of England. Two served Charleston, one Savannah, and four New Orleans. Mobile and other ports had intermittent packet service, but in the case of Mobile particularly the temptation to make the trade triangular discouraged the feature that made a packet line distinguishable as such: a schedule of sailings which, blow high, blow low, was really maintained, full or not full.

ABOVE. Havre was the terminal for two famous New York packet lines. Some features of this unidentified painting of an American ship making sail suggests that she is a Havre packet, and that the time is the early 1840s. BELOW. New Orleans, terminal for the coastal packets. The first line was established in 1831, and three others followed. The four employed nearly a hundred ships. The Megarey view, painted by W. J. Bennett from a sketch by A. Mondelli.

Transition
to Steam

The large colored lithograph reproduced above, sold in three sections
and measuring more than 2 x 5 feet,
was the work of Thomas Thompson
about 1828. The scene is New York
harbor, from the walk just east of
the Battery, looking toward Castle
William a little to the left of center. Two Black Ball packets are
discernible, with the distinctive
symbol on their foretopsails. One
little steam ferry appears in the
right-hand panel. Otherwise the
scene belongs to sail. The hard-
driving Yankee packets had attained a remarkable reputation and
were to hold it for two more decades despite the steady improvement in steamers, until the steamship men realized that reliability of
schedules was the most significant
factor in the competition. When the
Cunard Line commenced its regularly scheduled sailings in 1848, the
heyday of the canvas-propelled
Yankee packets began to fade.

ARTIST AS PIRATE

The extremely rare print below celebrates the "ARRIVAL OF THE GREAT WESTERN STEAM SHIP, OFF NEW YORK ON MONDAY 23rd APRIL 1838." It resembles the work of Robert Cruikshank. The suggestion has been made that the largely Pickwickian characters in the foreground are there to celebrate the arrival in New York of Charles Dickens on his first reading tour. If so, the print was published four years after the event its label celebrates. No publisher's name appears at the usual point, but the sign at the left bears the name of W. & H. Cave of Manchester, Engravers. A comparison with the picture at the left develops the pleasing coincidence that nearly every vessel present in New York harbor ten years earlier had returned to welcome the *Great Western*, and had managed to get back into the same spot on the same tack. Appropriately, the principal Black Baller of the Thompson picture has been replaced by the competing steamship.

De Bry expected his public to accept this scene as a picture of the building of a caravel by the shipwrecked Lope de Olano, on the Veragua coast of Panama, in 1510.

T IS NOT SURPRISING THAT ARTISTS LIKE TO DRAW WHAT THEY CAN clearly see, especially when fulfilling assignments in which they may be criticized for technical inaccuracy. The initial illustration at the left appears frequently in old nautical books, with minor changes of style and clothing, and often reversed to indicate that the copier worked directly on wood. No harm in that: some casters of the lead were lefties, and some had to behave as if they were. But an artist dependent upon an earlier model may misrepresent details of the vessel itself, in a later context. This was done by the poor methodical soul who used a century-old English model for the picture on page 117, to promote the building of an American ship of the line in the late 1790s.

For those who seek the elusive truth of nautical history in pictures, the main difficulties arise when an artist of superior talents chooses a poor model in his very search for accuracy. The two engravings facing each other above provide an example. The one at the left, by De Bry, has been reproduced in a number of books with the inference that it is the earliest, or one of the earliest, scenes of shipbuilding in the Americas. Published in the 1594 edition of the *Collectio navigationum in Indiam Occidentalem . . .* , it purports to show Lope de Olano building a caravel in Panama in 1510 from the timbers of his own wrecked vessel. E. Keble Chatterton, in *Old Ship Prints,* says of it: "Possibly de Bry got his details from some Flemish shipyard, where he sketched the ship in frame, the callipers, the axes, and the fire as they actually stood. But, in any case, this is just the print one is glad to possess if one really desires to have first-hand information about the sixteenth century and its sea adventures."

De Bry's source was not a shipyard. The engraving at the right, of which his is a partial mirror image implying direct copying on the metal, is the work of J. Sadeler, published eight years earlier than the De Bry. Moreover, Sadeler did what De Bry omitted to do; he acknowledged his source. Beneath the feet of the principal figure appears the credit line "M. de vos figur"—and the original painting by De Vos is one of a series of

Noah and his sons building the Ark. A print published eight years earlier than De Bry's. Engraved by J. Sadeler from a painting by M. De Vos. Note that De Bry, where he did not copy exactly, transmuted some of the forms of his model, the ship's timbers being heaped somewhat in the fashion of the pile of logs.

biblical scenes, this one of Noah and his sons building the Ark, an enterprise somewhat removed in time, space, and technology from Olano's remarkable achievement in Panama. The tools in use comport well enough with those in less fancifully conceived scenes of early shipbuilding. The frame seems a bit quaint.

In spite of its absurdities, De Bry's picture merits close study as an embodiment of several aspects of the problem of historical veracity. We might well begin with his own protestation in his introduction to Hariot's *Briefe and True Report* . . . , 1588. "I ask most earnestly that if anyone else should be found attempting to pirate this book of mine (for nowadays there are many dishonest people who try to get the benefit of another's work), that no credit should be given to the counterfeit copy, for I have put many secret marks in my drawings which will certainly cause confusion if omitted."

Yet his own later work contains instances not only of the sort of partial copying evident in the Olano plate, but also entire plates nearly identical with those of earlier engravers. Note his mirror-image pirating (page 20) of what Chatterton calls an "unseamanlike" allegorical plate of Columbus, with its "anchor lying foul of a gun." (The best work on prints pertaining to America, prepared by I. N. Phelps Stokes and Daniel C. Haskell, confuses the record concerning this Columbus plate in its very first entry. Describing the Vespucci plate engraved by Collaert [page 21], Stokes and Haskell identify it as belonging to a set of four, including one of Columbus, and go on to refer to "An interesting picture of Columbus" by De Bry without any hint that it was pirated from the one they have just mentioned.) Except for a slight difference in the facial expression of Columbus, and the omission of the name CHRISTOPH. COLVMB. from the deck, the De Bry plate is a close inverse copy of Collaert's.

In the fascinating world of De Bry we have to find our own balance between truth as he personally thought he observed it, artistic selection as all able artists consciously prac-

231

tice it, conventionalities taken for granted by viewers of his era—and on top of all this the fallibilities of a vastly productive worker who did not always practice what he preached. In much that he produced, De Bry had nothing to guide him but a traveler's terse narrative, as was the case with the Olano scene. He had to be completely imaginative or to follow a model that came to hand. His choice, this time of a silly one, was made easier by the Renaissance habit of portraying classical or biblical persons in contemporary European garb: not a conscious falsification, not even a failure of research, but more probably a device of realism. We can perhaps forgive De Bry for duplicating the absurd frame. The tools are all right. But in the human beings he departed wildly from his own script. That he tried to follow it elsewhere with care is all the more reason for noting this. The truth of the scene, as the account De Bry himself printed along with it explicitly states, is that the men who built the caravel were starving to the point of cannibalism. The exceedingly well-fed Flemings who had originally posed for De Vos, in the guise of Noah and his sons, were poor models for castaways in Panama. They should have been left behind with the stork-surmounted castle.

Another convention is brought to notice by the wrecked vessel at the right. Are we really to believe that these castaways, who had brought their caravel to an advanced stage of construction, had left a wrecked vessel nearby with her sails set and her rigging intact? Would these not have been salvaged? Would there have been time and men for the simultaneous construction of houses, and for the development of agriculture? These details are one of the many instances, in old pictures, of collapsed time. It was not until photographers established our new habit of looking at pictures as being of simultaneous occurrence in all their parts that other artists gave up the ancient practice of putting a sequence of events into a single scene. Here the wreck is shown at the moment of striking; her timbers are being salvaged below, after she had shattered; the houses are going up on a later day; the husbandry is caught still later; and the shipbuilding occurs last of all. This was not falsification of the scene—it was the expected treatment, but we need to be aware of it to offset our post-photographic provincialism.

One who wishes to compare De Bry's engravings conveniently against some of their

A change of sex. The pirate Mary Read, killing a man in a duel (*Pirates Own Book*), becomes Captain Kidd in the *Pearl Songster* of 1849.

The picture on the opposite page is a detail from a print of the *Chesapeake-Shannon* action by W. Elmes published in London about two months after the event. It is referred to by the great collector A. G. H. Macpherson as the rarest print of the War of 1812. He called it "rather a crude aquatint." The equivalent portion of an undated mirror-image mezzotint from a painting by W. B. Walker, turned by an unnamed engraver into an even cruder print, follows many details of the probable original.

models may do so in *The New World,* 1946, a handsome book edited and annotated by Stefan Lorant. Here the John White watercolors of Virginia are reproduced in color together with the engravings De Bry made from them. "I copied exactly," De Bry claimed, "from the originals themselves." The copies are faithful to the data, but White's easy naturalism has been replaced by formal, balanced groupings. A sense of rude geometry is suggested in some of the native structures drawn by White. De Bry has made them geometrically precise. Six strings of beads on the model become four—a sort of change which might be disturbing to the inquiring nautical technologist if it were made, for example, in the rigging of a vessel he was trying to identify. The distinctly Indian faces drawn from the life by White are in De Bry's prints Europeanized.

Such factors mar the accuracy of many old pictures that may have been prepared with no intent to falsify. The artist as pirate is sometimes only trying to help us. The Dickensian print of New York harbor on pages 228 and 229 perhaps shows a commendable impulse to use with precision the most recent data available. Nevertheless, all of these considerations reinforce the advisability of holding as closely as possible to the contemporaneous view prepared by an eyewitness, or by an artist who had to satisfy a patron or purchasers who would be critical of any error.

The plate at the left, by George Cruikshank, was published in *Greenwich Hospital* in 1825. The partial piracy at the right is from Samuel F. Holbrook's reminiscences, published in 1857.

THE NAVY
BETWEEN WARS

IKE MOST FIGHTING SERVICES WITH NO FIGHTING TO DO, THE UNITED States Navy went in for spit, polish, and ceremony in home waters and became embroiled in truculent episodes afar in which some of its less self-disciplined disciplinarians worked off their frustrations. The brief interlude of the war against Mexico offered no opportunities for glory on the seas. One of the first historians of that conflict judged that Mexico's only chance for a successful resistance was thrown away when the Navy landed 12,000 troops without any opposition at Vera Cruz. There is a picture of the operation on page 239.

The superfrigate *Liberator* was built in 1826 by Smith & Dimon for Greek revolutionaries who could not pay the bill. Political pressures seem to have been employed to unload her on the Navy, which was unappreciative of her substantial virtues as a result. Renamed the *Hudson,* she was permitted by the annoyed commissioners to make but one cruise, from which she is here shown returning. BELOW. The city of Washington prior to 1833, with the Navy Yard at the right. One of the sparkling Bennett series of views of American cities.

The death of Commodore Bainbridge in 1833, which brought forth this memorial print, was symbolic of the death of the old Navy of prideful independent initiative. Congress, as so often has been the case, had been authorizing more generously than it had been appropriating. Although he had commanded the Philadelphia and Charleston Navy Yards, and had ended his ardent service as Chief of the Board of Naval Commissioners, it was only in the year of his death that the Navy got the first of the dry docks he had wanted. The stone dry dock of these lithographs, at the Gosport Navy Yard, was begun in 1827. The *Delaware*, 74, laid down in 1817 and commissioned in 1820, was the first of our naval vessels ever to enter a dry dock belonging to the United States. The date was June 17, 1833, and the event was celebrated in a pair of progressive-action prints from sketches made by Joseph Goldsborough Bruff, dedicated to Colonel Loammi Baldwin, in charge of construction. Note the men at the capstan in the upper print, drawing the ship into the dock with a cable.

Vessels of the United States
Mediterranean squadron in the
roadstead off Naples, 1835.

The construction and use of the first-rate ship *Pennsylvania*, 120 guns, the largest sailing vessel ever to join the United States Navy, are a commentary upon the state of the service. She spent her first fifteen years getting built, before her commissioning in 1837, and was laid up in ordinary much of the time afterward, not excluding the day in 1861 when—to prevent capture—she burned at the Norfolk Navy Yard, together with the frigate *United States* and nine other naval vessels.

Bainbridge, the early Navy's youngest captain, was probably most distinguished career officer. Commodore Charles Stewart (below) served creditably without having the luck to encounter a first class antagonist at sea. Shown here in 1840, aged sixty-two, he still had a long career ahead. He was made a rear admiral twenty-two years later, during the Civil War. LOWER LEFT. A seaman and passed midshipman of the early 1840s. They seem conscious that the Navy had little at the time to do.

Low ebb for the valiant repute of the United States Navy, afloat and ashore, occurred on December 1, 1842, and in the months thereafter during which the establishment closed ranks and exonerated a timorous fanatic named Alexander Slidell Mackenzie who was so alarmed by an alleged plot of mutiny among the youngsters under his command on a training cruise that he hanged three of them from the main yard of the United States Brig *Somers*. No actual mutiny had occurred. The oldest of the three plotters was seventeen. Most of the boys aboard were even younger. Commander Mackenzie had exacerbated them, as the court-martial testimony indicates, by the stupid brutalities of a martinet. They worked off some of their resentment by schoolboy plottings of dire revenge. There was no comfort to their families in wondering what would have happened if one of Preble's boys had been in command. But a career service seems unable to avoid the occasional acquiring of a Sterett or a Mackenzie.

ow. The United States frigate *Macedonian* in New York harbor, August 1843. This is not the ship captured by the *United States* but an entirely structure built with appropriations provided to repair her. This may be reason why she took four years, 1832 to 1836, to complete at the Nor- Navy Yard. She was very fast but overgunned, and eventually cut down corvette.

ABOVE. The Yankee tar, in the uniform of the 1840s, lithographically sentimentalized in the aura of victories of his father's day. The naval action under his tarred hat is a fairly close mirror image of Birch's picture of the action between the *Constitution* and the *Guerrière*.

Seven years to the month before Commodore Perry's visit that changed the destiny of Japan, Commodore James Biddle made a preliminary attempt. Fresh from negotiating the first United States treaty with China, he entered the Bay of Yedo on July 20, 1846. "The commanders were politely requested to land their guns, ammunition, muskets & everything in the shape of a weapon, which request was as politely refused. . . . The visit altogether was one of the most novel kind. The people polite, amiable and exceedingly jealous of their customs, and adhered strictly to the long established one of not receiving the slightest remuneration for anything that they gave. The visitors were politely informed that as soon as their wants were made known they would be attended to and that done they were desired to leave and never to return again. . . . hundreds of Japanese visited the Ships and, to hasten their departure, formed a line of several hundred boats to tow the vessels out to sea, and left rejoicing that they had rid themselves so easily of such a number of barbarians." So says the graceful script of the label, identical on both pictures. As for authority, they are identified as having been drawn and lithographed from sketches by John Eastley, an eyewitness. The ships are the *Columbus*, 74, and the *Vincennes*, a ship-sloop of the second class. The former, second of her name in the service, was laid down in 1816, built in the quick time, for the period, of three years, and burned in the general holocaust at Norfolk in 1861 that did so much to terminate the sailing Navy. The *Vincennes*, built in 1825–1826, survived the Civil War only to be sold at Boston in 1867.

During the war made by the United States against Mexico in 1846, the Navy had almost no opposition afloat. Many of its ships were used to transport the troops commanded by General Winfield Scott which took Vera Cruz as a coastal base and then fought their way up to the high valley of Mexico. The lithograph above shows a phase of the landing, on March 9, 1847. Commodore David Conner directed operations from his flagship, the *Raritan* frigate, which had been twenty-three years on the stocks before launching in 1843. The two little steamers, at the center and the far left, were the *Spitfire* and the *Vixen*—detailed to cover the landing in water shallower than feasible for the sailing ships to enter. It must also unhappily be admitted that the larger *Princeton,* steam sloop of war, had led the armada of about a hundred vessels toward the beaches with the sailing flagship in tow. General Scott was aboard the steamer *Massachusetts.* The fleet was the largest yet assembled under the United States flag. The operation marked the first use of American naval steamers in warfare. The landing was unopposed. About two weeks later Conner was relieved by Commodore Matthew Calbraith Perry, who—restive under the task of blockading an enemy incapable of offering any resistance afloat—decided to assault Tuxpan, about 150 miles north of Vera Cruz, on a narrow river. Sail again was subordinate. Steamers hauled gunboats across the bar. Perry led the expedition (below) in the steamer *Spitfire*. Having taken the town and demolished the forts, he left the ship-sloop *Albany* and the gunboat *Reefer* to garrison the position.

NAVAL OPERATIONS in the WAR Against MEXICO

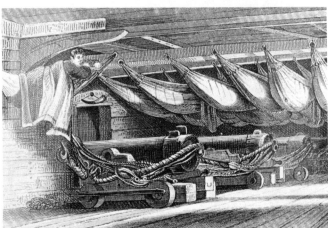

Space had to be intensively utilized in a fighting ship. Men and guns shared sleeping quarters.

The Gosport, later the Norfolk, Navy Yard in 1853. Eight years later the better part of the sailing Navy was burned here to prevent its use by the rebels.

SAVANNAH.   PRINCETON.   POWHATAN   SHIP HOUSES.   FRIGATE COLUMBIA.   NAVY YARD ENTRANCE.   GOSPORT.
ALLEGHANY.   UNITED STATES.

VIEW OF THE UNITED STATES NAVY YARD, AT GOSPORT, OPPOSITE NO

1. Furling sail
2. Poop on quarter-deck
3. Bobstays
4. Figurehead
5. Lowering a cask
6. Surgical inspection
7. Captain's cabin
8. Captain's dining saloon
9. Galley
10. Midshipmen's cabin
11. Sailors' berths
12. Exercising the guns
13. Officers' cabins
14. Wardroom
15. Dressing a wound
16. Musket exercise
17. Sailors' mess-room
18. Mending sails
19. Provision room
20. Sick bay
21. Lowering boat
22. Sail and cordage room
23. Prison
24. Shot magazine
25. Spirit room
26. Powder magazine
27. Blocks, pulleys, etc.
28. General store-room
29. Casks and tanks
30. Dunnage

Gleason's magazine, of Boston, provided its readers in 1854 with carefully charted views of both the externals and innards of naval vessels. A substantial reduction in the size of the picture of the United States line-of-battle ship at upper left makes it seem inadvisable to append the list of technical information to which more than 150 little figures and letters refer the curious and diligent. Above is a woodcut of "an American man-of-war cut open amidships."

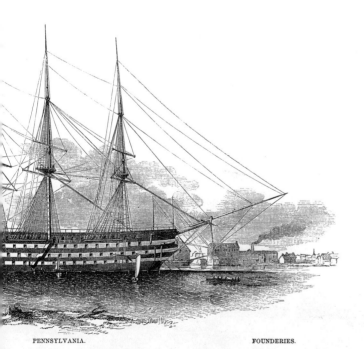

PENNSYLVANIA. FOUNDERIES.

Deck of an American line-of-battle ship.

The United States sloop of war *St. Louis* lying in the harbor of Smyrna on July 2, 1853, beside the Austrian brig of war *Huszar*. A Hungarian revolutionary named Martin Koszta, after taking the first steps toward becoming a United States citizen, had been seized by the Austrians and confined in chains in the *Huszar*. When diplomatic protests proved vain, Commander Duncan C. Ingraham of the *St. Louis* announced that at four o'clock, if Koszta had not been released, he would open fire. The lithograph shows the prisoner coming over the side, in good time. Ingraham, who despite violent protests from Austria was sustained by his government and voted a medal by Congress, abandoned his allegiance eight years later and attained the rank of commodore in the Confederate Navy. LEFT. Commander Ingraham. BELOW. The *St. Louis* at Spezia, a month later, together with the heavy frigate *Cumberland* which had been launched only in the preceding year, although work had begun on her in 1825. The depicted grand ball aboard her was so well attended by minor royalty that an old tar reported, "I beg pardon, commodore, but I thought you'd like to know as how one of them 'ere blasted kings has fell down the hatchway." In a time of accumulating naval-diplomatic incidents, it is fortunate that the "blasted king" was uninjured. The *Cumberland*, razeed to a sloop of war, was sunk by the rebel ram *Virginia* in the general death of the sailing Navy.

242

1856:
The Navy
AFAR

Again, the rough charm of the primitive. "The Perilous Situation of the U.S. Frigate SAVANNAH, off Fort Santa Cruz, Rio Janeiro, at 9.15 P.M. July the 5th, 1856." She was one of the delayed 44s, on the stocks twenty-two years before her launch in 1842. A print made from drawings by John Fuller and Augustus Bunse, evidently crew members. LEFT. The *Macedonian* II off Hong Kong, February 2, 1856. Compare the picture on page 237, made before she had been razeed to a ship-sloop, her armament reduced from 36 to 22 guns. BELOW. The ship-sloops *Portsmouth* (first class) and *Levant* (second class) attacking the barrier forts below Canton during the T'ai P'ing Rebellion. The *Levant* went missing in 1860. The *Portsmouth* was not sold out of the service until 1915.

COMMODORE TATNALL VISITING THE BRITISH ADMIRAL IN THE MIDDLE OF THE ACTION.

"BLOOD IS THICKER THAN WATER"

THE FAMOUS PHRASE DOES NOT APPEAR IN THE FIRST DISPATCH FROM THE U.S.S. *Powhatan,* dated June 29, 1859, and printed in *Harper's Weekly* for October 8th. The Pei Ho forts, destroyed in actions in which the *Portsmouth* and *Levant* had earlier participated, were rumored to have been secretly rebuilt as an aid to nullifying the treaties forced by the West upon China. Some British gunboats under Rear Admiral Hope probed the Pearl River to find out. They were so badly shattered that Hope, wounded himself, sent to ask the American Commodore Josiah Tatnall to tow the British reserves up to the scene of action. *Harper's* quotes Tatnall's reasoning:

"If I tow up the reserves, I at once engage in a hostile act against China, with whom my country is at peace. If I refuse, I leave the wounded admiral and his handful of men at the mercy of ten thousand treacherous cowards . . . Away with every consideration save those of humanity! I cannot stand quietly and see such wholesale butchery."

Having complied, "The Flag-officer . . . got into his barge to visit the wounded Admiral. . . . Round shot and grape tore the water along the boat's course . . . at the side of the *Cormorant,* . . . one of the former struck her on the quarter, wounded mortally the cockswain, and blew away the whole stern."

Harper's woodcut was made "from a sketch by our own correspondent." As a result of Tatnall's co-operation, the "wholesale butchery" which he had sought to prevent was redoubled. The relieving force was smashed as badly as the first one.

Harper's noted editorially that even if the government censured Tatnall "it must, at the same time, applaud him for services rendered in the cause of humanity"—evidently identifying "humanity" with persons of European extraction. Of those who were trying to defend their coasts against the opium sellers primarily, it concluded, "When will the masses of the western world arrive at a true idea of Chinese duplicity and rascality?"

Fortune plagued Tatnall with opportunities for other calamitous choices. Some may have been unavoidable, but in the basic one there was again an element of blindness toward the humanity of persons who did not chance to be white. Like Ingraham, in 1861 he joined the rebellion against the Union he had sworn to defend. Later he had to destroy his command, the Confederate ram *Merrimack,* to avoid capture. His defense of Savannah was unsuccessful, and he was obliged there to destroy his entire fleet.

Some Wrecks & Rescues

"Dreadful wreck of the Mexico on Hempstead Beach, Jany. 2nd 1837." Probably the first print by N. Currier. It seems to have been an advertisement for a new addition to "Haningtons Dioramas."

Wreck of the *Bristol,* also in 1837, near Rockaway, Long Island. An oil by Thomas Chambers.

A Currier lithograph of nine years later. Wreck of the ship *John Minturn* on the New Jersey coast, February 15, 1846. Of the fifty-one persons aboard, thirty-eight were drowned or frozen to death in the rigging while looters prowled the beach. The artistry, still crude, is improving.

The caption of this picture (right) of the Liverpool packet *Cornelius Grinnell,* published in *Gleason's Pictorial* in 1852 when she was two years old, called her "by all odds the strongest ship of her size ever built" in the vicinity of her home port, New York. Actually she was built in East Boston, Massachusetts, by Donald McKay. Her sturdiness was proved when *Gleason's,* a year later, published the opposite picture of her wreck on Squam beach, noting "the vessel will probably be an entire loss." But McKay built strong ships indeed. She continued in service for twenty-eight more years.

Strength was no guarantee against fire. McKay built the *Ocean Monarch* for Enoch Train's White Diamond Line of Liverpool packets. She had been in service scarcely a year when an emigrant lit a cooking fire in a ventilator. It roared out of control. Still in the sight of the English coast, she burned with a loss of about four hundred lives.

246

The interest of Currier & Ives in matters nautical developed a pair of mutually inconsistent trends. One was the sentimentalized, incomparably unrealistic scene, often treated in balanced or sequential pairs (why sell one print when you can just as well unload two?); the other an increasingly strict and careful delineation of the structure of particular vessels. The difference came, of course, from differing perceptions and abilities of their several artists, and from an appreciation of what was wanted by different sorts of buyers.

SHIPWRECK OF THE PACKET SHIP CORNELIUS GRINNELL, ON SQUAM BEACH

Boston early became known as the "market town of the West Indies." Toward the middle of the nineteenth century its citizens, with an enlarged confidence, adopted a local writer's phrase: "Hub of the Universe." This is part of a print made in 1841 by Robert Havell, three years prior to the establishment of a new spoke for the Hub, its first transatlantic packet line. In this activity, the center of the universe lagged twenty-six years behind the port that had long ago become the real hub of American commerce: New York.

Georgetown in British Guiana, on the Demarara River, in 1840, a thriving port at the end of one old spoke thrust seaward from the hub of Boston. Rosenberg's aquatint after Huggins.

Enoch Train brought Boston into the regular Liverpool packet competition in 1844, employing a rising mechanic named Donald McKay to build six ships. The first of them was the *Joshua Bates*.

A New Spoke for the HUB of the UNIVERSE

The Major and a Minor Terminal for New York's Packet Lines

LEFT. Passengers coming ashore from a Black Ball packet at Liverpool in 1841. A line engraving by Carter after Chambers. ABOVE. The famous Black Ball packet *Yorkshire* in the Mersey off Liverpool, 1846—the year in which she made the uphill voyage to New York in 15 days. BELOW. The coastal packet service from New York to Mobile was less regular than that to New Orleans, partly because it was economically desirable to operate a triangular trade in which the ships took cotton and passengers to Europe before returning to New York. This is the water-color drawing by William Todd from which W. J. Bennett made an engraving in 1842 for his series of views of American cities.

A Bostonian Wedding of Sail & Steam: 1845

Robert Bennett Forbes of Boston was an inveterate, empirical Yankee experimenter, often credited with having been the original inventor of a double-topsail rig. In this packet, the *Massachusetts,* launched in 1845, he tried double topsails and a screw propeller too, at a time when practically all sizable steamers still used paddle wheels. Note the odd structure of the afterdeck, another view of which can be had below. She was crippled on her first return voyage to her home port, but made better time than any of the paddle-wheelers in that boisterous season. Her engine was intended mainly as an auxiliary, for use in getting into and out of port.

ODDITIES Of 1846 And 1847

It is a fair inference that this sort of primitive lithograph, dated 1846, is probably more accurate than a reworked and artistically better finished one because the lithographer seems to have followed a painstaking eyewitness sketch. Note that the picture brings together two scenes different in their timing. Leonard A. Curtis is being shot aboard the whaler at the same moment when his coffin is being conveyed toward the church. Lest a doubt arise, the print bears beneath the boat and church the small label "Funeral of Leonard A. Curtis." Captain Isaac Ludlow is credited on another occasion with having lost an entire whaling season in order to carry a hundred British castaways to a place of adequate safety.

The Chinese junk *Keying* turned up in New York harbor in 1847, on July 8th or 9th. The news accounts vary, probably because of the difference between sea and land time. Her Chinese crew promptly attached her in court. When this difficulty was settled by payments of from $100 to $200 apiece, she was exhibited at New York and Boston before sailing for London. She is said to have crossed the Atlantic in 21 days. She measured over 750 tons, not counting her 9-ton mainsail of matting. At the wharf is a newly arrived immigrant ship, if we may judge by the label on one of the boxes, PAT MURFY for AMERIKY.

GOLD!

Few clippers were in port to be diverted from the China trade in the early days of the Gold Rush. The luckier argonauts went out in sturdy little ships like the *Mechanics' Own*. I find no record of her time on her first voyage, carrying genuine forty-niners, but she is later reported as having made voyages of 150 and 155 days, about average for the better vessels of her size. She measured 541 tons.

Early in the Gold Rush the harbor of San Francisco was crowded with ships deserted by their crews. The streets were sparsely peopled too, because no-one lingered any longer than he had to on the way to the diggings. This chromolithograph was published in London by M. and N. Hanhart. No date is given, but 1849 is likely.

California soil was valuable not only for gold dust. Building lots at the bay's edge were costly. More of it was made by dumping fill around stranded ships which before long found themselves situated well inland. BELOW. Those who had abandoned their vessels to rot in the mud often discovered that the gold they had won would not buy them a passage home again. N. Currier seems to have anticipated the situation in this print published in 1849.

THE WAY THEY COME FROM CALIFORNIA.

Experiences of those who found time, after the gold fever had abated a bit, to take the bouncy voyage out to the Farallones, off the Golden Gate, for a visit to the sea lions.

On the belly of this "used-up man" the words are written—"My Claim failed. Will you pay the tax." A large proportion of the sailors who deserted their ships ended with nothing to show for their labors, or were quickly relieved of what they got by the more cannily enterprising gold diggers of San Francisco. From *Pen Knife Sketches; or Chips of the Old Block,* a charming paperback published in Sacramento in 1853 for Alonzo Delano, who turned from gold panning to selling cabbages and quickly became a banker.

CLIPPER SHIP GENIUS

PERHAPS THE MOST SIGNIFICANT FEATURE OF THE PERIOD WHICH HAS LONG BEEN CALLED the "Clipper Ship Era" is the swiftness and confidence with which the new American kind of man effected a change in marine architectural principles. The validity of the change has been argued ever since. Its spectacular effectiveness stands on the record. When we have done with the nonsense of trying to decide which was the first clipper, and who invented it, we can turn to a more serious inspection of the quality of the achievement. Some ships had hollow bows long before John Willis Griffiths so changed the structure of the vessel's head, above water, that this hollowness became suddenly evident. Some ships had been made with sharply rising floors, others relatively flat. Some had been unusually long in proportion to their breadth. Such factors, and others, entered into the development—it was not an invention—of a group of famous ships produced at mid-century in America. Yet a point as significant as any is their mutual differences. There was no standard model. Many combinations of elements were tried. What then were the elements that made a vessel deserving of the name clipper? Those elements of design, precisely, which tended to increase her speed. A sharp entrance, but not necessarily a hollow-cheeked one, was advantageous for lessening the resistance of the water to forward motion, but perhaps more importantly for reducing the buoyancy forward which in earlier models had caused an excessive pitching up and down. The clipper stayed more nearly parallel to the horizon as she drove forward. A high ratio of length to breadth was the main factor in reducing forward resistance. Clippers usually had a ratio of more than 4.5 to 1. A few had a ratio of 6 to 1. Many older kinds of merchantmen had a ratio of 3 to 1. The clipper was heavily sparred, able to carry a great deal more canvas than former vessels in similar uses. These were the major differences, but it was the speed and authority with which a process of general experimentation changed the general concepts of shipbuilding that truly made the Clipper Era.

In choosing Donald McKay as representative of the special American qualities of talent and enterprise which developed the briefly brilliant clipper ships as a type, I have no wish to argue that he was the "greatest" or "most successful" builder of wooden ships.

Launch of the *Flying Cloud* in 1851 at Donald McKay's yard in East Boston, Massachusetts. The first of her innumerable publicists had no doubts about her beauty and her promise. Reporting the scene a few days later, a writer for *Gleason's Pictorial,* on the front page of the new publication's second issue, called her "beyond a doubt, the most beautiful specimen of the Yankee clipper style of building, that has yet been turned off the stocks. . . . Not only is she the longest and largest clipper ship in the world, but she has the sharpest ends, and is considered by all who have seen her, as possessing great beauty of model. . . . If the *Flying Cloud* does not prove true to her name for speed and excellent sea qualities, then we are no judge of maritime matters." He closed by "bearing testimony to the minute exactness of this excellent representation, by our artist . . ." Her career was crowded with triumphs, the most famous being her never equaled 89-day run from New York to San Francisco. She was sold abroad in 1862, for the usual war-time reasons, and was lost in 1874.

A similar, although a different, case can be made for William H. Webb—and there are others, less productive than either, some of whose ships performed in the same order of excellence. When judging ships by their recorded performances, one must take into consideration their captains, the instructions of their owners, the services in which they were employed, and the variables of meteorology. Samuel Hartt Pook's *Red Jacket,* with a different assortment of these aspects of luck, might have done better than McKay's best. She did well enough to rank high up among the sailing immortals.

Both Webb and McKay were recognized abroad, in their own time, as builders of the first rank. Webb was largely patronized by foreign governments, McKay by one particularly daring British shipowner, James Baines. The only preponderant basis for a choice between them is the consistency with which McKay's great clippers turned in records for speed and for maximum day's runs. Carl C. Cutler, author of the definitive work on clipper ships, *Greyhounds of the Sea* (1930), published in 1952 a new study—*Five Hun-*

Donald McKay

dred Sailing Records of American Built Ships. In it he evaluated the evidence, much more carefully than had ever been done before, and came up with several important revisions of earlier claims and assumptions. It is hardly conceivable that many different shipmasters, at widely separated times and places, by a remarkable conspiracy, falsified their logs for the single purpose of enhancing the repute of one shipbuilder. This, which has never seriously been argued, seems the only alternative to acceptance of Mr. Cutler's conclusions. The evidence was not recorded under controlled scientific conditions. It is only as good as most of the other evidence which we have to trust in making what we call history: testimony of the individuals involved, examined as carefully as possible for symptoms of falsehood. The evidence accepted by Mr. Cutler implies:

(1) That of twelve occasions when a sailing ship credibly recorded a speed of 18 or more knots, the three with the highest rates of speed all were built by McKay: The *Sovereign of the Seas,* 22 knots; the *James Baines,* 21 knots; the *Champion of the Seas,* 20 knots. (A 20-knot claim is also tentatively accepted for Pook's *Defiance,* on less valid evidence.)

The *Sovereign of the Seas,* one of Donald McKay's great racers which as a group had almost a monopoly upon the claim to days' runs of better than 400 miles. The evidence has been called into question in recent years, chiefly by knowledgeable shipmasters with an experience of fast runs in the huge steel barks built early in this century. It was thrashed out in 1957 and 1958 in a number of issues of the *Mariner's Mirror* to a conclusion (Volume 44:328–331) which seems to validate some of the old claims on the basis of evidence as good as that which we accept for many other generally credited "truths of history." Carl C. Cutler, who had carefully re-examined most of the evidence for a work published in the spring of 1952, assigned to the *Sovereign of the Seas* the fastest rate of speed, 22 knots, credibly recorded. She seems also to have been the only clipper except the *Lightning* to have logged 410 miles a day or better on two different occasions. The *Sovereign of the Seas* was launched at East Boston, Massachusetts, in 1852, and was commanded for a time by her builder's brother Lauchlan. It is to be noted that her two highest rates of speed were claimed by different commanders.

(2) That of the twelve records, nine were made by McKay ships.

(3) That only one ship, McKay's *Sovereign of the Seas,* appears to have made such a run on two different occasions. On both occasions the evidence is credible that a speed of 20 knots or more was attained a number of times on the same day, and on one occasion the *Champion of the Seas* appears to have made a noon-to-noon *average* of 20 knots.

(4) That in the thirteen occasions when ships have sailed more than 400 miles in a day, ten were McKay ships.

(5) That of these, McKay's *Champion of the Seas* heads the list with 465 miles.

(6) That McKay's *Lightning* did it three times, with day's runs of 436, 430, and 421 miles; and his *James Baines* also did it three times, with runs of 423, 407, and 404 miles.

Records of this sort are not the measure of the best vessel for general use, yet it is to be noted that all of these were made during normal commercial voyages, and that McKay's ships, despite the merciless driving to which they seemed to tempt a variety of commanders, British as well as American, also turned in a superior record for durability.

It is pleasant to note that both McKay and William H. Webb learned their craft from

Donald McKay's shipyard in East Boston. This view of the birthplace of great ships is reproduced from a daguerreotype made in 1855.

the latter's father, master builder of packet ships, Isaac Webb. For $2.50 a week McKay agreed, in articles of indenture signed in 1826 when he was sixteen, to have nothing to do with taverns, playhouses, or matrimony. Later he hung out his own shingle at Newburyport, Massachusetts, where in 1842 he built his first ship, the *Courier,* 392 tons. Webb, six years younger, had taken over his father's yard when Isaac died, in 1840. McKay gained assurance less rapidly, although his *New World* in 1846 was larger than any packet so far built by Webb. Between 1845 and 1850 McKay built five packets for Enoch Train's new Liverpool Line.

The packet, at this period, was a developed type—steadily enlarging but offering little scope for brilliant experimentation in design or construction. A concurrent phenomenon of the 1840s, however, gave McKay his chance for ultimate and spectacular triumph. Modest ships, especially designed for the tea trade with China, had been developed by John W. Griffiths, designer of the *Rainbow* and the *Sea Witch,* by the shipmaster-designer Nathaniel B. Palmer, and others. These had to meet two special conditions among others more usual: they had to be suited to all weathers, the boisterous Western Ocean; the happy trade-wind belts; the exasperating doldrums, horse latitudes, and Calms of Capricorn; the Roaring Forties—and they had to be fast to keep fine teas from becoming moldy on a long voyage through all climates.

Donald McKay, creator of great ships (standing in center foreground, wearing tall hat), and his medium clipper *Glory of the Seas,* on her launching day in 1869. She was the last large sailing vessel built by McKay.

When the news of California gold fired the eastern seaboard, the clipper model seemed just what was wanted for the California trade; but it now needed to be much more capacious, and to stand a cruel plunge into the even more loudly roaring Fifties off Cape Horn. McKay's first response to the new challenge, the *Reindeer* of 800 tons, launched in the middle of 1849, was almost too prudent: sharp, not hollow-bowed, sturdy. But a year later he produced the famous *Stag Hound,* about twice as large, a true clipper. The *Flying Cloud* followed in 1851, probably the most admired of all sailing ships.

The summary of performances from Carl C. Cutler's monograph is a sufficient indication of what followed. Further information about a number of McKay's more important ships will be found in the captions to pictures. Like other eminent men who gave the height of their creative talents to the enterprise of American sail, Donald McKay was deprived of opportunities for the fullest application of his genius by the panic of 1857, the calamity of the Civil War, and the rise of steam as a competitor. His greatest reach was the *Great Republic,* originally of 4,555 tons, for decades the largest wooden sailing vessel. But after her launch, burning, and diminished rebuilding in 1853, his clippers dwindled in size and performance. The last two, the *Mastiff* and the *Minnehaha,* were launched in 1856. A year later the Clipper Ship Era which he did so much to create was over.

The Owner's Portrait

A RECURRENT DIFFICULTY, IN THE TASK OF SELECTING PICTURES FOR A BOOK OF THIS SORT, is raised by what, during my otherwise happy excursions into the pictorial archives, I have come to think of as the owner's profile portrait of his ship. Zephaniah W. Pease, in his preface to Clifford W. Ashley's *The Yankee Whaler,* states the problem succinctly when he refers to "patrons who had very definite ideas about what they wanted and set up a standard to which the painters of the period adapted themselves. The whaler must be broadside, with her hull drawn to scale and every rope of the rigging must show. These ship portraits were likenesses, maybe, and demonstrated skill in draughtsmanship—but they were not art." Ashley himself, who saw ships with an intimate love and comprehension, noted that too many ship paintings had been executed with the eye of the owner "held like a filter before that of the artist."

The owner seldom had much regard for the ship's people, except as exasperating, unreliable items of expense. He wanted a view of his ship in prospering circumstances, with nothing unpleasant on the horizon. A stiff breeze was admirable, more so than a Chinese anchorage, because it meant prompt dispatch with safety. The owner had worries enough. Why should he hang over his mantel a view of his ship on her beam ends in a squall? Such views were more commonly commissioned by captains, but the owner wanted an exact profile, yards braced well up with all plain sail drawing, full and by. Harry T. Peters, in his huge bibliography of Currier & Ives prints, notes that, "Many of the marines . . . were drawn by staff artists from sketches or plans obtained from builders or owners." Although the exact date of issue of such prints is sometimes difficult to determine, a mid-nineteenth century version of Madison Avenue appears to have deftly coordinated the issuance of an "owner's portrait" with the launching date of many a new clipper "up for California." Some of the original sail plans exist. Laid beside the lithographs, or the woodcuts in *Gleason's* and other periodicals, they leave no doubt of what it was the artist worked from, in advance of the actual rigging of the vessels. Later representations of the same vessels celebrate events of the voyages they had made. Invariably these are the more satisfying pictures, for composition and originality.

The idealization of a ship in the owner's eye records an important if repetitious fact of social history which should be reproduced here for that reason alone. The best examples of the owner's portrait have an abstract charm that merits more than a glance, but I have used the type sparingly. If, as has happened on the ocean, an occasional well-known ship "turns up missing" in this book it may be because I could find no historically reliable picture except yet another "owner's." My main test always has been, "What was it like to be alive in the great age of American sail?" The answer calls for a human dimension in addition to the often fascinating geometry of a complex machine, the sailing ship.

TOP. The *Surprise,* a medium clipper embodying the ideas of young Samuel H. Pook, an independent designer. She was built in 1850 by Samuel Hall at East Boston, Massachusetts, and measured 1,261 tons. Her original commander was the famous Philip Dumaresq. She made consistently fast passages both in the China and California trades, and proved extremely durable as well. CENTER. The *Monarch of the Seas,* a full-bodied merchant ship of 1,971 tons built at New York by Roosevelt & Joyce in 1854. Like so many others, she was sold abroad during the Civil War. She went missing during a voyage out of Liverpool in 1866. John A. Burgess, a notable clipper captain, was one of her commanders. She was chartered as a supply ship during the Crimean War. BOTTOM. The *City of Mobile,* 1,715 tons, was built at Greenpoint, Long Island, New York, in 1854. In 1856 she brought into the East India Docks the largest cargo of wheat that had ever been shipped anywhere in the world. She carried Hodge's double topsails.

Three Owners' Portraits

Artists commissioned to do owners' portraits of ships seem often to have felt an urge to vary the standard pattern just a little. In many cases they prevailed upon the owner to allow one sail to be brailed up, or at least the weather clew of the mainsail to be hauled up. The best marine artists were careful as a rule to supply backgrounds of interest. The above vessels, in left-to-right pairs, are: The *Betsey* of Stonington, Connecticut, first ship from that port to sail around the world, in 1797–1798. The bark *Henry Buck,* built in Searsport, Maine, in 1852 by John Carver, leaving Venice in 1857: Giovanni Luzro was the painter. The *Indiana* entering Leghorn in 1831: a cotton trader built at East Haddam, Connecticut, in 1825, and employed for a time as a Mobile packet. The *Empress of the Seas,* built by Donald McKay at East Boston, Massachusetts, in 1853: a reliable but not spectacular clipper, burned at Port Phillip in 1861. The bark *J. C. Kuhn,* built at Portland, Connecticut, in 1859, painted by D. McFarlane in 1860. The *B. Aymar,* a painting on glass showing her entering the Texel, October 16, 1840. She was one of the 37 vessels built by John Carver between 1824 and 1864, and was Searsport, Maine's, first full-rigged ship. Later she was commanded for a time by Joshua Slocum. Here she is to be seen crossing her own stern.

ABOVE. Antitheses of the owners' portraits. Above, an unidentified clipper snugging down for a hurricane. Oil painting by James E. Buttersworth who did many of the preliminary studies for Currier & Ives nautical prints. Note the 28 men fisting the foremast canvas. RIGHT. The smaller of the two Currier & Ives prints of the clipper *Comet* in a hurricane off Bermuda, when bound for San Francisco on October 2, 1852. She was built by William H. Webb at New York in 1851, and measured 1,836 tons. British buyers later renamed her the *Fiery Star*, unhappily, because she burned at sea in 1865, with only 18 of her 98 people saved.

The Chinese Anchorage Picture

THERE IS AN OLD STORY ABOUT A YANKEE CAPTAIN WHO SENT A PAIR OF WORN-OUT PANTS to a Chinese tailor with the stipulation that he wanted another pair made exactly like them. The new pair arrived with frayed cuffs and patches in the seat precisely like those of the model. The same extraordinary fidelity was practiced by the abler Chinese marine artists. They abandoned their own conventionalized artistic tradition to draw American vessels at anchor in Chinese harbors with a micrometric objectivity. Marine artists of high repute in the West usually have done their best work when they painted ships in action. Buttersworth's view of the yacht *America* on page 1 and his clipper on page 263 are examples. Possibly because of the shift to a style expected of them by their visitors, the Chinese marine artists seem to have been able to paint well only from a posed model. These are still lifes, but they probably as a group are the most faithful representations of ships in service that have been made since the days of the van de Veldes.

Chinese penalties seemed so odd to Westerners in some instances, and so savage in others, that extraterritoriality treaties covering crimes committed by aliens were forced upon China as soon as it was militarily feasible.

Two sorts of close observation of the same ship: the *Nightingale,* designed and built as a clipper yacht to carry passengers to the London World's Fair of 1851—and, not quite coincidentally, to advertise the wares of her builder, Samuel Hanscom, Jr., of Portsmouth, New Hampshire, in the foreign market. She measured 1,066 tons. Her career varied greatly from her builder's plans. She was promptly sold to discharge building costs and was put into the China trade. For a while she sailed out of Rio as a slaver, until captured by a United States cruiser. She was armed for service during the Civil War and afterward sailed under the Norwegian flag. She was abandoned at sea in 1893.

The anchorage off Hong Kong. Undated, but the rig of the sailing steamers suggests the 1870s.

At a quick glance one might suspect that the Currier & Ives print of the *Nightingale* off the Battery at New York had been done on stone as a mirror image of the painting. It is possible, as the ship had made two voyages to China before that date and may have had the painting aboard. But a close inspection indicates differences beyond such casual ones as the disposition of the boats. The height of the transom and the rake of the stem are different enough to be ascribed to different observers of the object itself. In these particulars the Chinese was probably the more accurate draftsman.

The Chinese anchorage picture has a disability comparable to that of the owner's portrait. It is almost always a profile of a ship at anchor with her sails unbent or snugged smartly into harbor gaskets. Although it rewards the specialist with intricacies of detail in rigging and tackle not to be found elsewhere, each example to the casual viewer is almost exactly like all of the others. The one perhaps most frequently reproduced is of the *Sea Witch*. I have chosen that of the *Nightingale* because a number of pictures of her have been published that are obviously doctored copies of the Currier & Ives print, done into oils and mistaken for originals.

The yacht *America*, "wung out"—one boom to starboard, the other to port—crossing the finish line at Cowes. This lithograph, published a month later, excellently exemplifies the virtues of the well-observed contemporaneous view. The loss of the jib boom is evident, as is the laced foot of the mainsail which caused comment in the British press.

THE AMERICA AT COWES

JOHN C. STEVENS, COMMODORE OF THE NEW YORK YACHT CLUB, WAS PERSUADED LATE IN 1850 that a yacht exemplifying the virtues of American design should be sent to England at the time of the projected International Exposition in the following year. William H. Brown, shipbuilder, examined a resulting model made by the commodore's friend George Steers, and was so impressed that he offered to build her either for $30,000 or for nothing, the latter choice to come into effect if a British vessel of the same size should beat her. Steers at the time was chiefly known as a designer of very fast pilot schooners. The *America* took a little longer to build than had been foreseen. She did not do very well in her trial runs against the *Maria* and was not delivered until June 18, 1851. Three days later she sailed, carrying her racing spars. Dick Brown, a New York pilot who had cruised on and off Sandy Hook for years in calms and hurricanes, was in command of her. He took her into Havre exactly a month after her departure, where she spent ten days refitting and then sailed for Cowes, about midway on the English Channel coast.

For a $10,000 purse, Commodore Stevens first challenged the Royal Yacht Club to a race against any number of schooners, then to race vessels of any rig whatever. There were no takers, so he entered the *America* in the Royal Yacht Squadron Regatta which would sail a course around the island of Cowes on August 22nd. At one point a question arose whether the *America* had wandered inside the course limits. Since her skipper and crew were newcomers, the point was waived. During the race her jib boom snapped in two (her huge jib repeated this performance several times on later occasions), but the wreckage was cleared in about fifteen minutes. As she ghosted over the line in light airs at the end of the fifty-three-mile course, the famous question was asked and answered:

"Who's second?"

"There is no second."

LOOK OUT FOR SQUALLS!

The proprietors of *Punch* ribbed their country-men hard and well in a series of issues, beginning with the cartoon at the left, and continuing with several nursery rimes:

"Lullaby, Johnny, upon the tree-top;
When thy ships fail, thy Navy will drop;
When thy fleets yield, thy glory will fall,
And down comes JOHNNY, and Commerce and all."

Reactions to the Victory of the Yacht AMERICA

The Illustrated American News printed this much-reduced copy of the *Punch* cartoon within the month. Other publications happily noted *Punch*'s spoof advertisement: "Timber For Sale. —A great quantity of Planks, Sticks, Masts, and Spars, to be had cheap. —Inquire at the Royal Yacht Club House, Cowes." *Punch* also reported that British agents had bought an American steamer "to tow The Cunard packets over." BELOW. On October 11th *The Illustrated American News* presented a suggestion that British naval architects were beginning to pay attention to American design.

Yankee Doodle had a craft, a rather tidy clipper,
And he challenged, while they laughed, the Britishers
Their whole yacht squadron she outsped, and that on the
Of all the lot she went a-head, and they came nowhere

News of the *America*'s victory reached New York in time for this wood engraving to be made and published in *The Illustrated American News* less than five weeks after the event. Compare the headsails at the right with the single forestaysail she was wearing (page 267) at the close of the race, having snapped her jib boom. BELOW. Currier & Ives made use of the coincidence, which was not unplanned, of the *America*'s performance with the great London trade fair.

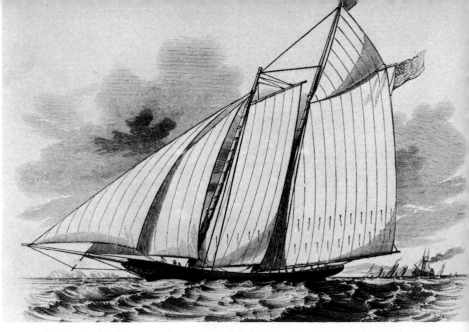

E GREAT EXHIBITION OF 1851.

AMERICAN DEPARTMENT.

Above is John Carlin's painting "After a Long Cruise." Below is R. C. Woodville's "The Sailor's Wedding." The two pictures are unrelated in their origins, but the expressions of those who are interrupting the magistrate at his impromptu lunch perhaps justify the joint caption, "One Thing Leads to Another."

Clippers & Packets of the GREAT '50's

The naval architect and historian William Armstrong Fairburn has called William H. Webb "probably the most versatile and practical builder of wood vessels that the world has ever known." In 1831 he went to work in the shipyard where his father, Isaac Webb, built more than a dozen fine packets and many other vessels. At the age of twenty-four, in 1840, Webb took over the business when his father died. It was still called Webb & Allen, but two or three years later Webb was building ships under his own name. Here are three of his many sturdy productions. *Gleason's* first marine specialist, William Wade, covered the launch of the clipper ship *Challenge* (right, above), 2,007 tons, in 1851. The old practice of getting the masts into a vessel after she was afloat seemed too slow in the days of the great clippers. She was built to be commanded by the hard-driving Captain Robert H. Waterman, but despite the pummeling he gave her she lasted for 25 years. The *Young America* (right, center), shown here in a Currier & Ives print, was ready for sea in the spring of 1853 when Webb, nettled by praises of McKay's *Sovereign of the Seas,* offered to bet $10,000 on a race between the two. The wager was not accepted. The *Young America* was consistently fast, making five voyages to San Francisco in 117 days or less. She lasted 33 years. Two of Webb's Black Ballers, below, the *Harvest Queen* (left) and the *James Foster,* also were durable—lasting 22 and 24 years on the racking run to Liverpool. The former is seen in a typical "owner's portrait" by J. Hughes. The latter's picture, slightly modified for variety, is by the same specialist.

Newburyport, Massachusetts, birthplace of the famous clipper packet *Dreadnought,* and of one of the last ships to be responsibly classified as clippers, the *Reynard.*

This N. Currier print of the *Dreadnought* locates her off Sandy Hook on February 23, 1854, only nineteen days from Liverpool. Excellent time, but four days more than the record set by the old *Yorkshire* packet eight years earlier. Luck was a large factor in all such records. The *John Stuart,* when she all but tied the *Yorkshire*'s record in 1852, reported that she had been becalmed for four days off Long Island.

It seems evident from her figurehead that the ship in this Currier & Ives print entitled "A Squall off Cape Horn" is meant to be the *Dreadnought,* 1,414 tons, built by Currier & Townsend at Newburyport in 1853. It was off Cape Horn that she concluded her great voyaging in 1869.

The *Reynard,* a late clipper representative of the curtailment in size dictated by the tapering off of the California and Australia boom days. She still was a very sharp and narrow ship, although the length-to-breadth ratio which had been touching 6 to 1 in the extreme clippers had dropped to what mechanics called a whisker under 5 to 1. She was built at Newburyport, Massachusetts, by George W. Jackman in 1856, and measured 1,051 tons. Her service covered three full decades. A painting by J. Hughes.

Some concepts, sentimentalized and corrective, of the foremasthand. LEFT. From the recollections of Captain George Davis. BELOW. "The Boatswain," a lithograph published by J. Baillie in New York.

JACK ASHORE.

BILL CHAPMAN IN HUDSON STREET.

THE JOLLY JACK TAR OF FICTION.   THE POOR JACK TAR OF REALITY

Fo'c's'le conditions did not change notably until strong maritime unions arose in the twentieth century. What did change during the great climacteric of sail was the career aspect of seamanship, which came to offer less and less to the competent.

The *Tornado*, built by Jabez Williams at Williamsburg, New York, in 1852, registered 1,802 tons. Despite a life of tremendous buffetings she succumbed at last not to the winds or waves but to fire at New Orleans in 1875. The episode here depicted, in an illustration from *Gleason's Pictorial*, occurred in September 1852 while the clipper, commanded by Captain Oliver R. Mumford, was on passage from San Francisco to New York. In the Pacific not far from Cape Horn, as *Gleason's* reported, "The vessel was struck by a whirlwind . . . which broke the bowsprit off at the knight-heads, carried away her foremast by the deck, and seriously injured her rigging and sails. . . ." Mumford's somewhat uneager crew repaired the damage sufficiently to make New York under jury rig in 100 days from San Francisco, despite the accident: excellent time for a normally rigged ship that had not got into trouble.

The *Electric*, 1,274 tons, was built by Irons & Grinnell at Mystic, Connecticut, in 1853. She lasted nineteen years.

The clipper ship *Golden West*, 1,441 tons, was built by Paul Curtis at East Boston, Massachusetts, in 1852. Like so many others, she was sold to the British in the great rush for safety that eliminated most of the best American sailing ships during the Civil War. Her 20-day run from Japan to San Francisco in summer may have been the record, but her voyages out around the Horn were about average.

The *Typhoon*, 1,611 tons, built at Portsmouth, New Hampshire, in 1851 by Fernald & Pettigrew. The painting by Samuel Walters celebrated her arrival in the Mersey River in 13 days and 12 hours after her departure from Portsmouth on her maiden voyage—the record. She was reported off Cape Clear two days earlier but met with fog. She was sold during the Civil War and later listed as the British ship *Indomitable*.

SHIP-WORK DONE.

COPPER NAILS.

COPPER.

FRANCIS HARLEY,
No. 78 *South Front-street, (West side,)*
PHILADELPHIA

The *Shackamaxon* of George McHenry & Company's Philadelphia and Liverpool Line. The lithograph is undated, but it was made in Liverpool by John R. Isaac from a painting by C. P. Williams. The *Fanny McHenry* of the same line was in operation in 1854. Not many prints were made of the packets from ports other than New York and Boston. This one is something of a rarity.

Clipper ship *Adelaide*, 1,831 tons, built by A. C. Bell at New York in 1854. D. McFarlane's painting shows her hove to off Rio de Janeiro to aid a British ship in distress. The captain in command at the time, Ned Wakeman, had earlier defied a sheriff to take an attached steamer from New York to California, by way of the Strait of Magellan.

The clipper packet *Staffordshire* built by Donald McKay at East Boston, Massachusetts, in 1851, for Enoch Train's Liverpool line. She measured 1,817 tons and was for a time the largest packet afloat. She was lost after two years near Cape Sable, on Christmas day, 1853.

The *James Baines* embarking passengers at Liverpool, as painted by Samuel Walters and lithographed by Picken. She was built by Donald McKay at East Boston in 1854 for Baines's line of Liverpool packets, at a time when enterprising British shipowners were willing to by-pass their own shipbuilding industry in recognition of the fact that, for a brief period, the American yards were the best in the world. The *James Baines* established the permanent record of 12½ days from Boston to Liverpool, port to port. She measured 2,515 tons.

The marine specialist for *Gleason's Pictorial* who signed his wood blocks "Warren" and who engraved the view of the launch of the *Great Republic* shown on page 12, had this second look at Donald McKay's big clipper when she was fully rigged. Nearly forty years were to pass before the building of the giant wooden schooners that exceeded her tonnage in proportional loaded displacement.

The End of Greatness

The *Syren,* built by John Taylor at Medford, Massachusetts, in the earlier part of the Clipper Ship Era, had the distinction of outlasting all of her later and larger contemporaries. Just how long she lived is uncertain, but she was still afloat and at work in 1920, renamed *Margarida* of Buenos Aires, and carrying bark rig. At that point she was sixty-nine years of age. She made several creditable passages out to California, but broke no records, except that for longevity.

BELOW. The last of the outstanding clippers was given a name almost too appropriately prophetic: *Twilight.* She was built by Charles Mallory at Mystic, Connecticut, in 1857. Her tonnage, 1,482, was the largest of the year. Nautical reporters, used to a decade of astonishing ships, remarked her for her outstanding beauty. It was as if fate conspired to make the last example of one of man's defiantly excellent achievements a worthy one. The clippers were an extreme sort of answer to a transient set of commercial problems. Economics put them to death as a class of merchant vessels soon after they had attained their own variety of perfection. Many individual examples fell prey to the sea raiders of the Civil War. More were sold abroad to escape the hazard. Americans turned their eyes inland in the twilight of the great age of American sail.

The *Dashing Wave,* 1,180 tons, built durably by Fernald & Pettigrew at Portsmouth, New Hampshire, in 1853. Her hull was still in first-class condition in 1920, when she was in service as a barge. She was lost that year.

ABOVE. J. W. Hill's charming view of Portland, Maine, in
1855, with a beflagged sailing ship about to be launched.
RIGHT. A crude lithographic reworking of the same
scene, ten years later, distinguished chiefly by the enlargement of hoopskirts and the substitution on the ways
of a fat-cheeked paddle-wheel steamer.

Decade of Transition

The steam sloop of war U.S.S. *Monongahela,* with stu'n's'ls set. She was launched in 1862.

278

Lieutenant Maury's Trade Wind Chart of the Atlantic Ocean, in which an alternative graphic method is used to indicate more clearly the general behavior of the wind over larger areas. As may be seen by the pale regions of no evidence and the darker ones where the evidence was abundant, Maury's mathematics revealed an unforeseen pattern for the three calm belts between which the trade winds had been known for centuries to blow all year in a fairly constant direction. Shipmasters frequently had reported "picking up the trades" at a latitude higher or lower than expected. Maury discovered that the "calm belts" known to sailors as the horse latitudes, doldrums, and calms of Capricorn were more serrated than belt-like. It was an advantage to change course to follow northeast trades down the deep dip of the "belt" at about 38° west, then to steer into the region of the variables to keep some sort of wind rather than a preponderant calm until the final nip into an upreaching hump of the southeast trades. In Chapter XVII of his *Physical Geography of the Sea*, 1855, Maury analyzed the logs of the *Archer, Flying Cloud, Wild Pigeon, John Gilpin, Flying Fish,* and *Trade Wind* to show, with pardonable satisfaction, that those who had the stamina to hold to his instructions even when they seemed improbable had made much the fastest voyages.

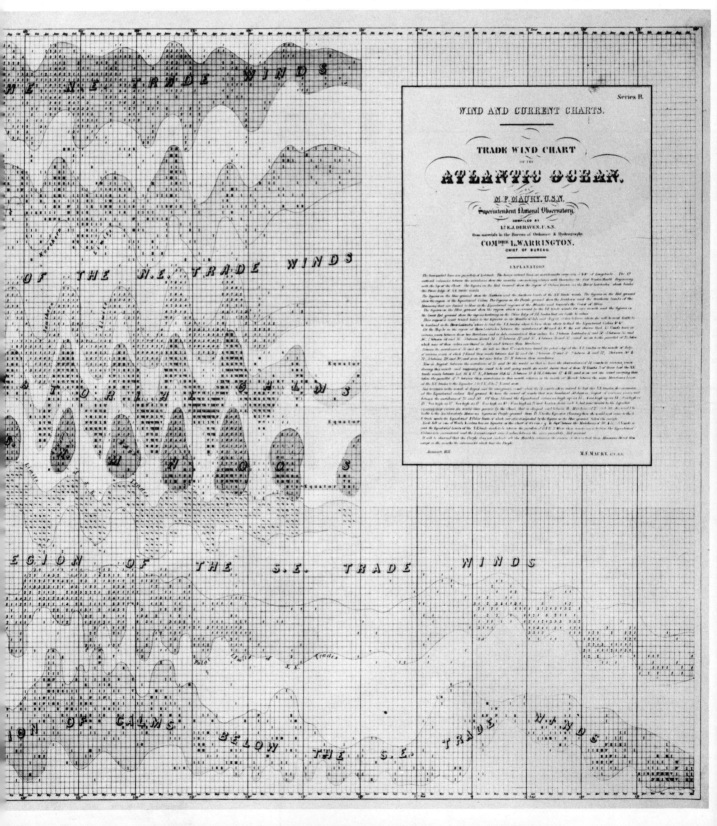

Not content to map only the winds and currents, Lieutenant Maury evolved whale charts, for which the one partially reproduced above is a "Preliminary sketch," of 1851. The detail at the left more clearly indicates its symbolism. Again relying upon the principle that scattered exact information, though possibly misleading in the particular instance, when organized is in most instances more reliable than guesswork, he put into his usual 5° rectangles of ocean such reports as he could find in available logbooks. The letters refer to the seasons ("v" for Latin spring, the rest as in English), with two spouts for right whales, one for sperm. Two of the same species in a rectangle denoted unusually good fishing there. Spouts alone were for stragglers rather than herds. BELOW. The double spout of the right whale is noted on the earliest printed map of northern waters, the Olai Magni Carta Gotha Marina of 1539. The "orcha" is probably meant to be a killer whale.

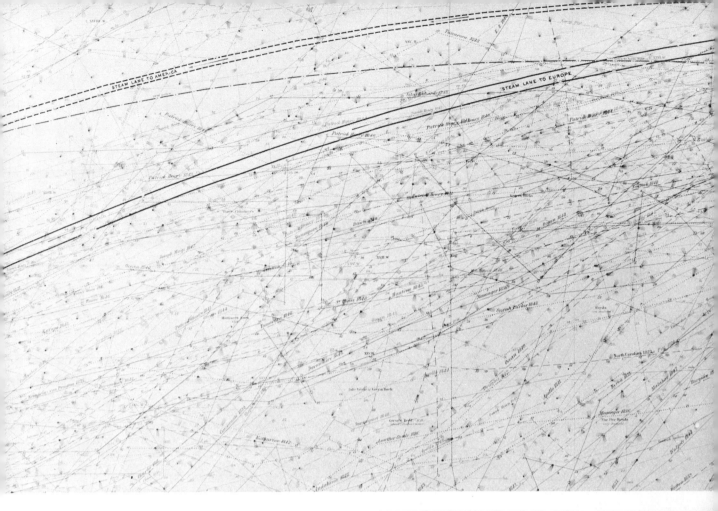

Above is a portion of another sort of Maury chart, upon which he has plotted the courses of many ships from their logbooks, with what he called "small brushes" to indicate the reported winds. The curved solid and dotted lines are his recommended paths, as of 1849, for the best steamship lanes to and from Europe. BELOW. Much of Maury's effort was turned toward the keeping of ships as long as possible in "flying fish weather," in the trade winds. Here is how it had seemed to De Bry, who found his somewhat odd models in Rondelet, labeled "L'Arondele de Mer."

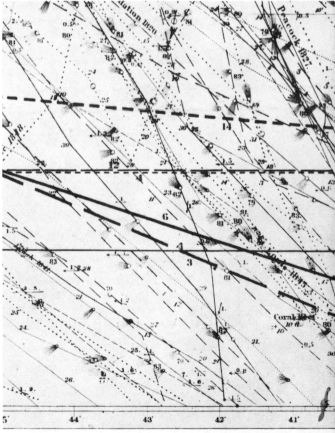

A closer look at Maury's "wind brushes" from an 1852 chart. They point as if blown by the wind. The black or white circles indicate its strength and the width of the brush its reported variation. Included are tracks of the *Congress, Constellation, Guerrière, Peacock,* and *United States.*

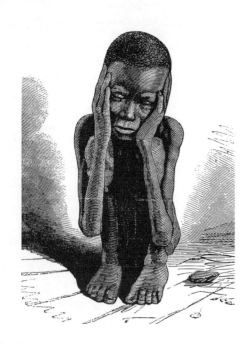

The INFAMOUS Traffic

In 1853, at a world conference in Brussels, representatives of the navies and merchant marines of almost all trading nations paid unexampled honor to an American, Matthew Fontaine Maury, a mere lieutenant, putting him in charge of the co-ordinating of meteorological and hydrographic information for the entire world. In the same season American shipmasters, from the North and the South, offset the great humane efforts of Maury upon the seas by persisting for personal gain in the most infamous seaborne traffic the world has ever known. The sugar islands, such as Grenada (below, as its port of St. George's appeared in 1852 to Captain H. A. Turner), had demonstrated for more than a decade the falsity of the always sinful contention that their economy was indispensably linked to slavery. But the southern states insulated themselves from all argument. When hostilities commenced over what the public recognized as centrally the cause of slavery, Matthew Fontaine Maury was one of the officers who offered their services to the side that supported that evil cause.

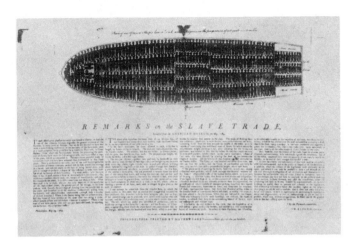

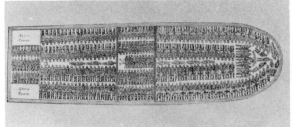

The arguments had been in the open for more than half a century. The faded broadside at the left was issued by Matthew Carey in the year of the Bill of Rights, 1789. The almost identically packed "Lower Deck of a Guineaman," below, was sketched by Commander Andrew H. Foote, U.S.N., on the coast of Africa in 1850.

The United States brig *Perry*, Commander Foote, taking the American slave ship *Martha* off the coast of Africa, June 6, 1850. The *Martha* was owned in New York and had aboard "sundry papers, making curious revelations of the agency of some American citizens . . . little suspected of ever having participated in such a diabolical traffic." The captain jumped bail, and escaped. The mate received two years in jail.

Slaves in the open air. Periods of freedom from their fetters in the dark hold were found to be requisite. Otherwise too large a proportion of a costly cargo might have to be jettisoned because of disease. Most slaves at this period were destined for Brazil, but some were smuggled into the southern United States. Jamaicans had calculated, toward the end of the eighteenth century, that the best economic arrangement was to work a slave to death in seven years, and replace him.

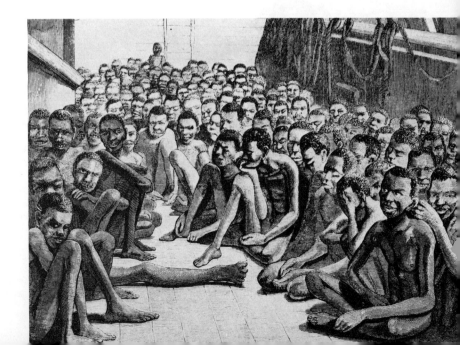

Newport, Rhode Island, seen from Fort Wolcott in the latter 1850s. The town, as an all-year open port accessible to the seaside distilleries of the rest of New England, had the vicious distinction in the eighteenth century of being one of the three indispensable angles of the traffic carrying sugar to New England to be made into rum for the purchase of slaves in Africa to be sold in the West Indies to grow sugar for New England. Casuists of course argued that the slave leg of the triangle, which never touched a New England port, was essential to the respectable trade in rum and sugar.

The contribution of free Negroes under American sail could be the subject of a separate study. Logs and letters are strewn with references which leave the impression that Negroes were neither better nor worse in competence than other seamen, and perhaps as a group more reliable. A "black seaman" in the whaler *Lydia* was discovered at the end of a successful cruise to have been "a woman who had ably performed her tasks." Richard Seaver, known as "Big Dick," served in the *Chesapeake,* was imprisoned at Dartmoor, and according to a romantic biographer later specialized as a Boston policeman in rescuing virtuous young women from procurers: a task at which he is here shown.

Post Script
upon an INIQUITY

JUDGED BROADLY, THE DOWNFALL OF THE GREAT ERA OF AMERICAN sail was the result of concurrent factors, largely technological and economic, but the corrupting practice of slavery was pervasive in the event. The best skills of designers and builders of medium-sized, weatherly craft were turned —knowingly or unknowingly—to this iniquitous business. A large number of vessels, built specifically for the slave trade, came from the yards of men who were equally ready to accept all commissions, regardless of the purpose. Others, like the schooner yacht *Wanderer* and the beautiful clipper ship *Nightingale,* were bought for the trade after they had demonstrated a tempting suitability in their primary uses.

Even while our builders of wooden sailing ships were engaged in a proud last challenge to steam in the early 1850s, a modest but excellent sort of steamer was being developed in Britain for the contrary purpose of catching fast American-built slavers on the Guinea Coast. The British Navy took very seriously, under both English law and international conventions, its duty to suppress the infamous traffic at its origins. The United States Navy, under similar laws and conventions, dawdled in the task. There were not many commanders like Andrew H. Foote. The poor performance can be related to the attitude of Secretary of State Daniel Webster, who was much more concerned with the formal preservation of a cancerous union than with the risky surgery that might make the Union worth saving. His cynical lack of vigor in implementing the slave-trade clause of his own Webster-Ashburton Treaty established its evasion as a precedent for his successors. As on a more recent occasion of moral muddle, Great Britain kept up a lonely fight, with little support, in the long interest of both nations. While doing so she learned useful lessons in the mechanics of recapturing from American

...nk Leslie's Illustrated News-...er for January 21, 1860, pre-...ted this picture of the "cele-...ted yacht Wanderer, formerly ...he New York Yacht Club fleet, ...rwards the famous slaver—now ...ed as a slave ship and in charge ...the Marshal of Boston." Few of ... many suspected northern slav-...were seized, and of these a sub-...ntial proportion were let go as a ...ult of pettifogging legalism. ...rthern participants in the slave ...de were of course the most ...ous of all because they did not ...n have the southerners' false ... apparently sincere belief that ...r regional economy depended ...n it.

This oil by Xanithus Smith summarizes succinctly the factors that put an end to fighting sail. At the right is the steam-propeller *Wabash,* variously listed as a sloop of war and as a steam frigate. She was built in 1855, measured 3,472 tons, and was conventionally armed. She served creditably, on one occasion towed another ship into action, was used as a flagship—but her sails had almost nothing to do. The *New Ironsides,* in the distance, was built in the first year of the war by Cramp at Philadelphia, with a wood hull and bolted iron plating. Her armament was mostly of Dahlgren guns. She "fought in more battles, stood up under severer shelling, and piled up more damage on Southern ships than any other vessel in the Union fleet." Here she is shown prior to her main engagements, for which Admiral Du Pont stripped her of her "anachronistic" masts and spars: an act of notable symbolism in the history of the Navy. In the forewater is the ironclad screw monitor *Patapsco,* a transitional gambit in the abolition of sail. She was built in 1862.

A story in *Harper's Weekly* for July 11, 1863, describes these scenes as piracy. Lieutenant Charles W. Read, who had sworn as a graduate of the United States Naval Academy in 1860 to defend the Union, accomplished more against it, with less, as a commerce raider, than any of the other rebel seamen. Starting in a prize brig off Brazil, with two boat howitzers and 24 men, he bettered his luck by captures until he had the sizable bark *Tacony* under him. Then, in about two weeks, as shown at the right, he took nineteen vessels, including two transatlantic passenger steamers.

A scarce print of the little naval base developed at Port Royal, South Carolina, after its capture by Commodore Samuel F. Du Pont early in the Civil War. Its defender, Commodore Josiah Tatnall, preferred this time that water should not be thickened, at least by his own blood. At the first shot that came his way, he "scurried for safety into nearby Skull Creek."

shipyards their short-lived repute as the world's most ingenious and best.

Beyond these significant but secondary matters the major one was the Civil War itself. Many students, a generation ago, convinced themselves and some others that slavery was a minor economic issue among more important ones—and that economics explains all. Those who speak for their own motives, in private documents of the day, seem to me to give contrary evidence.. A proportion far more than sufficient to swing a seesaw balance finally, for the winning side, discarded economic comforts to risk their economically irreplaceable lives as volunteers specifically to abolish slavery. It was a boundary drawn where slavery preponderated that resulted in the burning by its defenders, in April 1861, of a large part of the sailing Navy at Norfolk, to prevent the capture of 10 sailing vessels by the rebels. Champions of a "peculiar institution," which they were embarrassed to call by its honest, evil name, went to sea in the *Alabama* and other raiders which sank so many of the finest sailing ships that most of the others were sold to foreign owners to remove them from the hazard.

The sailing Navy was finished by a war that centered upon slavery. A few ships were kept in technical commission, and two still survive as reconstructed objects of sentiment. But sail was never employed again in the Navy's primary functions.

Our merchant marine was badly shattered by the war. Most of the famous ships were gone. The survivors were more conservatively sparred. Smaller but excellent British iron and steel clippers that had begun to appear in the late 1850s set new standards of fine performance under conditions which no longer encouraged spar-smashing voyages. Economics, in abeyance as always during a war, reasserted a normal effect upon an American merchant marine in difficulties—and the Congress refused to bail it out.

Short of ammunition, young Captain Read went boldly into the harbor at Portland, Maine, seized the revenue cutter *Caleb Cushing,* and got her out to sea. When he was followed in force, he blew her up and was captured.

If our eyewitness rule is valid, the sea fight between the U.S.S. *Kearsarge*, Captain John A. Winslow, and the C.S.S. *Alabama* should be more accurately shown in Lebreton's Paris lithograph (below) than in the American woodcut at the top, because the latter's egregious captain, Raphael Semmes, made it a written-challenge match in sight of Cherbourg. Semmes even invited a party of ladies to come out in a yacht to watch him slaughter people. He was unaware that concealed chain armor protected the *Kearsarge*'s boilers, the factor which turned his intended display of prowess for the ladies into a calamity for his British-built raider. His impulse to stage a last romantic single-ship challenge duel had a soggy ending. While the *Kearsarge* and her two unsmashed boats were busy picking Semmes's crew out of the water, he himself was scooped up by his friends in the *Deerhound* (the yacht may be seen in both pictures) and spirited off to England. No gallant passing over of the sword: perhaps he knew that Secretary of the Navy Gideon Welles wanted to try him, when caught, as a common pirate, not merely as a traitor. A year and a half later Semmes was finally arrested on a charge of treason, but one of President Johnson's amnesty proclamations saved his neck. Owing partly to the dependence of British manufacturers on raw cotton, Matthew Fontaine Maury and other southern agents had had little difficulty in procuring evasion of the laws and orders which restrained Englishmen from providing the rebels with instruments of warfare. The most serious contribution took the form of commerce raiders, of which the *Alabama* was the most effective. The sailing Navy was already finished as a real weapon, but this commerce raider played a dominant part in the destruction of the United States merchant marine, under sail, from which it never recovered. The seventy vessels destroyed by the *Alabama* are only a partial measure of her effectiveness. While "in being" she caused the sale abroad of a great many more. Her original illegal departure from British waters was the chief basis for the "Alabama Claims," for which an international court assessed Great Britain $15,500,000. The sum—enormous for the times—was promptly paid into the United States Treasury, setting a new precedent in international law for the dignified admission of wrongdoing by a major power.

ABOVE. Even as steam triumphed, the symbol of sail was hard to eradicate. Above is an advertising lithograph prepared in 1868 for the Atlantic Works of Boston: "Vessels of War and Merchant Steamers, Built or Supplied With Steam Machinery" by that firm. The two nearest monitors evidently are intended for the *Nantucket* and the *Casco,* built entirely by Atlantic, which also supplied turrets for four others and engines for five naval steamers. But it is the symbol of sail that continues to be central and dominant, even for cylinder and piston merchants, purveyors of the latest cheesebox version of the sort of vessels once miscalled "Jefferson's gunboats." BELOW. Old Ironsides, the most durable symbol of the sailing Navy, ready for relaunching from the dry-dock railway after one of the numerous repair jobs which have kept her in existence. A photograph taken on May 27, 1858, at Portsmouth Navy Yard.

Before and after the great days. New York harbor in 1833 and in 1867. There is not much change in the general aspect of this haven for the world's shipping. In the earlier view, above, an English brig and a Dutch leeboarder are visitors. One of the few surviving United States frigates is prominent in the later. But there is an unseen difference. In the great days the larger part of New York's imports and exports was carried in American-owned vessels. After the Civil War it became a minor and dwindling fraction.

VALENTINE'S TITLE PAGES

ALL OF OUR INFORMATION ABOUT SOME PARTS OF THE HUMAN PAST HAS HAD TO BE INFERRED from surviving pictures. The process of inference can also enlarge our comprehension of well-documented times. During the Civil War, when American sail was being hunted from the oceans by rebel commerce raiders, what was the attitude of citizens who should have been greatly concerned: residents of our largest seaport? One curious sidelight upon that attitude is reflected from the pictorial title pages of D. T. Valentine's *Manual of the Corporation of the City of New York*. It was to this happy oddity in a category of useful but invincibly dull municipal publications that the Common Council of the City of New York, in 1841, directed the energies of its clerk—David Thomas Valentine. In a moment of executive expansiveness they authorized him, not only to present current statistics, but also to enlighten New Yorkers with some documentary and pictorial recovery of their past.

Valentine, a pack-rat amateur of history, came up with a strange jumble of tedious utilities and imaginative riches. With the first issue's appearance it was too late for the councilmen to retract: their manual caught on as nothing of its kind has ever done since. Printing orders rose, from the too hopeful few hundred usual in such cases, well up into the thousands. The editor, eventually, was allowed 2,000 copies for his personal bestowal in addition to a fee, magnificent for the times, of $3,000 a year for the job. It is clear that Valentine knew his public and remained sensitive to its responses.

At the end of his manual's first decade, the compiler brought it into conformity with a general trend toward the symbolically pictorial title page. Such T.P.s, in periodicals such as *Godey's Lady's Book* and in separate novels, were reciprocal with the values and taste of the times. They were the equivalent of magazine covers of a century later, that have built large circulations by giving the public pictorial images of virtues and foibles which it is most pleased to recognize in itself. Valentine's first pictorial T.P. symbolized with a deliberate balance the large concerns of a great port. Ready beforehand in the official seal at the top there was a heritage of contact with Indian culture, posing beside a romanticized seaman in contemporary attire. The midget locomotive, a relative newcomer to the city's transit, was balanced against the well-established river steamer across the page. But both were puny beside the bark-rigged ocean steamer, probably intended for one of the brand-new Collins liners, sharing the main emphasis with the sort of manufactory which produced much of its cargo. In the lower corners were placed the products and symbols of husbandry. The city hall in its ornate frame was negligently draped with what might have been mistaken for a curtain.

Valentine and his public seem to have been well pleased. The first T.P. appeared unaltered in ten annual issues. In the next to last of these the editor noted, "The tastes of our people are essentially maritime." Then came the Civil War—and a sudden urge to reinterpret the city to its citizens. A formerly benign Indian of the great seal shares with everyone else the aspect of armed truculence; his counterpart, the prettified seaman, has become a hard-bitten foremasthand. Trains have improved, eight-windowed carriages replacing those with only six. The ocean steamer is getting along with much less canvas. Husbandry has come to the fore— but the great change is a consciousness of distances, central emphasis upon the ocean port of New York. A crumple of vague drapery has become the indubitable stars and stripes, which may also be seen flying in miniature, along with the city's own flag, atop the formerly non-patriotic city hall. But this pictorial interpretation of the new spirit proved to be usable only twice, in 1862 and 1863. As if in recognition of the driving from the oceans of our merchant marine, Valentine's T.P. was again redesigned.

In the 1864 lithograph, the city as a port has been pushed almost out of the top of the page, and half-eclipsed at that by an arc of type. Attention is turned away from the uncomfortable present toward an amiable Dutch-Indian past and the promise of a better future through education. The brief hardiness of both Indian and seaman on the great seal of the

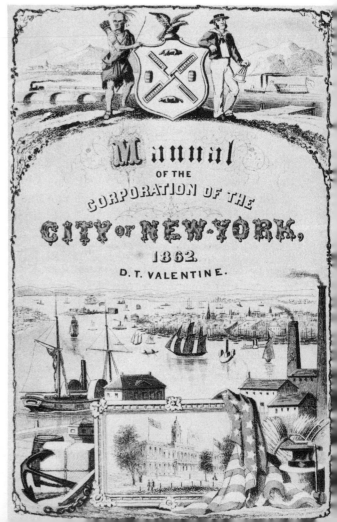

city has vanished. They have decided to sit down. An ever-improving locomotive emerges into greater prominence. Self-conscious artistry, with its palette and brushes, finds itself a spot below the cowcatcher. A more portentous new note, the sentimental wildwood, usurps the lower left corner.

Yet another new design for 1865 confirms and furthers these shifts. For the first time, however, the viewer is not looking seaward across lower Manhattan at the huge world; he is looking introspectively at his own city, from the bay. No matter what is happening between the Union and the Confederacy, relations between the Dutch and the Indians are getting better all the time. Our ships may not be making much use of the great globe, but our teachers are. The locomotive has puffed well into the foreground. The seal has shriveled, which is just as well, seeing that its once upright figures now are lounging in indolence. The wildwood beckons as the anchor diminishes. A new gearwheel announces the shape of some things to come.

In the last shift of concept, for 1866, the introspective eye has reached the city's center. The harbor, with an ocean crisscrossed by ship lanes just beyond it, has dwindled to a pond in Central Park, sustaining one small pleasure boat with a nicely scalloped awning. And this too was the notable turning point at which old New-York discarded its hyphen.

For an attentive eye that wishes to see more clearly the shape and subtleties of the past, there are other pictures in this book which will similarly reward a close inspection. The pair that celebrates the opening of the Gosport dock provides another instance. A sufficient gathering of the prints of Currier & Ives will serve as a social history of the preoccupations of a people, and will reinforce the inference of this year-by-year revelation in Valentine's T.P.s— that Americans, with a vast inland to exploit, were for the most part turning their backs upon the broader scene of their triumphs, the sea.

BELOW. Among many reproductions of documents and pictures from earlier periods of the life of New York, *Valentine's Manual* presented a sampling of contemporaneous scenes such as this one and the one on page 295, from the days when at the foot of most streets spars were in evidence, squared or acockbill.

COFFEE HOUSE SLIP AND NEW YORK COFFEE HOUSE.

Transatlantic MIDGETS

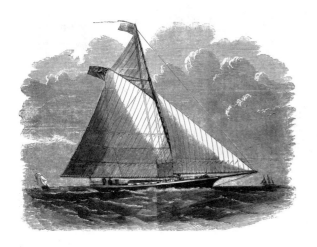

Reporting on December 4, 1858, that the 45-ton cutter *Christopher Columbus* (above) had reached Southampton, *Harper's Weekly* remarked, "A more frail-looking bark in which to cross the stormy Atlantic it is scarcely possible to conceive." A mysterious Captain Donovan found the conception, if not the performance, possible, eight years later, when he vanished into the Atlantic in the one-ton brig *Vision* (right). In 1866 a ship-rigged metallic lifeboat of 2.38 tons register, the *Red, White, and Blue* (below), made it in the very respectable time of 38 days, by one account, 35 by another. The veracity of the voyage was disputed at the time. There was one story that the *William Tapscott* had carried her almost all the way across. The preposterously difficult rig was a reason for doubting Captain William Hudson's story. But his log stands up under close inspection. It seems likelier that Captain Hudson was ridiculed because there was then no precedent, as there is now, for believing that what he claimed could possibly be true.

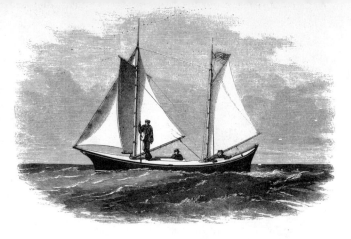

The almost successful voyage of the *John T. Ford* (above) went unquestioned. Captain Gould (the original caption is in error) spoke several vessels along the way before foundering near the Irish coast. Three of her crew drowned. The fourth, after clinging to her for 87 hours, was rescued. Then she drifted ashore. The *Nonpareil* (right), weirdly constructed upon three rubber cigars, made a successful seven-week passage in the same year, 1867. John Mikes, her skipper, spoke many vessels. He got from one a chicken, described by a visitor at the end of its passage as "a common brown, dowdy, grandmother-looking hen" which he considered "very odd and incongruous, tethered to the deck by a bit of tarred lanyard." Several small-craft skippers, including the redoubtable William Andrews who tried the Atlantic five times and once crossed single-handed in a 14′ 6″ folding canvas sloop, similarly testified to an inability to kill any live creature, where the world of the living was so small. Slocum's testimony on this point is beautifully reticent. The *City of Ragusa* (below) was a British lifeboat, rebuilt by an American, John C. Buckley, for the first attempt in so small a craft to make the uphill passage, westward. He and she succeeded, in 84 days. She returned in 38 days, apparently under command of Buckley's mate, an Austrian, Nicholas Primcraz. She was the smallest vessel (two tons) ever to clear formally at Liverpool, whence she sailed on June 3, 1870.

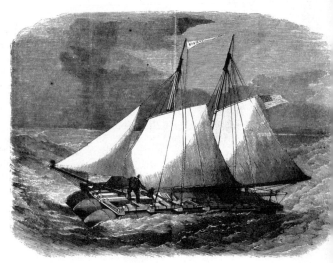

These are a few of Thomas Fogarty's illustrations, commissioned by the *Century Magazine* when it serially published Captain Joshua Slocum's account of his single-handed voyage around the world in 1895 and 1896 in the twelve-ton sloop *Spray*. He sailed first for Europe, thence took the hard route southwestward via the Straits of Magellan, thence through Polynesia to Australia and Cape Town, and so home to New England. An acquaintance gave Slocum command of the decrepit *Spray* as a joke. Since no better employment offered, for even so extraordinary a master in sail, he took the joke and rebuilt her into the most famous of

all small sailing vessels. At the right he is receiving the expected derision of the local nitwits. Below, Fogarty portrays the ingenuity with which Slocum met crises beyond the reach of plain seamanship. Needing sleep, in Patagonian waters, he strewed his deck with carpet tacks and turned in. The natives who, as he had foreseen, came aboard to capture his vessel "howled like a pack of hounds" and plunged over the side.

The achievements of Joshua Slocum have been approximated by one later single-handed circumnavigator, Alain Gerbault, and have been paralleled in part by others. Slocum remains the lonely pioneer, one of the very greatest of American seamen, marked in his writing by a whimsical modesty that is possible only for those who are serenely sure of themselves.

SAMOAN SEA-NYMPHS AT PLAY.

The natives of Samoa paid him kindlier sorts of visits. At this point in his story, Joshua seems a bit diffident about the exact particulars.

Like many another merchant seaman, Joshua Slocum vainly petitioned his government for redress of losses occasioned—as he thought—by a failure of our diplomatic energies abroad. The picture above, taken in 1907, shows him in the *Spray* during one of his fruitless voyages up the Potomac. LEFT. Slocum, surely America's most notable yachtsman, is only one of a number of merchant-marine skippers who continued in sail for the love of it. Samuel Samuels of the clipper packet *Dreadnought* was one. In the transatlantic yacht races of 1866, 1870, and 1887, he commanded the *Dauntless,* the following yacht in this picture of the start of the third race, won by the *Coronet* in 14 days, 19 hours, 56 minutes.

302

G. L. Lorillard, of the New York Yacht Club, who had entered the *Vesta* in the first transatlantic yacht race (1866) was also owner of the *Meteor* (above). Her measurement, 293 tons—123 more than the *America*, which she superficially resembled—indicates the seriousness with which yachting was taken after the *America*'s victory, as an advertisement for the egos of the wealthy.

A tendency to crowd the bay racers with canvas was early evident in the *Sylvie* (above), 105 tons, an American adaptation of the British cutter, laid down by Steers in December 1850, the same month in which he began work on the *America*. Against the right margin is Buttersworth's oil of sandbaggers racing in Great South Bay, New York. These extreme craft, kept upright only by the shifting of sand ballast to windward, were soon ruled out of competition. LEFT. Frederick Cozzens's water color of the *Mischief* and the *Atalanta* racing in 1883. BELOW. Another Cozzens painting, dated 1890, of the *Bedouin, Katrina,* and *Emerald,* taking the wind out of a catboat's sail.

BEFORE THE CIVIL WAR. The New York Yacht Club's 1854 regatta. The *Ray* is filling away on the leg to leeward. The *Una* is gybing at the mark. The *Alpha* is preparing to gybe. The next big white sloop is the *Irene*. Crowded last to windward is the famous *Maria*, which had consistently beaten the *America* during her shakedown races three years earlier. A typically knowledgeable Buttersworth scene, lithographed by Parsons for Currier & Ives. BELOW. The schooner *Haze*, centered in this woodcut from *Harper's Weekly,* made the best time in the 1860 regatta: one of two—the other is the *Alpha* off the *Haze*'s starboard quarter—identified in both pictures.

1854
FOUR
1860

1869
REGATTAS
1872

AFTER THE CIVIL WAR. Regatta pictures issued after the war reveal a change of emphasis. The actual races were as spirited as ever, but the printsellers—who were makers and followers of the public taste—evidently thought that they could do better with pictures stressing the social aspects of the sport of tycoons. The Currier & Ives lithograph above is of the start of the 1869 race. The ocean racer *Dauntless* is given the position of prominence just to the right of the flagstaff. The white schooner is the *Palmer*. BELOW. The *Palmer* visited Newport with the squadron in 1872. She is anchored in the left forewater, with the *Dauntless* just beyond.

The Down-Easters

AN UNDERSTANDABLE OVEREMPHASIS UPON THE GLAMOUR OF THE CLIPPER SHIP ERA HAS tended to divert the attention of all but specialists from a group of American deep-water traders built twenty or thirty years later that had their own kind of excellence. The measure of a ship, in any place and era, is its success under the conditions of the particular trade for which it was designed. It is unfair to judge the last big schooners by their poor performance in deep water; very few were built for it, and these merely confirmed the general finding that the rig was unsuited to such uses. The successful sizable deep-water sailing vessel, for about three centuries, continued to be a three-masted square-rigger: a ship. The clipper was an extreme development of the type, suited to extreme but transient demands. It is just as foolish to deride the clippers, as some sober-sided marine historians have done, for having their own brief merit, as it is to underrate the Down-Easters for lacking clipperly qualities which their trades did not call for and their designers deliberately did not provide.

In a book concerned centrally with the particular American contribution to the history of sail, on the other hand, it should not be claimed that the group of ships generally referred to as Down-Easters was in any important sense a contribution. These vessels represented the best adjustment that prudent men could make to the increasingly difficult task of keeping sail alive in the seaports of a country which had turned its preponderant energies inland. The legislators seemed not to care what happened to the merchant marine, except as a steam auxiliary to a steam navy. The wooden-ship builders after the Civil War consequently were most successful, not in their multiplications of schooner masts, but in their prudent retrenchment from the particular, transient merits of the clipper in all respects except average size.

The bark *Kennard,* launched in 1877 at East Machias, Maine.

An example of the best that emerged from this long rearguard action against destiny was the ship *Gov. Goodwin,* shown in photographs on later pages. But the *Gov. Goodwin* was not, if we respect usage, a Down-Easter. She was built a little too far "up west" for that, near Donald McKay's East Boston yard. A proper Down-Easter had to be built in Maine. The marine architect and historian Howard I. Chapelle believes that some Down-Easters were "the highest development of the sailing ship." The very fact of their persistence, earning their way for two or three decades of the cruelest competition even after steam had clearly triumphed, is in itself a proof of Chapelle's point. The only comparably successful vessels in this period were also a product of Maine—the big schooners. But whereas these were pushed past virtues of design into absurdities of false economy, the similarly large wooden square-riggers were well-crafted outgrowths of both the packet and clipper experiences. Some of the earlier ones were called half-clippers, or medium clippers. The term had a magic which made shipowners reluctant to abandon entirely the distinction it still gave to any vessel. Some durable Down-Easters—the *Benjamin F. Packard* (page 13) is one— were later publicized in ignorance or by promoters as "the last of the clippers"—and some of them did make passages better than the average for clippers as a group between some ports. But high speed was not their function.

William Hutchinson Rowe has stressed the point that the Down-Easters emerged and endured as a general type because of a sort of gold rush in reverse. The particularly hard wheat which grew in the dry California climate would keep in good condition during a long ocean voyage, when most wheat would commence to ferment. Large, capacious ships, to carry this new kind of California gold to Europe, were suddenly in demand. They had to be strong. Speed was all to the good, but not essential. In these vessels, as in the schooners, the town economy of Maine made it possible to save some expense in the building and operating which ordinarily would have vanished into the money market.

The type was in full production by 1880. Down-Easters of that period include the *Benjamin F. Packard,* the *A. J. Fuller,* the *Tacoma,* the *Henry B. Hyde,* and the *Llewellyn J. Morse.* They were built in Thomaston, Searsport, Rockland, Waldoboro, Machias, Eastport, and many even smaller places. It is significant that single "great" builders did not emerge— no McKay, no Webb. Perhaps fifty locally trusted master builders had real charge of the design and production of large square-riggers in the period of revival that began in 1873. On this occasion the American contribution of imagination and individualism was not intensely symbolized in a single person—such as a Phips or a Nat Palmer; the special quality of life along the myriad-harbored Maine coast instead had produced communities, any one of which could bring forward, on short notice, a master builder whose talents were of the first order. And the small community itself sustained the enterprise. It has been claimed that the people of Searsport never allowed the ships they built to be owned anywhere else. The overstatement is worth reiterating, as indicative of special conditions that sustained Maine shipbuilding long past the time when the production of similar vessels became completely uneconomic anywhere else. The nearness of suitable timber continued to be the basic condition upon which the others rested, but timber was there both before and after the periods of heavy production of big ships. The master builders and the fisherman-farmer-shipwrights provided the decisive elements in the equation. Some of the many skillful Maine shipbuilders were Nathaniel L. Thompson of Kennebunk, George Russell of East Deering, Lyman Walker of Yarmouth, John A. Briggs and Charles Cushing on the Harraseket, Enos C. Soule of Freeport, Arthur and Edward Sewall of Bath—the list could be stretched into dozens with the names of others as capable.

Ship *Benjamin Sewall,* launched at East Brunswick, Maine, in 1874, aground on the China coast.

The breath-taking incongruity of the picture below tells us a great deal about America's commercial penetration of the world. Captain Frank Irving Pendleton came from Searsport and traded to Japan. A man who could "sit" with a straight face for such a portrait could be counted on to handle almost any odd situation into which the needs of commerce might bring him. The *William H. Connor,* the last Down-Easter built at Searsport, was Pendleton's most important command. The town is said to have supplied 10 per cent of all American captains at sea in 1889. Little Searsport, a town of 2,000 people, supplied 77; and of these, 33 were captains of Cape Horners.

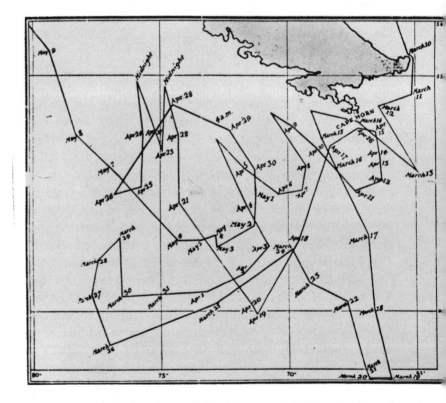

Track of the *Edward Sewall,* beating around the Horn in the spring of 1904. A good ship, competently commanded, required 61 days to regain latitude 55° S., on the Pacific side. The weather that year was unusual. Yet similar if less-prolonged frustrations sometimes befell one of two ships sailing almost in company, when the other, a few miles and hours away, had little difficulty.

The Northwest Down-Easters

By a device of organization not unlike that which permitted the Yankee whalers to endure for so long, the Alaska Packers Association kept square-riggers at work upon the ocean long after they had become economically calamitous in all other American trades. The Packers bought sturdy and capacious old ships for combined use as transports, freight haulers, and floating warehouses. The elimination of any one of the three functions would have made the vessels more costly than steamers to run. The empty hull of a sailing ship represented only a trifling expense when she was tied up during the winter in Californian waters. On the spring run to Alaska, a steamer would have had to carry fuel for the round voyage or buy more at a high rate. Both the space and the expense were saved in a sailing ship. Speed was of little importance. Cannery workers were crowded into the sailing ships, along with tin plate and box shooks; but whereas the whalers did their manufacturing aboard ship, the salmon canneries operated on the Alaskan coast. Their products slowly filled up the ships which again could afford to loiter because the investment was low. The plan worked so well that it was ended, not by inherent failure in the operation, but by the dying off of competent commanders and the unwillingness of the dwindling number of experienced foremasthands to ship out for such long voyages to such unalluring ports.

The Alaska Packers Association pooled the resources of independent packers at a time when such amalgamations were worrying the trust busters. Individual members and firms had been buying many Down-Easters in the last decade of the nineteenth century and the early years of the twentieth. These vessels, mostly of wood, retained their original names in the new service. The first such ship purchased was the *George Skolfield* with which the fleet was established in 1893. Others, in the order of purchase, were the *Llewellyn J. Morse* in 1895; the *Centennial, Santa Clara,* and *Sterling* in 1896; the *Bohemia* in 1897; and the *Indiana* and *Tacoma* in 1898. The individual packers began to buy British iron and steel ships in 1901. In 1907 the *Star of Russia* was acquired for the business, and thereafter all of the metal square-riggers were renamed as "Stars." Most had been built in Europe, but five of the nine steel square-riggers built in the United States eventually joined the Packers' fleet. These were all shipentines, carrying square sail on four masts rather than three. Representative American-built vessels of the Alaska Packers' fleet are shown on these pages. The operation was discontinued in favor of steam in 1929, another of the several dates which might be given as the end of the era of commercial sail.

Bark *Star of Finland*, launched as *Kaiulani* in 1899 at Bath, Maine, for Williams, Dimond & Co., specifically for the San Francisco–Honolulu run. Sold in 1907 to the Alaska Packers Association, she was used in World War II as a fore-and-after, competent square-rig men being unavailable.

ABOVE. The wooden ship *Tacoma,* launched in 1881 at Bath, Maine, and sold to the Alaska Packers in 1898 for $40,000. She was lost in the ice in Alaska in 1918. LEFT. Launched at Brewer, Maine, in 1877, the wooden ship *Llewellyn J. Morse* was operated for ten years mostly in Far East trade. In 1888 her Bangor owners sold her to John Rosenfeld, San Francisco. She joined the Alaska Packers salmon fleet in 1895.

Loss of the *Dauntless*

Several notable vessels have borne the name *Dauntless,* including the Medford clipper of 1852. The slightly larger but less sharp *Dauntless* of these pictures was built by Maxson, Fish & Company of Mystic, Connecticut, in 1869, for the California trade, and has been described as "yacht-like." She was the last of the Mystic-built square-riggers. At one time she ran from Manila to Boston in 96 days. On the coast of Africa, in 1883, she was driven from her anchorage in a gale and was smashed to pieces.

DEPARTURE
OF THE *GOV. GOODWIN*

Setting the main topsail.

Hoisting the main upper topsail yard.

Catting the anchor.

MOST OF THE EARLY ACTION PHOTOGRAPHS TAKEN ABOARD SHIP ARE EVIDENTLY THE WORK of amateurs coping with inadequate equipment or of more skillful photographers who, as crew members, were unable to exercise the necessary patience and care in waiting for the best moments: when something exciting or spectacular was happening, the chances were that they were tailing onto a rope themselves. The photographs that follow are an exception. I believe that eight are here being offered in a book for the first time. (The last one was included in *American Merchant Ships,* Volume I, by Howe and Matthews.) They were taken when the *Gov. Goodwin* was getting under way in New York harbor on June 10, 1891.

She was built of wood at East Boston in 1877 by Campbell & Brooks and launched in July for M. F. Pickering & Company of Boston. Her net tonnage measurement was 1413.99. She was named for Ichabod Goodwin, who had been governor of New Hampshire during the Civil War—one of the rare politicians of the times to take a strong interest in maritime affairs. Her first master was William Lester, who was succeeded by a Captain Norton. Lester had learned the finishing touches to his trade as mate under Coggin in the fine Mallory clipper *Pampero.*

Although she was comfortably far from a clipper in model, the *Gov. Goodwin* made a number of Cape Horn passages as good as those made by the great clippers in an off season and better than the best that some vessels, classed as clippers, ever were able to make. On her maiden voyage she went out to San Francisco from the Delaware in 119 days, and later made it in 108 days. Her average for five eastward Cape Horn passages from San Francisco to North Atlantic ports was 117½ days—the best being 98 days. She ran four times to Europe from San Francisco in an average time of 114½ days. Under Captain Charles C. Oakes, whose picture is given here, she made the run from Manila to Boston in 102 days, with a best average speed of 10½ knots throughout 24 hours. She was wrecked in Sunda Strait in 1896, bound from New York to Chefoo with case oil. Examination of the details of these pictures reveals a well-maintained ship in which the owners took pride. But the odds had turned heavily against such enterprises, in the twilight of American sail.

ABOVE. Setting the *Gov. Goodwin*'s main staysail. Note that the nearest seaman is wearing his knife where it belongs, to reduce the chance of a foul-up in the running rigging. LEFT. Captain Charles C. Oakes, who bought a 6/64 interest in the *Gov. Goodwin*. His first mate, for six years until the loss of the ship, was Frank E. Young, who had been master of a larger ship than the *Gov. Goodwin*—an indication of the dwindling of opportunities for competent masters in sail.

The pilot with Captain Samuel Pray of Foster & Pray, owners of the *Gov. Goodwin* after 1890.

Man at the wheel in the *Gov. Goodwin*.

The *Gov. Goodwin* photographed from the pilot boat off her weather quarter.

The *Lucile,* hove down at a San Francisco pier. She was a ship of 1,394.29 tons, 200.2′ x 40′ x 23.9′, built at Freeport, Maine, in 1874.

New Bedford and some of its Yankee whalers in the 1860s.

THE WHALE FISHERY

CETACEANS WERE FOUND BY EARLY EUROPEAN VOYAGERS TO BE AN ITEM in the food supply of seaboard peoples throughout the world—a fact that did not surprise them because whale meat and oil had long been staples in France when the Biscayan whales were exterminated in the sixteenth century. The Dutch of the following century were dominant in this as in other maritime pursuits. A pleasantly inaccurate engraving from Friedrich Martens's account of their Spitsbergen fishery appears below. But the Dutch, with a fleet finally numbering above 250 vessels, likewise hunted the nearby seas bare, and gave up. The British then extended their fishery into more distant waters by the political device of a bounty. Their whalers were still dominant in the early part of the nineteenth century.

What then was the American contribution that has so fully identified whaling with two small places in New England? It was like most of our other marine achievements. The

LEFT. American Indians catching whales, as engraved by one of the De Brys. The Latin text accompanying the original published in 1602 does not reveal the source of the information. BELOW. Dutch whaling near Spitsbergen, as engraved for an English translation of Friedrich Martens's account of operations in the latter seventeenth century.

The mastheadman (above, left) with an eye out for spouters was a popular figure with readers of the middle part of the last century. This particular reproduction is taken from J. Ross Browne's *Etchings of a Whaling Cruise,* 1846; but close copies of it turn up in other books. The whaling scene below can be exactly dated, which is unusual for older engravings. It is from the "Poli Arctici" plate of Hondius, which appeared without such corner illustrations in his English atlas of 1636. But the scene was added when the same plate was used for a German appendix of the same year.

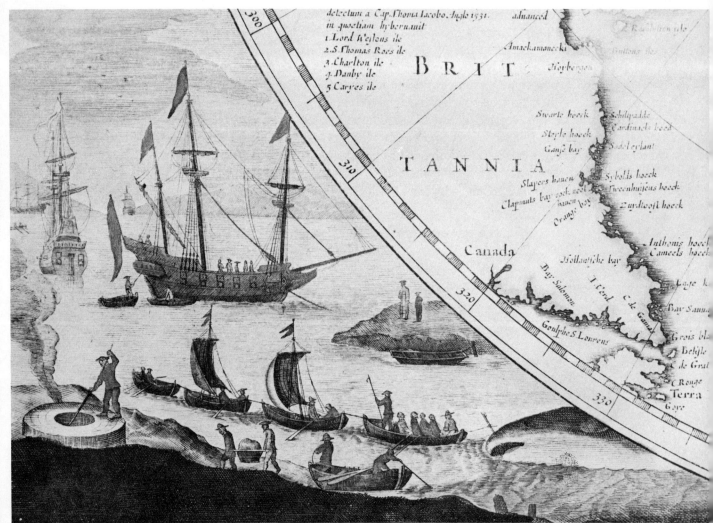

special ingenuity of free men, in voluntary association, brought to a full development something already in existence which had been hampered elsewhere by privilege and monopoly. Since they lacked capital from aristocratic or military accumulations of wealth, American enterprisers made every crew member an investor in the voyage, sharing by prearrangement in its risks and its profits. Knowledge and ability were primarily recognized. The provider of a ship and its stores got more or less for his investment in the same proportion as the boatsteerer or harpooner who provided courage, skill, and three or four years of his sometimes abruptly terminated life. As I have earlier noted, the ultimate contribution was the development of a practically self-sufficient floating village that could continue to exist indefinitely, anywhere in the world of water, with an internal unity of purpose based in the interdependence and mutual respect of its members. There were rascally and tyrannical whaling captains, but such attributes did not make for success in an enterprise that depended so critically upon the periodic, utmost exertion of voluntary daring and skill. It was feasible, in the brutal days of the Yankee packets, for bucko mates to drive a crew mercilessly to the first port, at which they were expected to "run," or jump ship, paid or unpaid—and preferably the latter. Similar conditions made a dark stain across the record of the last Down-Easters, from which men with much more pay due them were driven to desert in the ports of the Far East. Voyages of a few weeks or months could be so managed; in a forty months' voyage it did not work.

The whaling "grounds" receded farther and farther from Nantucket and New Bedford until it was taken for granted that little oil could be secured nearer than the waters off Japan. Later, the Pacific Arctic was the only profitable ground for large-scale operations out of New England.

These circumstances largely account, I believe, for the development, around 1850, of Nantucket and New Bedford fleets which between them were far larger than previous totals for all other ports in the entire world. A decade or so later, in the general decline of American sail, the evils of decadence became prevalent in the whalers as in other ships. "A Roving Printer's" *Life and Adventures in the South Pacific* indicates that normal capitalization had become dominant before 1861 in the engaging of crews. Charles Nordhoff, five years earlier, had given an account of some owners' positive preference for greenhorns who could be swindled at outset and whipped into shape at sea. Two pictures on this page, from Nordhoff's *Whaling and Fishing*, illustrate the device to which a real sailor was driven in order to get a berth in a whale ship.

The two views at right, of the same man, illustrate Charles Nordhoff's story of his friend who was turned down by the owner of a whaler because he looked too much like a merchant seaman, but who was quickly accepted by the same man when he returned, transformed by the shipping master into a country bumpkin. The scene opposite from Hondius's "Poli Arctici" plate reveals one reason why the vast Dutch fishery followed the French into oblivion. The trypots were always erected on the shore, where the coopering also was done. The British and their American colonists, by transferring these operations into the whale ships themselves, made the world-wide fisheries possible.

Americans take over. In 1824 the bounty which had stimulated British whaling for almost a century was withdrawn. Thereafter, as the American fishery increased, the British declined. Shipowners who had accustomed themselves to one of the devices of privilege were unable to compete with the co-operative investment system of the Nantucketers and New Bedford men. It was at about the time of this shift that W. J. Huggins, one of the most faithful of the British marine painters, produced his well-known scenes of the whalers off Greenland and Bouro. How faithfully he followed details of the specifically named ships it is now not possible to determine, but the trustworthiness of the "American" whalers depicted by the piratical American lithographer J. Baillie in the pair of scarce prints at the right can be easily inferred. Little is changed but the flags. These prints, like Valentine's title pages, reward the close viewer. Note, for example, the process of "cutting in" and the whalebone arches. Baillie's "South Sea Whale Fishery," since it is not a mirror image, may have been pirated from an intermediate pirated print.

NORTH SEA WHALE FISHERY.

Pub by J. Baillie 87 St near 3rd Avenue N.Y.

The Head of a large Whale in the Agonies of Death.

Pub by J. Baillie 87 St near 3rd Avenue N.Y.

A Boat destroyed by a wounded Whale.

SOUTH SEA WHALE FISHERY.

The *John Carver* as a bark

When this picture of the whaler *Maria* of New Bedford was published by *Gleason's* in 1852, she was identified as the oldest vessel owned in the United States: built for use as a Revolutionary privateer, bought by William Rotch of Nantucket in 1783. It was claimed for her that she was the first merchant vessel to wear the Stars and Stripes in a British port. On this voyage her owner is reported to have said, "Captain Mooers, it would be more conducive to our safety for thee to take in some sail; thee had better do so." The captain replied, "Mr. Rotch, I have the deck, you have the cabin." One account credits Mooers as having been first to display the American flag in England in the *Bedford,* when peace had been announced but not yet ratified. The *Maria's* first whaling voyage ended on September 26, 1795. Her twenty-seventh and last such voyage under the United States flag began 64 years and 3 days later. A sailmaker named Harditch, of Fairhaven, who had worked on a suit of sails for her in 1792, went to work on another suit for her in 1856. During the Civil War she sailed under the safety of the Chilean flag, renamed *Maria Pachaco.* Her early service included voyages to the Falklands in 1785, to Greenland in 1788, and a Nantucket-to-Dover passage in the good time of 21 days. She ended her service in 1872 at Vancouver, aged ninety.

The bark *John Carver* is shown at the left above as she appeared to the Antwerp artist P. Weytz who painted her on glass "off Flushing." Like the *B. Aymar,* she was built at Searsport, Maine, by John Carver, the master shipwright whose name she was given. She was launched in 1842 for a group of owners, including her builder and John Pendleton. For a while she was owned in Maine. During the Civil War she was taken by the raider *Jeff Davis* but appears to have been repurchased or redeemed by the Maine firm of Walsh, Carver & Company, given by Lloyd's as her owners for 1864 to 1866. Starbuck notes that she was "bought from New York" in the latter year by T. Knowles & Company and sent into the Pacific on a four-year cruise under Henry F. Worth. A second four-year cruise for the same owners, under Captain Jacob L. Howland, followed. She returned on July 2, 1874, and sailed again for the Indian Ocean on June 1, 1875, under Captain Aaron Dean who died during the voyage. She was still out in 1877 when Starbuck's account ends, but Lloyd's still lists Knowles and others as her owners two years later. She met what was, for the times, a typical whaler's end—in the Bering sea, on June 21, 1886. Her owners of record were then William Lewis and others, her official number 13005, and her signal letters HLBN. Certain structural differences in addition to the new rig can be noted in her appearance as a bark, on glass, and as a ship, in the oil painting on canvas, above. Both are now in the collection of Clifford N. Carver.

Perils of Whaling.

The *John Carver* as a whale ship

"Perils of Whaling" (opposite page) is from Nathaniel Hawthorne's *American Magazine of Useful and Entertaining Knowledge*, 1839. (Below) Going on a sperm whale. From the lithograph "The Chase," by Benjamin Russell, the mid-nineteenth-century New Bedford painter of whaling scenes whose carefully detailed work reflected a knowledge gained by personal experience.

Life in a Whaler

ABOVE. "Life in the Forecastle."
LEFT. "Scramble for Salt-Junk."
BELOW. "Flogging."

Light and dark aspects of an existence which as a rule kept a group of about thirty men within a space the size of an average farmhouse for three or four years with only rare and brief visits ashore. These three pictures and the middle one opposite are from J. Ross Browne's *Etchings of a Whaling Cruise*, 1846.

There are three well-known instances of ships having been sunk by whales. Less well known is the almost-sinking of the *Pocahontas* of Tisbury. When a whale smashed one of her boats, the captain steered for the angry animal with harpoons ready. He was out-maneuvered by his adversary which "struck with such force as to start one or two planks and break one or two timbers . . . causing the vessel to leak at once at the rate of 250 strokes an hour." The *Pocahontas* ran for the nearest port, leaving the ocean to the winner.

ABOVE. Lancing a harpooned whale. RIGHT. The *Horatio*, a particularly successful late Nantucket whaler.

What seems to have been the longest-range rescue operation on record was hatched between the subversive Irish patriot John Boyle O'Reilly and H. C. Hathaway, New Bedford police captain. As a result of their plot the bark *Catalpa* (above) was equipped for a whaling expedition in the South Pacific and two secret agents were sent out to Australia in a passenger vessel. Of those aboard the *Catalpa*, only Captain George S. Anthony knew the true purpose of the cruise, which was to rescue six other Irishmen who had behaved treasonably toward their queen and had been committed for life to imprisonment at hard labor in the Fremantle penal colony. A whaler was chosen as the least likely sort of foreign vessel to be suspected of plotting sad tricks against the authorities on the West Australian coast. After some routine whaling, Captain Anthony had himself rowed ashore at the prearranged time and place. The Fenians, who had run for it from their labors in the woods, were waiting with one of the agents, John J. Breslin. So was a storm. The escaping whaleboat could not find the ship for more than twenty-four hours. Then a nerve-racking bit of luck occurred. As they at last sighted the *Catalpa*, a British cruiser came alongside her. The officials satisfied themselves that the felons were not aboard—and they did not spot the boat in the steep seas. As they steamed away, as shown above, a police boat under sail approached. The oarsmen bent their backs and reached the *Catalpa* with only seconds to spare. Captain Anthony defied the armed boat and headed for New Bedford.

ABOVE. The bark *Greyhound* of New Bedford, built in 1851: a five-boat whaler. The captain's boat is at the stern. BELOW. Whalers at New Bedford.

The jaunty little bark
Swallow of New Bed-
ford, built in 1856, had
fairly fine lines for a
whaler.

BELOW. Sperm whaling
scene from a water
color by a New Bed-
ford whaleman.
OPPOSITE PAGE, LOWER
PICTURE. An enraged
sperm whale in action.

Cutting in a sperm whale from the cutting stage of the bark *California*. From a photograph taken in 1903. Much the same methods of cutting in had been used for many decades. This work was usually done by the mates; most foremast hands were too green for it.

Handling blubber at the tryworks in an Arctic whaler.
The man at the left is wearing Eskimo boots.

The single event that seems in retrospect to have doomed the sailing whaleship was the loss at one time and place of thirty-one New Bedford vessels. The pictures below, and following, are portions of a series of proof lithographs celebrating a singularly triumphant sort of disaster in the Bering Strait, in September of 1871. They merit a close inspection because they were prepared for distribution in the first place under the scrutiny of a community of experts. There was hardly a New Bedford family that was not involved in some way in the calamity. The illustrations explicitly identify thirty of the trapped whaleships and all seven rescuers in open water. Considering the place and the occasion, there is a minimum of doubt that they have been shown with the accuracy of the contemporaneous view.

KOHOLA.   EUGENIA.   WAINRIGHT INLET.   AWASHONKS.   THOS DICKAS
                       JULIAN.

Whaling ship *James Arnold*, built in 1852. This photograph, taken about 1910, shows her leaving New Bedford after being sold to Chilean owners.

MINERVA.   WM. ROTCH.   VICTORIA.   MAR

A few whalers with auxiliary steam power, which was used mainly for maneuvering in the ice, were built for New Bedford's whaling fleet. At the left is the steam bark *Mary and Helen, 2nd,* built in 1882, from a painting done in the same year by Charles S. Raleigh.

Whaling schooner *Margarett*, built in 1889. Up to the 1920s, during the last marginal period of whaling out of New England ports, such schooners operated on the Hatteras grounds and off the Azores and Cape Verdes, often making a swing back through the South Atlantic to the West Indies. There they might transship their cargo so as to stay out another season.

EUROPA.   DANIEL WEBST

SHIPS RECEIVING THE CAPTAINS

MIDAS.   CHANCE.   ARCTIC.   PROGRESS.   LAGODA.

RS AND CREWS OF ABANDONED SHIPS.

Whale fishery, adapted to a peculiarly American pattern, persisted through a series of vast calamities and died with its feet on the deck. In the Revolution the British made a great effort to absorb the Nantucketers and their ships. For a while they appeared to have succeeded. Then the Nantucketers came home. In 1812 the island base of the industry again was made untenable, and most of its ships captured or sunk. Its strongest revival followed. At the outset of the Civil War forty-five whalers were acquired by the federal government as a "stone fleet" to be uselessly sunk in an effort to stop up the approaches to Charleston and Savannah. Storms and currents quickly opened new channels around the obstructions. Confederate raiders worked an extensive reprisal against whalers particularly, because many could be caught homeward bound from long voyages, unwarned of the war.

It was the special advantage of the American whaling system that took it to its two ultimate disasters. Blubber in the early days had always been tried out ashore. The development of a factory ship, with its own try works and cooperage facilities, when combined with incentives of the share system of recompense, allowed the American whalers to range anywhere. When the whales were hunted out of all other waters, the surviving herds retreated into Bering Strait. There, in 1871, the ice closed upon an entire fleet of 32 ships. Five years later, 12 ships out of a fleet of 20 were crushed. This proved to be the final portent. The last great enterprise which had relied wholly upon sail for power succumbed to the evident need for steam auxiliaries if hunting were to continue where whales in quantity could still be found.

The 1876 disaster was in one sense not only a portent, but also an aftermath. It occasioned the deaths of many men who preferred the temporary safety of their trapped ships to the perils of attempted escape by whaleboat through the clashing floes. Something remarkably different had happened when nearly three times as many ships had been crushed in 1871. The last series of pictures here reproduced is taken from a set of original proofs of five lithographs issued in impoverished New Bedford to celebrate, amid economic disaster, perhaps the most triumphant of all sea rescues. Whaleboats under sail, badly overloaded, carried 1,219 of the ships' people through eighty miles of gullies in the shifting ice and put them aboard another group of whalers in open water, under stormy conditions that made any contact between a small craft and a ship hazardous. A number of women and children were aboard the rescue fleet. Not one person was lost in transit. Only one, by an oversight, was left behind. He was found alive in the following year aboard the *Minerva,* the sole ship out of 32 that had not been splintered. A crew levied from the new fleet put her to rights and used her as a freighter to carry oil to New Bedford.

If a date must be chosen for an end to the heroic age of American sail, can a better one be found than the 15th of September, 1871, when 180 lugger- and sloop-rigged whaleboats completed their feat of faultless seamanship through the ice floes, in a wind so strong that five of the seven waiting whalers had had to cat their anchors and get under way?

"So ends, &c—"

The delicately carved and colorful sternboard of the whaling bark *America,* built in 1818 at Duxbury, Massachusetts. Removed when the *America,* after long service, was dismantled in the 1860s, the sternboard measures 14 feet in length and 3 feet in height.

Acknowledgements and Sources of Pictures

Multitudinous generosities enter into this sort of book. My colleagues at the Dartmouth College Library have shown, during its three years in the making, a concern with someone else's odd problems that should not be taken for granted merely because it is one of the graces of their profession. They all know why I single out Professor Virginia Close and Mr. George Dalphin for central thanks. About a third of these pictures were found in the book, print, and map collections of Dartmouth College. Many supplementary volumes were brought here for my use on interlibrary loan. Mr. Emil Rueb has advised me in the choice and behavior of photocopying equipment. Mr. Shirley Spaulding has been endlessly patient as I hovered over his developing trays. I am further indebted for photoprocessing to Mr. Aubrey Janion and Mr. Frederick Wood. Most of the prints concerned with our sailing Navy are in the superb collection of Mr. Irving S. Olds, to which Mr. J. H. Osmers served as my hospitable guide. Photocopies of these and of many other subjects were supplied by Mr. Harry Shaw Newman, upon whose friendly interest much of the best in this book depends. Mr. Robert J. Friedrich put unique pictures in my way that I would otherwise surely have missed: the endpaper painting is one. Special gratitude is due to correspondents abroad who located rarities and saved me from some descriptive blunders: Mr. M. S. Robinson, Curator of Pictures, National Maritime Museum, Greenwich, England; Prof. J. G. van Gelder, Kunsthistorisch Instituut der Rijksuniversiteit, Utrecht; Mme. D. de Hoop Scheffer, Rijksmuseum, and Dr. G. A. Cox, Nederlandsch Historisch Scheepvaart Museum, both of Amsterdam, Netherlands; Sr. Ricardo Magdaleno, Director, Archivo General de Simancas, Spain. The sources of prose quotations have been acknowledged in the text.

I list gratefully, along with their institutions, the names of some individuals who have done more for my book than any author has a right to expect:

MARINE HISTORICAL ASSOCIATION, Mystic, Conn.: Mr. Edouard A. Stackpole, Curator; Mrs. H. C. MacDonald, Registrar

MARINE SOCIETY OF THE CITY OF NEW YORK, New York, N. Y.: Capt. P. B. Blanchard; Capt. J. H. Hagan

MARINERS MUSEUM, Newport News, Va.: Mr. Robert H. Burgess, Curator of Exhibits

MUSEUM OF THE CITY OF NEW YORK: Mr. W. M. Williamson, Curator, Marine Gallery; Miss Grace Mayer, formerly Curator of Prints

337

NEW YORK PUBLIC LIBRARY, Print Room: Mr. Karl Kup, Curator
PEABODY MUSEUM OF SALEM, Mass.: Mr. M. V. Brewington, Assistant Curator
PENOBSCOT MARINE MUSEUM, Searsport, Me.: Mr. Clifford N. Carver, President; Mr. Edgar Thorne, Curator; Mr. Robert B. Applebee, Historian

SAN FRANCISCO MARITIME MUSEUM: Mr. Karl Kortum, Director; Mrs. Matilda Dring, Photos
WHALING MUSEUM OF NEW BEDFORD, Mass.: Mr. Philip F. Purrington, Curator

Additional important maritime collections appear in the specific acknowledgments that follow. Some, surprisingly absent, were not drawn upon only because examples in certain categories already had been chosen elsewhere. The names of individuals who have been helpful also appear alongside references to pictures they kindly supplied. My thanks to all of them, particularly to Capt. Arthur J. Elliot, master and master-builder of schooners, and Mr. John Pray Wadham, both of whom allowed me to copy rare photographs. I am indebted to Mr. Charles Malik for translating an inscription in Arabic; to Mr. Ward Melville for making possible my use of the frontispiece; and for various kindnesses to Mr. James M. Landis, the Misses Elizabeth A. and Helen H. Livingston, Commander W. J. L. Parker, Mr. Edward Pinkowski, Mr. Stephen T. Riley, Miss Ethel M. Ritchie, and Professor David B. Tyler. My wife Veronica was equal sharer in the seven labors of proofreading. The fullness and precision of the indexing are her contribution; its shortcomings are my own.

A.L.
Hanover, N. H.
Labor Day, 1961

Kennedy Galleries, Inc., New York.
Endpapers. Pages: 3, 50B, 56-57, 58B, 59, 139, 144, 158BR, 166B, 222B, 228T, 237TL, 237BL, 245M, 252B, 263T, 265B, 271BR, 273T, 275B, 290T, 292B, 294, 303MR, 303B.

Some other sources that supplied several pictures apiece are identified below by symbols:

MCNY: Museum of the City of New York
MHA: Marine Historical Association, Mystic, Conn.
MSNY: Marine Society of the City of New York
NYPL: New York Public Library
PMS: Peabody Museum of Salem
Frontispiece: Courtesy of Suffolk Museum at Stony Brook, Long Island
Pages:
x & xi, NYPL
1, Museum of Art, Rhode Island School of Design
4 & 5B, MHA & PMS
Color plate at p. 10, Historical Society of Pennsylvania
11B, MHA & PMS
13, MSNY
14T, Whaling Museum, New Bedford, Mass.
14B, Mr. Walter Magnes Teller
16, Mrs. Graham L. Schofield
18B, Mr. Rudolph Ruzicka & PMS
21, NYPL
32-33, Archivo General de Simancas, Spain
38, NYPL, Phelps Stokes Collection
42, Mr. Aubrey P. Janion
44, Mr. William Doerflinger & NYPL
47, Mrs. William Tudor Gardiner
51T, Courtesy of the New-York Historical Society, New York City
51B, NYPL
54, (Coins) Mr. Aubrey P. Janion
58T, MHA & PMS
91, PMS
92, Massachusetts Historical Society
93T, 96B, 97, 98, PMS
107B, Enoch Pratt Free Library, Baltimore, Barker Collection
120, Courtesy of the New-York Historical Society, New York City
121, NYPL
122, PMS
136, MCNY, Marine Museum
137B, PMS
183, NYPL
Color plate at p. 190: top, PMS; bottom, Seamen's Bank for Savings in the City of New York
192B, NYPL
197T, Algemeen Rijksarchief, Leupe 1353, The Hague, Netherlands
200B, Mr. Myron Hilton
202, MHA & PMS
205B, Mariners Museum, Newport News, Va.
206, Sun Oil Co.
207, MSNY
208, 209, 211, Capt. Arthur J. Elliot

212, Mrs. Graham L. Schofield
221R, MCNY, The Edward C. Arnold Collection lent by the Metropolitan Museum of Art
222T, New York State Historical Association, Cooperstown
227B, 228B, 229, 234B, NYPL
239T, Courtesy of the New-York Historical Society, New York City
239B, Courtesy of the U. S. Naval Academy Museum
246TR, 247T, MCNY, H. T. Peters Collection
248T, 249B, NYPL
251T, MCNY
253B, Courtesy of the M. H. de Young Memorial Museum, San Francisco
257, India House, New York
258-259, PMS
261M, MHA & PMS
262TR, Penobscot Marine Museum
262BR, Mr. Clifford N. Carver
262BL, MHA
263T, Seamen's Bank for Savings in the City of New York
264T, MHA & PMS
268B & 269B, MCNY
270T, McCaughen & Burr, Inc., St. Louis, Missouri
270B, Courtesy of the Walters Art Gallery, Baltimore
Color plate at p. 270, PMS
271M, MHA & PMS
271BL, India House, New York
272T, NYPL
274BR, MHA & PMS
275T, Mr. John Pray Wadham
275ML, (From Bowditch: *New American Navigator*, 1826)
277MR, 277BL, MHA
278T, NYPL
278MR, Maine Historical Society
278B, MSNY
293B, Official U. S. Navy Photo
302T, Courtesy of Mr. Winfield Scott Cline & Mr. Walter Magnes Teller
305T, MCNY, The J. Clarence Davies Collection
306, 308T, MSNY
308M, Capt. P. B. Blanchard
308BL, Penobscot Marine Museum
309, 310, San Francisco Maritime Museum
311T, MHA & PMS
311B, MHA
312-315, Mr. John Pray Wadham
316T, Capt. Arthur J. Elliot
316B, San Francisco Maritime Museum
317T, MSNY
Color plate at p. 318 [top and bottom], Whaling Museum of New Bedford
322TR, 323T, Mr. Clifford N. Carver
323B, 327T, 328-329, 330T, 331T, 332T, 333T, Whaling Museum of New Bedford
327B, MSNY
337, Seamen's Bank for Savings in the City of New York

INDEX of Vessels

Sailing vessels of the United States Navy are given their original gun ratings, in bold type, preceded by (1st), (2nd), etc., when more than one bore the same name. "U.S.S." signifies a naval steamship, with or without sail; "c" means caption.

INDEX of Persons